# Jokowi's
# Indonesia
## and the
# World

# Jokowi's Indonesia
## and the
# World

### Ahmad Ibrahim Almuttaqi
*The Habibie Center, Indonesia*

**World Scientific**

NEW JERSEY • LONDON • SINGAPORE • BEIJING • SHANGHAI • HONG KONG • TAIPEI • CHENNAI • TOKYO

*Published by*

World Scientific Publishing Co. Pte. Ltd.
5 Toh Tuck Link, Singapore 596224
*USA office:* 27 Warren Street, Suite 401-402, Hackensack, NJ 07601
*UK office:* 57 Shelton Street, Covent Garden, London WC2H 9HE

**British Library Cataloguing-in-Publication Data**
A catalogue record for this book is available from the British Library.

**JOKOWI'S INDONESIA AND THE WORLD**

ISBN 978-981-121-407-3

For any available supplementary material, please visit
https://www.worldscientific.com/worldscibooks/10.1142/11658#t=suppl

Typeset by Stallion Press
Email: enquiries@stallionpress.com

Desk Editor: Karimah Samsudin

*Dedicated to the people of Indonesia*

# Contents

# Acknowledgements

This book would not have been made possible without the support, kindness, and inspiration of a number of individuals to whom I am tremendously indebted to. Whilst there are too many to name them all individually, several warrant special mention.

First and foremost are my beloved '*Abah*' and '*Ummi*', Abdurrahman and Zaiedah Almuttaqi. I cannot thank them enough for the love and care they have given me at every stage of my life and for raising me into the person I am today. Whilst a parent's sacrifice for their child is truly immeasurable, I hope I can go some way in repaying that sacrifice by making them proud of what their son has achieved. Likewise to my siblings, Imran and Hannah, who though I may not always express it well, have always counted among my closest companions.

Beyond my family, I would like to express my gratitude to the inspirational Rahimah Abdulrahim for taking a risk on me and giving me my first proper job in the think tank community. I count myself among the luckiest of people to be able to do what I love and to be compensated for it. There has never been a truer proverb than to 'Do what you love, and you'll never work another day in your life'. I am further indebted to her for constantly encouraging me to write — from short opinion articles for newspapers to academic papers for conferences — sparking what has become a passion for writing that has culminated in this book.

I would be amiss not to acknowledge all my friends and colleagues at The Habibie Center who have also been part of that journey. Special mention should go to Anissa Dini who helped enormously in getting the initial manuscript over the proverbial finish line and for kindly assisting me in navigating the difficult stage of submitting the manuscript to potential publishers.

In this regard, I would like to express my thanks to World Scientific Publishing for placing their trust in this book. Special mention should go to Karimah Samsudin for her patience, understanding, and efficiency in making the entire publishing process as smooth as possible, especially for this inexperienced author.

Lastly to Than Tha Aung, who has been with me from the very beginning of the writing process to the very end, I would only like to say: *Chit tae.*

# List of Acronyms and Abbreviations

| | |
|---|---|
| 1MDB | 1 Malaysia Development Berhad |
| ADMM | ASEAN Defense Ministers Meeting |
| AHKFTA | ASEAN–Hong Kong Free Trade Agreement |
| AJCEP | ASEAN–Japan Comprehensive Economic Partnership |
| AKFTA | ASEAN–Korea Free Trade Agreement |
| APEC | Asia-Pacific Economic Cooperation |
| ARF | ASEAN Regional Forum |
| ARSA | Arakan Rohingya Salvation Army |
| ASEAN | Association of Southeast Asian Nations |
| BNPB | Badan Nasional Penanggulangan Bencana, or National Disaster Mitigation Agency |
| Brimob | Brigade Mobil or Mobile Brigade |
| CEO | Chief Executive Officers |
| CEPA | Comprehensive Economic Partnership Agreements |
| COC | Code of Conduct |
| Densus 88 | Detasemen Khusus 88, or Special Detachment 88 |
| DMZ | Demilitarized Zone |
| DOC | Declaration on the Conduct of Parties in the South China Sea |

| | |
|---|---|
| DPD | Dewan Perwakilan Daerah, or Regional Representatives Council |
| DPR | Dewan Perwakilan Rakyat, or House of Representatives |
| DPRD | Dewan Perwakilan Rakyat Daerah, or Regional Legislative Council |
| EAS | East Asian Summit |
| EEZ | Exclusive Economic Zone |
| e-KTP | e-Kartu Tanda Penduduk, or e-Identity Cards |
| FPI | *Front Pembela Islam* or Islamic Defenders Front |
| G20 | Group of 20 |
| Gerindra | Partai Gerakan Indonesia Raya, or Great Indonesia Movement Party |
| Golkar | Partai Golongan Karya, or Party of Functional Groups |
| Golput | *Golongan Putih*, or White Group (refers to a section of the electorate that opt to abstain during an election) |
| GOP | Grand Old Party (refers to the U.S. Republican Party) |
| Hanura | Partai Hati Nurani Rakyat, or the People's Conscience Party |
| HTI | *Hizbut-Tahrir Indonesia* |
| IDR | Indonesian Rupiah |
| IHSG | *Indeks Harga Saham Gabungan* or Indonesia Composite Index |
| IJEPA | Indonesia–Japan Economic Partnership Agreement |
| IMF | International Monetary Fund |
| Indomalphi | Indonesia–Malaysia–the Philippines |
| INKA | PT Industri Kereta Api (a state-owned train manufacturer) |
| INTERPOL | International Criminal Police Organization |
| IOC | International Olympic Committee |
| IORA | Indian Ocean Rim Association |
| IUU Fishing | Illegal, Unregulated and Unreported Fishing |

| | |
|---|---|
| JAD | *Jamaah Anshar Daulah* |
| KIH | *Koalisi Indonesia Hebat*, or Awesome Indonesian Coalition |
| KMP | *Koalisi Merah Putih*, or Red and White Coalition |
| Koopsusgab | Komando Operasi Khusus Gabungan, or Joint Special Operations Command |
| Kopassus | Komando Pasukan Khusus, or Special Forces |
| KPK | Komisi Pemberantasan Korupsi, or Corruption Eradication Commission |
| KPU | Komisi Pemilihan Umum, or General Elections Commission |
| KRI | Kapal Perang Republik Indonesia, or Republic of Indonesia Warship (a prefix denoting a commissioned vessel of the Indonesian Navy similar to U.S.S. for the U.S. Navy) |
| LGBT | Lesbian, Gay, Bisexual, and Transsexual |
| MD3 | Legislative Institutions (consisting of the MPR, DPR, DPD, DPRD) |
| MIKTA | Mexico, Indonesia, South Korea, Turkey, and Australia |
| MPR | Majelis Permusyawaratan Rakyat, or People's Consultative Assembly |
| MRT | Mass Rapid Transit |
| MUI | Majelis Ulama Indonesia, or Indonesian Ulema Council |
| NasDem | Partai Nasional Demokrat, or National Democratic Party |
| NLD | National League for Democracy |
| OIC | Organisation of Islamic Cooperation |
| OOC | Our Ocean Conference |
| PAN | Partai Amanat Nasional, or National Mandate Party |
| Pansus | Panitia Khusus, or Special Committee |
| PBB | Partai Bulan Bintang, or Crescent Moon Party |

| PCA | Permanent Court of Arbitration |
| --- | --- |
| PDI-P | Partai Demokrasi Indonesia — Perjuangan, or Indonesian Democratic Party of Struggle |
| Perindo | Partai Persatuan Indonesia, or United Indonesia Party |
| Perppu | *Peraturan Pemerintah Pengganti Undang-Undang*, or regulation in lieu of law |
| PKB | Partai Kebangkitan Bangsa, or National Awakening Party |
| PKI | Partai Komunis Indonesia, or the Indonesian Communist Party |
| PKS | Partai Keadilan Sejahtera, or Prosperous Justice Party |
| PPP | Partai Persatuan Pembangunan, or United Development Party |
| PTIK | Perguruan Tinggi Ilmu Kepolisian, or Police Staff College |
| PTUN | Pengadilan Tata Usaha Negara, or State Administrative Court |
| RCEP | Regional Comprehensive Economic Partnership |
| SME | Small- and Medium-sized Enterprises |
| SOE | State-Owned Enterprises |
| SOP | Standard Operating Procedure |
| TNI | Tentara Nasional Indonesia, or the Indonesian Military |
| TPP | Trans-Pacific Partnership |
| U.N. | United Nations |
| U.S. | The United States |
| USD | U.S. Dollars |
| UUD | *Undang-Undang Dasar*, or the Constitution |
| WB | World Bank |

# Prologue

# The Beginning of Jokowi's Indonesia and the World

## 1. Introduction

On October 20, 2014, Susilo Bambang Yudhoyono officially stepped down as the sixth President of the Republic of Indonesia after serving his maximum two terms in office. After a decade at the helm, Yudhoyono's place was taken over by Joko 'Jokowi' Widodo who was sworn in as Indonesia's new President for the period 2014–2019 having secured 53.15 percent of the votes during the July 9, 2014 Presidential Elections. The change in personnel at the highest executive office of state naturally raised questions about the likely changes in government policies between that of the outgoing Yudhoyono Government and that of the incoming Widodo Government. This was especially so in the area of foreign policy given that: (a) Yudhoyono was widely lauded for his efforts and achievements on the international stage; and (b) the general perception that Widodo lacks sufficient foreign policy experience and knowledge. Chief among those questions were: Will Indonesia's foreign policy change with the new Government? If so, how will Indonesia's foreign policy change and why? If not, how not and why won't Indonesia's foreign policy change?

It was in this sense that the author undertook a reflective review of the Yudhoyono Years and a prospective look at the next Government, contributing a chapter entitled, 'Indonesia's Foreign Policy: Reflections on the Yudhoyono Years and Prospects for the Next Government' for *THC Review* (Vol. 2/2014), an annual journal produced by the Jakarta-based think tank The Habibie Center. A critical examination of the Yudhoyono Government's foreign policy over the decade he was in charge — spanning from 2004 to 2014 — identified five key lessons/challenges that the newly-elected Widodo would likely have to face. Then, the author decided to once again contribute a chapter to *THC Review* (Vol. 2/2015), this time entitled 'Indonesia's Foreign Policy in Jokowi's First Year: Few Friends, Many Enemies?' This second contribution aimed at evaluating how the new President coped in his first year in office, in particularly *vis-à-vis* the five key lessons/challenges previously identified. Unfortunately, further chapter contributions were not made and there would be no follow-up evaluations of President Widodo's achievements and failures in each of his year in office. The desire to fulfill this gap thus serves as the key rationale behind this book, continuing what the author started back in 2014.

## 2. Explaining the Book's Approach

It also explains the way the book was written, with each chapter not only covering each of Widodo's year in office (with the exception of his fifth and final year due to time constraints) but crucially written soon after each of Widodo's year was completed. As such, the style of the book contrasts somewhat with a political memoir or biography that would usually be written at the end of an individual's career, analyzing a person's achievements and failures from a reflective standpoint, long after events have occurred. The contemporaneous nature of this book thus differs greatly in the sense that President Widodo's achievements and failures are analyzed as they happened, during the actual time of his presidency. There are some advantages and a few drawbacks to such an approach. To coin a phrase from former U.S. Secretary of Defense Donald Rumsfeld,

> 'There are known knowns; there are things we know we know. We also know there are known unknowns; that is to say we know there are some things we do not know. But there are also unknown unknowns — the ones we don't know we don't know.'

In adopting a contemporaneous approach, the book is able to capture all the 'known unknowns' and 'unknown unknowns' that marked each year of the Widodo presidency. On the flipside, it less effectively captures what would now become 'known knowns.' For example, in his first year in office, Widodo lacked a majority in Parliament, with question marks over whether he would be able to push his legislative agenda through the House of Representatives. It was not known back then that by the end of his presidency, a number of political parties would join the ruling coalition to the point that President Widodo would not only command a parliamentary majority but was so emboldened that he, at times, threatened to pass regulations in lieu of law (*Peraturan Pemerintah Pengganti Undang-Undang* or Perppu). Thus, with the book's contemporaneous approach, the chapter covering the President's first year is able to encapsulate the genuine fears and concerns that were present in 2014 that may have been downplayed or altogether omitted if it was written reflectively in 2019.

On the downside, it does mean that undue attention and space was perhaps given to covering certain fears and concerns that ultimately did not transpire. One example would be the rumours of a planned coup against the President that were making the rounds in late-2016 but which, in the end, proved unfounded. Nevertheless, upon considering the advantages and drawbacks outlined above, the author took the view that a contemporaneous approach was the best option — particularly because it allows the reader to trace the ways issues that affected Widodo's presidency developed over time. For example, the developments in Indonesia's relationship with the United States (U.S.) can be traced from the time Jakarta had a special connection with Washington D.C. given the then-U.S. President Barack Obama's childhood in Indonesia, to the understandable uncertainty that surrounded the U.S. Presidential Elections in November 2016, to the stunned disbelief when it became clear Donald J. Trump had won the race, to the outright confusion when the new U.S President listed Indonesia among a list of countries to be investigated for running a trade surplus with the U.S. Each stage is more aptly captured as a result of adopting a contemporaneous approach to the book, whereby each chapter was concluded shortly after each year of Widodo's presidency.

Here, it should be explained that since Widodo was inaugurated on October 20, 2014, each year is counted with reference to that date. In this sense, an event that took place at the beginning of October 2015 would count towards Widodo's first year in office, whilst an event that took place at the end of October 2015 would count towards his second year in office. Some flexibility was permitted but only where it made sense. For example, the results of Widodo's approval ratings that was published on October 23, 2018 was included as part of the President's fourth year in office, even if technically it was already the fifth year. This was justified on the grounds that the survey would have been conducted — and thus measured/covered — Widodo's performance in the backend of his fourth year in office.

Mention should be made regarding the way President Joko Widodo is referred to throughout the book. Whilst the President is popularly referred to as 'Jokowi', the author made the deliberate decision to refer to him by his last name, as is the common international practice as well as out of respect for the office of the presidency (it is also the same reason why Susilo Bambang Yudhoyono is referred to by his last name in the part of this chapter that looks at the key lessons from his presidency). Only in the title of the book itself and the titles of each chapter is the President referred to as 'Jokowi'. For other Indonesian individuals, they were referred to by their full name in order to avoid the confusion caused by the Indonesian media's preference to call people by their first names and the international media's preference to call them by their last names. For example, the book refers to 'Prabowo Subianto' rather than the Indonesian-style 'Pak Prabowo' or the international-style 'Mr. Subianto.' Lastly, with regards to Indonesian words, these are italicized with the exception of state institutions and other important entities such as political parties, following the style of international media.

Now that the book's approach has been sufficiently explained, the rest of the prologue chapter shall proceed to outline the key lessons/challenges identified as a result of a critical examination of the Yudhoyono Government's foreign policy from 2004 to 2014 and serves as the 'Beginning of Jokowi's Indonesia and the World.'[1]

---

[1] To read the critical examination in its entirety, see the chapter 'Indonesia's Foreign Policy: Reflections on the Yudhoyono Years and Prospects for the Next Government' that can be found in Salim, Z. (2014). THC Review — Evaluasi Pemerintahan Presiden Jokowi. Vol. 3/2015 (Jakarta: The Habibie Center).

## 3. Key Lessons from the Yudhoyono Years/Challenges for the New Widodo Government

### 3.1. *Relationship with Parliament*

The Yudhoyono Years showed the importance of building and maintaining good relations between the Government and Parliament, in order for Indonesia to have a foreign policy that was active and assertive. The example of Parliament's anger over the Yudhoyono Government's stance regarding Iran's nuclear program at the U.N. Security Council was indicative of this point. Parliament's strong reaction to Yudhoyono's stance resulted in the Government taking cautious positions in its future foreign policy on the issue. Parliament was also very vocal with its opinions on the ASEAN Charter which it deemed insufficiently pro-democracy. As such, Indonesia was one of the last to ratify the ASEAN Charter which would have undoubtedly resulted in some embarrassment for President Yudhoyono among his ASEAN peers.

Since the *Reformasi* era, Indonesia's Parliament has emerged as a key actor in terms of Indonesia's foreign policy. Crucially it has not been afraid to use its powers. For example in 2008, the House of Representatives refused to accept I Nyan Lin as Myanmar's new ambassador to Indonesia citing the country's poor human rights and democracy record (*The Jakarta Post* 2008, March 8). Underlining the strong influence of the legislative branch on Jakarta's foreign policy, MacIntyre & Ramage (2008) stated that, as 'the Indonesian Government must take into account the views of the Indonesian Parliament, so must other governments seeking to collaborate with Jakarta.'

This was one area where the then-newly elected Government under Widodo was seen to likely face one of its biggest challenges. The coalition of parties that supported the presidential candidacy of Joko Widodo–Jusuf Kalla (PDI-P, Hanura, NasDem, and PKB) commanded just 207 of the total 560 seats in the House of Representatives following the April 9, 2014 legislative elections. That figure represented only 36.96 percent. Meanwhile the coalition of parties that supported the rival presidential candidacy of Prabowo Subianto-Hatta Rajasa commanded a majority with 353 seats or 63.04 percent of the House of Representatives. The situation of a Widodo Government and a Prabowo Subianto-dominated Parliament made likely that the 2014–2019 period would see a difficult Government-Parliament relationship, both in general government policy and specifically over foreign policy.

Indeed, the Prabowo–Hatta coalition signaled its intent to make life difficult for the Widodo Government. The passage of the Revised Law on Legislative Institutions (*Revisi Undang-Undang MPR, DPR, DPD, DPRD* or MD3) — where the Speaker of the House of Representative was no longer automatically chosen from the largest party at the legislative elections (in this case, Widodo's PDI-P) but instead up for a parliamentary vote (thus ensuring that a figure from the majority Prabowo Subianto–Hatta Rajasa coalition took up the role) — was indicative of the difficult dealings the Widodo Government would face from Parliament. Similarly the Prabowo Subianto–Hatta Rajasa coalition promised to form a Special Committee (Panitia Khusus or Pansus) of the House of Representatives to investigate alleged fraud surrounding the July 9, 2014 Presidential Elections in order to undermine the legitimacy of the next Government and consequently any government policy including in the area of foreign affairs.

### 3.2. Maximizing Parliamentary Support versus Commanding an Effective Ruling Coalition

Yudhoyono famously embraced a 'big-tent' cabinet with 20 of his 35 ministers in the United Indonesia Cabinet of 2004–2009 being affiliated to political parties (Liddle & Mujani, 2006). Despite Yudhoyono's initial pledge to form a cabinet dominated by technocrats, his desire to maximize support in Parliament saw Yudhoyono award cabinet positions to a wide array of political parties including those that did not support his presidential candidacy. However, by attempting to maximize parliamentary support, Yudhoyono arguably suffered from an unruly and unwieldy ruling coalition. As Liddle and Mujani (2006) observe, 'The bond between the president and all the legislative parties except his Partai Demokrat was tentative and weak' and, 'The policy agendas and priorities of PKS, PAN, and PBB [parties within the ruling coalition] were often at odds with those of the president' (Liddle & Mujani, 2006).

On several occasions during the Yudhoyono Years, the Government was unable to assert its will over its own ruling coalition. This was most clear when several parties of the ruling coalition voted in favor of interpellation regarding the Yudhoyono Government's stance on Iran's nuclear program at the U.N. Security Council. Demonstrating the 'tentative and weak' position of Yudhoyono *vis-à-vis* his ruling coalition, the then-President was unwilling in 2012 to expel Partai Golkar and PKS from the ruling coalition after they voted against the Government's key proposal to cut fuel subsidies.

As such, a key decision facing the then-new Government under Widodo was whether to maximize parliamentary support at the expense of an unruly and unwieldy ruling coalition. Given that the coalition of parties supporting the presidential candidacy of Joko Widodo–Jusuf Kalla commanded just 36.96 percent of seats in the House of Representatives, the Widodo Government was seen to have no choice other than to embrace a 'big-tent' cabinet like his predecessor in order for government policies (including on foreign affairs) to pass easily through Parliament. However, Widodo had publicly declared his firm commitment that cabinet positions would not be based on transactional politics and that appointments instead be based on merit.

Another point worth observing was Widodo's position within his own PDI-P. If the bond between Yudhoyono and his ruling coalition was 'tentative and weak' with the exception of his own Partai Demokrat — which he founded and serves as chairman — one wondered the bond between Widodo and PDI-P given that Megawati Sukarnoputri remains the party chairwoman. Indeed, there were genuine concerns expressed over the influence Megawati Sukarnoputri may have over the Widodo government and its policies, including in the area of foreign affairs.

## 3.3. *Appointment of Foreign Minister*

Despite Yudhoyono often being lauded for projecting a confident and more outward-looking Indonesia, a critical examination of the Yudhoyono Years instead showed the important role played by Indonesia's then-Foreign Minister Marty Natalegawa. This was obvious in Marty

Natalegawa's fact-finding mission to Myanmar in October 2011, the shuffle diplomacy mission following the outbreak of the Thai-Cambodian conflict in 2011, and the shuffle diplomacy mission following the unprecedented inability of ASEAN Foreign Ministers to issue a joint communiqué due to disagreements over the South China Sea in 2012.

As Connelly (2014, July 21) observed, 'Yudhoyono left much of the heavy lifting to his talented foreign ministers, Hasan Wirajuda and Marty Natalegawa.' Liddle and Mujani (2006) backed this view arguing, 'Yudhoyono appears as a legitimator of the acts of others...rather than a significant player in his own right.' While this is not a criticism of Yudhoyono himself, it nonetheless highlights the importance attached to whoever Widodo would appoint as his foreign minister. A likely option back in 2014 was for Marty Natalegawa to continue in his role as foreign minister. This would have ensured a sense of continuation and stability in very much the same way that Yudhoyono initially asked the then-foreign minister under Megawati Sukarnoputri's presidency, Hasan Wirajuda to carry on. This sense of continuation and stability was seen as all the more crucial given that 2015 marked a significant year for Indonesia's foreign policy with the introduction of the ASEAN Community 2015.

At the same time however, the then-candidate Widodo announced several innovative ideas regarding foreign policy. For example, during a televised presidential candidate debate on June 22, 2014 Widodo pledged that if elected, he would ensure Indonesian ambassadors spent 80 percent of their time marketing Indonesian products overseas (*The Jakarta Post* 2014, June 23). The Joko Widodo–Jusuf Kalla '*visi dan misi*' (or vision and mission) campaign document also pledged to 'realize a free and active foreign policy and strengthen Indonesia's identity as a maritime nation'. As such it was also seen as more likely for Widodo to appoint a new foreign minister that could implement his innovative ideas. As such, it was interesting to note Santikajaya (2014, June 5) who highlighted the important role played by Rizal Sukma — Widodo's foreign policy advisor during the election campaign — who 'should be closely watched as a leading candidate to be the next foreign minister.' Another highly tipped for the job was the then-Deputy Foreign Minister Dino Patti Djalal although his chances was seen as limited having participated in Partai Demokrat's failed convention to find a presidential candidate.

## 3.4. *Translating Rhetoric into Concrete Actions*

The critical examination of the Yudhoyono Years revealed the need to translate rhetoric into concrete action as one of the key lessons/challenges. Indicative of this point was the ASEAN Charter where Yudhoyono had earlier promised a groundbreaking document incorporating Jakarta's democratic and human rights agenda, but was finally forced to accept a severely watered down version. Similarly, Yudhoyono's speeches at several major international conferences were lauded as strong in dramatic rhetoric and idealistic proposals but nevertheless highly unrealistic and driven purely by public relations considerations. The Yudhoyono government was at times left embarrassed when its rhetoric did not align with its actions. Illustrative of this point was Yudhoyono's keynote speech on climate change at the G20 Summit in Pittsburgh which contradicted the government's decision to build 35 coal power plants (Mietzner, 2010; MacIntyre & Ramage, 2008).

As Mietzner (2009) points out, 'While respected in the West as a symbol of a consolidating Muslim democracy, Indonesia has not been able to translate this appreciation into concrete diplomatic weight.' In other words, while the Yudhoyono Government had made the most of talking up its potential and credentials, at times it was not able to match this with concrete action that carry real weight. As such it was interesting to observe whether the Widodo Government would be able to manage this challenge. As touched on earlier, Widodo made much rhetoric about realizing Indonesia's identity as a maritime nation as part of its foreign policy. It remained to be seen in 2014 whether that rhetoric could be translated into concrete action and in what ways the Widodo Government would position itself *vis-à-vis* maritime issues such as the South China Sea, illegal, unregulated and unreported (IUU) fishing, and asylum seekers going to Australia, among others.

## 3.5. *Ensuring Cooperation with External Parties*

A final key lesson/challenge is ensuring the cooperation with external parties. During the Yudhoyono Years, Indonesia proposed a number of good initiatives to external parties but often found an unwillingness to cooperate. For example, Indonesia's proposal to send military observers to the Thai-Cambodian border never materialized due to its final rejection by Thailand, despite Bangkok initially welcoming the idea and informally agreeing to it. Similarly, Jakarta's strong advocacy for a groundbreaking ASEAN Charter incorporating Indonesia's democratic and human rights agenda met resistance from some ASEAN member-states unwilling to depart radically from the status quo, finally resulting in a severely watered down version.

Perhaps the best example of the need to ensure cooperation with external parties was in Indonesia's relationships with major powers in the region. The signing of the Lombok Treaty with Australia was meant to signal closer cooperation across a range of areas, yet senior Indonesian government officials including the President himself found themselves the victims of Australian spying, forcing Jakarta to officially downgrade ties. Similarly, despite the Strategic Partnership Agreement with China in 2005 (which was then upgraded to a Comprehensive Strategic Partnership in 2013), Indonesia has not been able to definitively resolve the uncertainty over Beijing's 'Nine-Dashed Line' claims over the South China Sea, especially the waters surrounding Indonesia's Natuna islands.

Therefore, a challenge back in 2014 for the new Government under Widodo was to ensure that cooperation from external parties was materializing, genuine, and consistent. This was one area where Widodo was seen as possibly excelling given his abilities for persuasive and conciliatory approach to dialogue. In the past Widodo had effectively used this approach to relocate hawkers off the streets of Tanah Abang or move slum dweller from the banks of the Pluit reservoir during his term as Governor of Jakarta. Thus, it was interesting to see whether or not Widodo would be able to apply his persuasive and conciliatory approach to ensure cooperation with external parties on issues of international politics.

## 4. Summary and Conclusion

During the period of 2004–2014, Indonesia's foreign policy grew ever more assertive and active. The Yudhoyono Years saw Jakarta enthusiastically act on its ambitions for a larger Indonesian role in international affairs. Led by an internationalist president, Indonesia notched up a number of foreign policy achievements during the Yudhoyono Years. These include — holding the chairmanship of ASEAN; serving as a non-permanent member of the U.N. Security Council; becoming a member of the G20; playing a greater regional role in ASEAN and the wider Asia-Pacific; playing leading roles in important international conferences; and enhancing its bilateral relations with major powers in the region.

However, a critical reexamination of the Yudhoyono Years revealed a number of shortcomings and failings in Jakarta's attempts to be more assertive and active in its foreign policy. From the critical examination of the Yudhoyono Years, a number of key lessons were identified that would likely be challenges back in 2014 for the next Government under Widodo. Chief among the major challenges for President Widodo were: (1) building and maintaining a good relationship with Parliament; (2) deciding whether to maximize parliamentary support at the expense of an unruly and unwieldy ruling coalition; (3) appointing a foreign minister that can both create a sense of continuation and stability as well as implement Widodo's innovative ideas regarding foreign policy; (4) translate rhetoric into concrete action by transferring Widodo's ability to achieve results at the local and regional level of government onto the national and international stage; and (5) ensure that cooperation with external parties is materializing, genuine and consistent.

Remembering the questions that were raised at the outset of this chapter — will Indonesia's foreign policy change with the new Government? If so, how will Indonesia's foreign policy change and why? If not, how not and why won't Indonesia's foreign policy change? — the answers depend very much on how Widodo managed the five challenges. Overall however, from the reflective review of the Yudhoyono Years and a prospective look at the then-new Widodo Government, it was clear that the past decade were a high point in Indonesia's foreign policy. Certainly the Yudhoyono Years will be remembered for an assertive and active Indonesia in the field of foreign policy. However, due to several shortcomings and failures, missing in this equation is 'effective'. Whilst the fact that Indonesia's foreign policy should be applauded for growing ever more assertive and active, it was somewhat meaningless if it was not always effective. As such, it was greatly hoped that in five (or ten years) time when Indonesians look back on the Widodo Years, Jakarta's foreign policy can be regarded as assertive, active, *and effective.*

Whether this ultimately transpired or not shall be seen in the following chapters.

# References

Connelly, A.L. (2014, July 21). 'Indonesia's Jokowi Eyes Mideast Involvement.' *CNN.* Retrieved from http://edition.cnn.com/2014/07/20/world/asia/indonesia-jokowi-analysis/

*The Jakarta Post* (2008, March 8). 'House rejects new Myanmar Ambassador.' Retrieved from http://www.thejakartapost.com/news/2008/03/07/house-rejects-new-myanmar-ambassador.html

*The Jakarta Post* (2014, June 23). 'Jokowi wins on Prabowo's turf.' Retrieved from http://m.thejakartapost.com/news/2014/06/23/jokowi-wins-prabowo-s-turf.html

Liddle, R.W. and Mujani, S. (2005). 'Indonesia in 2004: The Rise of Susilo Bambang Yudhoyono.' *Asian Survey*, Vol. 45, No. 1 (January/February 2005), pp. 119–126.

MacIntyre, A. and Ramage, D.E. (2008). *Seeing Indonesia as a Normal Country: Implications for Australia* (Barton ACT: Australian Strategic Policy Institute). Retrieved from https://www.aspi.org.au/publications/seeing-indonesia-as-a-normal-country-implications-for-australia/Seeing_Indonesia.pdf

Mietzner, M (2010). 'Indonesia in 2010: Electoral Contestation and Economic Resilience.' *Asian Survey* Vol. 50, Issue 1, pp. 185–194.

Santikajaya, A. (2014, June 5). 'Indonesia: Foreign Policy Under Jokowi and Prabowo.' *The Diplomat.* Retrieved from http://thediplomat.com/2014/06/indonesia-foreign-policy-under-jokowi-and-prabowo/

# Chapter I

# Indonesia's Foreign Policy in Jokowi's First Year: Few Friends, Many Enemies?

## 1. Introduction

A year has passed since the historic accession of Joko 'Jokowi' Widodo to the presidency of the world's third largest democracy.[1] Having secured 53.15 percent of the votes during the July 9, 2014 Presidential Election, there were high expectations on President Widodo to deliver on the promises he made during his campaign. In particular, to realize an Indonesia that was sovereign in its politics, independent in its economy, and distinct in its cultural character.

Despite the high expectations entrusted to President Widodo, there nonetheless remained some doubts about whether or not the new President would be able to deliver. In the area of foreign policy, especially, there were question marks over the direction the new President would take Indonesia. Given that his predecessor, Susilo Bambang Yudhoyono was widely lauded for his efforts and achievements on the international stage,

---

[1] See the Prologue chapter for an explanation of the contemporaneous approach adopted in this book. In short, each chapter covering a particular year of Widodo's presidency was written soon after each of Widodo's year in office was completed. For example, this chapter that covers Widodo's first year was completed soon after October 2015.

some pointed to President Widodo's perceived lack of sufficient foreign policy experience and knowledge. Early indications had suggested President Widodo would not continue his predecessor's 'a million friends and zero enemies' foreign policy approach and a number of observers feared the possibility of a more nationalistic Indonesia dealings with the outside world (Connelly, 2014). The President's strong stance on illegal fishing, uncompromising position on drug smuggling, and perceived indifference to ASEAN gave rise to such fears and has arguably alienated Indonesia with her neighbors — leaving President Widodo with few friends and many enemies (Poole, 2015, September 7).

While a year is too short a time to pass judgment on Indonesia's foreign policy under President Widodo, there has nevertheless been a number of incidents and issues that are worth exploring and may help give some indication as to whether Indonesia's foreign policy has changed with the new Government. It is in this sense that a reflective review of President Widodo's first year in government becomes an appropriate topic to study and serves as the motivation for this chapter, 'Indonesia's Foreign Policy in Jokowi's First Year: Few Friends, Many Enemies?'

## 2. Key Initial Challenges Facing President Widodo

A previous critical examination of the Yudhoyono Years had identified five key lessons or challenges that President Widodo would likely have to face in his first year in office. Namely, these were:

(1) the importance of building and maintaining good relations between the Government and Parliament in order for Indonesia to have a foreign policy that is active and assertive;
(2) deciding between maximizing parliamentary support at the expense of an unruly and unwieldy ruling coalition or maintaining a strong command of the ruling coalition at the risk of limited support in the legislature;
(3) appointing a foreign minister to carry out Jakarta's foreign policy;
(4) translating rhetoric into concrete action; and
(5) ensuring the cooperation with external parties to ensure the successful implementation of Jakarta's foreign policy initiatives.

With a year in office, it is worth observing how President Widodo has met these initial challenges. As such, this chapter shall go through each initial key challenge one-by-one and assess the strengths and weaknesses of the President's approach to resolve them.

## 2.1. *Challenge No. 1: Relationship with Parliament*

Upon assuming the Presidency, Widodo was faced with a Parliament where the composition of the 560-seat House of Representative was unfavorable to him. The coalition of parties that had supported Widodo's presidential candidate, *Koalisi Indonesia Hebat* (KIH, or Awesome Indonesian Coalition) numbered only 207 seats, whilst the coalition of parties that supported his rival, Prabowo Subianto, numbered 353 seats. In percentage terms, the President could only rely on a minority 36.96 percent of the House to support his policies, while a majority 63.04 percent of the House was part of the *Koalisi Merah Putih* (KMP, or Red and White Coalition) that had opposed his presidential candidacy.

Earlier on, there was a very real concern that the situation of a Widodo Government and a Prabowo Subianto-dominated Parliament would signal a difficult Government–Parliament relationship for the period 2014–2019. This was not only for government policy in general but also specifically over foreign policy. Initial indications suggested that the opposition KMP intended to make life difficult for the new Government. Having forced through the Revised Law on Legislative Institutions (*Revisi Undang-Undang MPR, DPR, DPD, DPRD*, or MD3), the opposition KMP secured for themselves the position of the Speaker of the House of Representatives, as well as other House Leadership positions (*The Jakarta Post* 2014, October 13). Despite being the largest party in Parliament, Widodo's PDI-P was shut out from the House Leadership.

The KMP also threatened to form a Special Committee (Panitia Khusus, or Pansus) of the House of Representatives to investigate alleged fraud surrounding the July 9, 2014 Presidential Elections (*The Economist* 2014, September 7). This was seen as an effort to undermine the legitimacy of the Widodo Government and consequently any government policy including in the area of foreign affairs.

However, only a few months after the swearing in of President Widodo, the KMP has arguably fallen into disarray. Two parties within the KMP have been split into rival factions whilst another has apparently left to join the ruling KIH coalition. Golkar, the second largest party in KMP with 91 seats in the House, has been divided into two camps, with the leaders of each camp claiming to be the rightful party chairman. A party congress held in December 2014 in Bali re-elected Aburizal Bakrie to lead Golkar; however, a rival party congress held in Ancol just days later elected Agung Laksono as the new party chairman. Complicating the matter is the fact that the leaders of the two camps crucially differ over the direction they wish to take Golkar *vis-à-vis* KIH and KMP. Aburizal Bakrie wishes for the party to remain with KMP — indeed as party chairman from 2009–2015, it was on his decision that Golkar backed the candidacy of Prabowo Subianto — whereas Agung Laksono intends to bring the party within the KIH fold. To date, the leadership of Golkar remains unresolved, with the Ministry of Law and Human Rights recognizing the results of the Ancol party congress, only for the Jakarta State Administration Court (Pengadilan Tata Usaha Negara, or PTUN) to annul the decision and rule Aburizal Bakrie as interim chairman. As a result of the rift, the KMP is unable to count on the support of its second largest party to oppose the Government.

A similar fate has affected another party within the KMP, PPP. With 39 seats in the House of Representatives, the party is divided between the rival leaderships of Djan Faridz and Muhammad Romahurmuziy, who both claim to be the legitimate party chairman. The former was the chosen successor appointed by previous party chairman, Suryadharma Ali, who himself had made the original decision to join the KMP. Meanwhile, the latter has stated his intention for PPP to join President Widodo's KIH. Indeed, it was based on Muhammad Romahurmuziy's pro-Government stance that a PPP cadre, Lukman Hakim Saifuddin, was appointed as Religious Affairs Minister by President Widodo. Like the fate of Golkar, a solution to the leadership rift is unclear, with the Ministry of Law and Human Rights recognizing the party chairmanship of Muhammad Romahurmuziy, only for PTUN to annul the decision. Curiously, PTUN did not declare who was the rightful party chairman after annulling the

Ministry of Law and Human Rights' decision, leaving PPP in a state of limbo.

In addition to the divisions that beset the KMP's Golkar and PPP is the decision of PAN to leave the opposition coalition and instead join KIH (*The Jakarta Post* 2015, September 2). Announced in September 2015, the decision is seen as significant, not least because with 48 House seats, the move tips the legislative balance in favor of President Widodo's coalition. Curiously, PAN Secretary-General, Eddy Soeparno, argued that PAN was merely supporting the Government, and that this did not necessarily mean the party had either left KMP or had joined KIH (Stefani, 2015, September 12). Nevertheless, the decision is significant given that Prabowo's running mate during the 2014 Presidential Election was then-PAN party chairman Hatta Rajasa. Arguably, PAN's decision to now support the Widodo Government symbolizes how far the KMP — unable to present a united bloc capable of opposing the Government — has fallen apart.

Despite the above, it could be argued that Parliament has only on a very few occasions strongly differed with President Widodo in the area of foreign policy. Certainly, there have been no incidents between President Widodo and the House akin to those that marked his predecessor, Susilo Bambang Yudhoyono's two terms in office. Indeed, on a number of occasions, Parliament reacted angrily to Susilo Bambang Yudhoyono's foreign policy (Almuttaqi, 2014). Parliament has for the most part supported President Widodo's assertive stance on addressing illegal fishing by foreign vessels and the 'state of drugs emergency' brought about by foreign smugglers, to name a few examples. That is not to say that Parliament is not willing to flex its muscles. Recently, the House Speaker, Setya Novanto, has found himself in a controversy after appearing at a campaign rally for the U.S. Republican presidential candidate Donald Trump, with the House Ethics Council demanding the Speaker explain his actions.

Overall, the main fear *vis-à-vis* the key initial challenge of the President's relationship with Parliament — that Widodo would face a hostile Parliament — has not been realized since firstly, the KMP has largely disintegrated; and secondly, Parliament has mostly not made much ventures in the area of Indonesia's foreign policy.

## 2.2. Challenge No. 2: Maximizing Parliamentary Support versus Commanding an Effective Ruling Coalition

In the run up to announcing his Cabinet, President Widodo had publicly declared cabinet positions would not be based on transactional politics and that instead, appointments would be based on merit. President Widodo had on a number of occasions promised to promote technocrats to his Cabinet and limit the number of politicians. This was seen as a break away from the criticisms levelled at his predecessor, Susilo Bambang Yudhoyono, who famously embraced a 'big-tent' cabinet with 20 of his 35 ministers in the United Indonesia Cabinet (*Kabinet Indonesia Bersatu*) of 2004–2009 being affiliated to political parties (Liddle & Mujani, 2006). By selecting a technocratic cabinet line-up, it was hoped that the President would not be afflicted by the problems faced by Susilo Bambang Yudhoyono who, at times, struggled with an unruly and unwieldy ruling coalition. The downside of a technocratic cabinet, however, was that his support in Parliament would likely be limited, which was all the more significant, given the KIH was a minority in the House of Representatives. President Widodo dispelled such fears stating,

'It's not a problem to have a minority. I had a similar experience in Jakarta and it was not a problem to get things done'. (Kapoor, 2014, October 7).

PDI-P Deputy Secretary, Hasto Kristiyano, added that the President would 'hold on to their promise in clinging on people's mandate and avoiding transactional politics' (*Tempo* 2014, October 3).

Demonstrating his commitment for a more professional Cabinet, President Widodo took the unprecedented decision to ask the Corruption Eradication Commission (Komisi Pemberantasan Korupsi, or KPK) to vet his proposed appointments. Indeed, eight candidates failed the KPK's vetting process due to graft concerns. Symbolically, the Cabinet was also given the name *Kabinet Kerja*, or 'Working Cabinet', to signify the President's intent that his Government would focus on getting to the task at hand rather than being distracted with political interests.

In reality, however, when Widodo's 'Working Cabinet' was announced, it drew mixed reactions with nearly half of positions going to political allies (Aspinall, 2014, November 1). In a Cabinet of 34 positions, 18 went to technocrats, with the remaining 16 going to political parties that backed Widodo's presidential campaigns. On the one hand, the appointment of eight women in the Cabinet drew plaudits as too his appointment of Indonesia's first ever female foreign minister, Retno Marsudi. On the other hand, the decision to appoint several controversial individuals seen as close to PDI-P's chairwoman, Megawati Sukarnoputri, was questioned. These included Ryamizard Ryacudu as Defense Minister, Rini Soemarno (Megawati Sukarnoputri's confidante) as State Enterprises Minister, and Puan Maharani (Megawati' Sukarnoputri's daughter) as Coordinating Minister for Human Development and Culture (Aspinall, 2014, November 1). According to one political observer, the Cabinet was 'overshadowed be political interests' whilst another described it as a 'Cabinet of compromise' (*BBC* 2014, October 27).

Tellingly, within less than a year, President Widodo reshuffled his Cabinet due to poor performance, especially in the economics sector. The President replaced six ministers in August 2015, with a number of key economic positions going to experienced technocrats. Whilst the reshuffle was hailed, some noted the fact that out of all the four Coordinating Ministers, only Puan Maharani remained unchanged, despite showing little major achievements (Kandi, 2015, August 12).

Much attention has also been paid to the influence Megawati Sukarnoputri holds over the President. It was noted by Liddle & Mujani (2006) that Susilo Bambang Yudhoyono's presidency was sometimes hindered because 'the bond between the president and all the legislative parties except his Partai Demokrat was tentative and weak.' Given this, it was speculated that if the bond between Susilo Bambang Yudhoyono and his ruling coalition was 'tentative and weak' with the exception of his own party, one wonders the bond between Widodo and PDI-P. This was especially so given that Megawati Sukarnoputri remains the party chairwoman.

Megawati has done little to dispel the notion that the President is beholden to her. On April 2015, Megawati delivered a speech at the fourth PDI-P national congress in what some described as 'her 'I am the boss speech'' (Rachman & Otto, 2015, April 11). With Widodo in attendance, Megawati Sukarnoputri reminded the President that he was merely a party cadre that should enforce the party's policy line. Megawati Sukarnoputri added that it was she who gave Widodo the mandate to run for President. In her closing speech at the national congress, Megawati Sukarnoputri again reminded that all party cadres in the executive and legislative branch — including the President — were merely an extension of the party and described them as *petugas partai* or party officials. She warned that if anyone did not want to be a *petugas partai*, they could simply leave the party (*Kompas* 2014, April 11).

In many ways, the PDI-P has acted as the main opposition to the President. A senior managing editor at *The Jakarta Post* wrote,

> 'Indonesians also felt frustrated because the PDI-P often acted in opposition to Jokowi's plans, despite the fact that the PDI-P leads the ruling Great Indonesia Coalition. PDI-P politicians in the House of Representatives seem eager to disrupt the government's activities.' (Purba 2015, March 29).

One explanation for PDI-P's antagonism with the President is the feeling that Widodo has not given the party enough positions in the Cabinet despite being the largest party in the House of Representatives, as well as the lack of influence PDI-P officials have in Widodo's inner circle. Arguably, the struggles between the President and his coalition — most notably the PDI-P — have spilled into the area of foreign affairs. For example, it was notable that during the 60th Asian-African Conference Commemoration, Megawati Sukarnoputri joined President Widodo for a re-enactment of the historical Bandung walk with foreign leaders. As such, the concerns expressed over the influence Megawati Sukarnoputri may have over the Widodo government and its policies, including in the area of foreign affairs, appears to be true.

## 2.3. *Challenge No. 3: Appointment of Foreign Minister*

The third key initial challenge facing President Widodo was deciding on who to appoint as foreign minister. While his predecessor Susilo Bambang Yudhoyono won plaudits for his internationalist outlook, it could be argued that his foreign minister, Marty Natalegawa, deserved a lot of credit for Indonesia's foreign policy achievements. Marty Natalegawa's fact-finding mission to Myanmar in October 2011, the shuffle diplomacy mission following the outbreak of the Thai-Cambodian conflict in 2011, and the shuffle diplomacy mission following the unprecedented inability of ASEAN Foreign Ministers to issue a joint communiqué in 2012, demonstrated the crucial role played by the then-foreign minister. It also served to highlight the importance attached to whoever Widodo appoints as his foreign minister.

It was initially predicted that President Widodo would opt for Marty Natalegawa to continue in his role. In August 2014, the *Jakarta Globe* newspaper ran with the headline, 'For Indonesia's Foreign Minister Post, Best Man May Already Be in the Job' (Dahal & Busyra, 2014, August 14). One observer argued,

> 'If they look at his [Marty's] track record — the achievements he's made as foreign minister — they would know better than to use their own people and let him go'. (Dahal & Busyra 2014, August 14).

With 2015 marking a crucial year for Indonesia's foreign policy, especially with the introduction of the ASEAN Community 2015, it was felt that re-appointing Marty Natalegawa would ensure a sense of continuation and stability in very much the same way that Susilo Bambang Yudhoyono initially asked the then-foreign minister in Megawati's Government, Hasan Wirajuda, to carry on. Other names that came under speculation were Rizal Sukma, Widodo's foreign policy advisor during the election campaign, and then-Deputy Foreign Minister Dino Patti Djalal.

Instead, President Widodo announced the appointment of Retno Marsudi, who was then the Indonesian Ambassador to the Netherlands, as his foreign minister. As was alluded to before, the appointment of Retno Marsudi was significant as she became the country's first female Foreign Minister. However, Retno Marsudi's appointment was not only based on her gender. In addition to serving as Indonesia's ambassador to the Netherlands, Retno Marsudi had also been the Indonesian ambassador to Norway and Iceland. She also held the positions of Director for Europe and America, Western European Director, and General Director for

America and Europe at the Foreign Ministry. In this sense, by appointing a figure from within the Foreign Ministry, President Widodo was sending a message of continuity in terms of Indonesia's foreign policy.

While Retno Marsudi does not have the same charisma or profile as Natalegawa, she has nonetheless impressed with her handling of certain foreign policy issues. These include the Rohingya migrant boat crisis, the negative response to Jakarta's strong policy of sinking foreign vessels caught illegally fishing in Indonesian waters, and Australia's anger at the execution of two of their nationals for drug smuggling, among others. Indeed, Australia, along with Brazil, and the Netherlands withdrew their respective ambassadors to demonstrate their anger, while French President Francois Hollande warned of diplomatic 'consequences' (Chrisafis, 2015, April 29). Meanwhile, Brazilian President Dilma Rousseff showed her displeasure by refusing to receive the credentials of the new Indonesian Ambassador to Brazil, Toto Riyanto (*Reuters* 2015, February 21). Indeed, 2015 has proven to be a difficult period for Indonesia's foreign relations.

In the area of protecting Indonesians abroad, Foreign Minister Retno Marsudi explained that 88,000 citizens had been assisted by the Foreign Ministry. These include 2,000 citizens who were evacuated from conflict areas, and a further 41 Indonesians who were freed from the death sentence in other countries (*Jakarta Globe* 2015, October 22). The fact that Foreign Minister Retno Marsudi kept her position after President Widodo reshuffled his cabinet in August 2015 suggests her performance has been satisfactory despite this difficult period. It should also be noted that unlike Marty Natalegawa, there has so far been no internal grumblings within the Foreign Ministry itself about Retno Marsudi's leadership. Former Indonesian ambassador to Switzerland, Djoko Susilo (2014, August 19), openly criticized Natalegawa in a *The Jakarta Post* opinion article, in which he blamed the then-foreign minister for '[t]he death of reforms in the foreign ministry.' To date, there have been no such open criticisms of Retno Marsudi from either within or outside the Foreign Ministry.

In her first Annual Press Statement, Foreign Minister Retno Marsudi reconfirmed Indonesia's commitment to the *"bebas-aktif"* (or free and active) foreign policy concept and that, '[i]n accordance with our constitutional mandate, Indonesia will continue to contribute and play an important role in safeguarding world peace and security' (Ministry of Foreign Affairs, Republic of Indonesia, 2015 January 8).

Describing Indonesia '[a]s a middle power country, with a population of about 250 million, as the world's third largest democracy, as the country with the largest Muslim population, as the largest ASEAN country and as a G-20 member', it was declared that Indonesia would continue to play a role in the regional and global environment (Ministry of Foreign Affairs, Republic of Indonesia, 2015 January 8).

Indeed, Foreign Minister Retno Marsudi dismissed any idea that Jakarta would neglect its responsibilities to the world and focus more on domestic concerns. She pointed to the fact that in the first two months of the new Government alone, Indonesia had participated in 12 international summits, and that President Widodo had held meetings with 21 of his counterparts (Ministry of Foreign Affairs, Republic of Indonesia, 2015, January 8).

With regards to ASEAN, despite declaring the regional organization as *a* priority in Indonesia's foreign policy, it was notable that ASEAN was no longer *the* priority. Traditionally, ASEAN was regarded as *the* cornerstone of Jakarta's foreign policy, yet it was notable that the word 'cornerstone' itself was omitted in Retno Marsudi's Annual Press Statement. Indeed, the Foreign Minister's Statement went on to detail Indonesia's foreign policy engagement in areas beyond ASEAN, most notably the South Pacific and also Palestine.

Overall though, President Widodo's appointment of Retno Marsudi as Indonesia's foreign minister appears to have been a good decision, with Indonesia managing to navigate its way through a difficult period.

## 2.4. *Challenge No. 4: Translating Rhetoric into Concrete Actions*

The fourth key initial challenge facing President Widodo was translating rhetoric into concrete action. At times, his predecessor Susilo Bambang Yudhoyono had failed to do just that with several major speeches at international conferences being criticized for being strong in dramatic rhetoric and idealistic proposals but nevertheless highly unrealistic (Mietzner, 2010; MacIntyre & Ramage, 2008). As one expert pointed out, '[w]hile respected in the West as a symbol of a consolidating Muslim democracy, Indonesia has not been able to translate this appreciation into concrete diplomatic weight' (Mietzner, 2009). In the area of foreign policy, President Widodo had announced a number of innovative ideas. These included the pledge that Indonesian ambassadors should spend 80 percent of their time marketing Indonesian products overseas (*The Jakarta Post*, 2014, June 23). President Widodo also promised to realise Indonesia's identity as a maritime nation and would position the country as the World's Maritime Fulcrum. As stated by the President in his Inauguration Address,

> 'The oceans, seas, straits and bays are our future. We have too long turned our backs on the seas, turned out backs on the oceans, turned our backs on the straits and the bays' (Hermawan, 2014, October 20).

Widodo continued by calling on Indonesians to remember the Javanese maxim, '*Jalesveva Jayamahe*' ('In the Seas, We will be Victorious'). Underscoring the new Government's commitment to maritime priorities, Widodo ended his speech by metaphorically portraying Indonesia as a ship, and describing himself as its captain that, together with the people, would sail towards Greater Indonesia.

President Widodo went on to outline his World Maritime Fulcrum initiative to a global audience when he spoke at the 25th ASEAN Summit in Naypyidaw on November 12, 2014. During his speech, President Widodo stressed that regional prosperity and peace would be determined by how ASEAN countries worked together and manage the seas. He went on to state,

> 'Indonesia hopes that sources of conflict at sea — such as illegal fishing, territorial violations, smuggling and territorial disputes — can be overcome through genuine cooperation' (Sekretariat Kabinet Republik Indonesia, 2014, November 12).

The commitment to Indonesia's waters would appear to mark a break from previous Indonesian governments that have tended to neglect the maritime domain and focused more on the land domain. However, one year into his presidency, the rhetoric of a World Maritime Fulcrum has yet to be implemented into anything concrete beyond the high profile sinking of foreign vessels conducting illegal fishing in Indonesian waters. To date, there has been no blueprint or government white paper produced that provides more details about the initiative (Manggala, 2015, March 22).

President Widodo has also made much rhetoric about making Indonesia more open to foreign investors. At the APEC CEO Summit 2014 that was held in Beijing on November 10, the President called on business leaders to invest in Indonesia. In a well-received speech, President Widodo told the audience frankly, '[w]e are waiting for you to come to Indonesia. We are waiting for you to invest in Indonesia' (*Jakarta Globe* 2014, November 11). President Widodo has made similar calls on his other overseas visits such as to Japan and China.

Despite this rhetoric, the Government has, on a number of occasions, introduced policies that have been criticized as economic nationalistic. These include a requirement for foreigners to be able to speak Bahasa Indonesia in order to receive a permit to work or stay in the country, as well as the sudden announcement in July 2015 that Indonesia would be cutting its beef import from Australia by a massive 80 percent, as part of the Government's drive for 'food sovereignty' (Otto & Sentana, 2015, April 1; Medhora, 2015, July 14). Exacerbating the situation is the tendency of the Government to reverse its decisions, serving only to create uncertainty among foreign investors (Rahadiana & Purnomo, 2015, July 8). For example, the language requirement was quickly dropped, and the Government requested 50,000 Australian cattle only a few weeks after it had decided to cut demand. In March 2015, the Government expanded visa-free policies to 30 countries, only for it to be scrapped a few days later after warnings that it would be in violation of the Immigration Law (Natahadibrata, 2015, March 23).

Perhaps most demonstrative of President Widodo's struggle to translate rhetoric into concrete action was with the project to build Indonesia's first high-speed railway. Connecting Jakarta with Bandung, the project saw Indonesia invite China and Japan to compete for the contract. As recently as July 2015, President Widodo had stressed the importance of building a high-speed railway. He explained, '[t]rains are a mode of transportation that is efficient, reliable and cheap. That's why its development must be prioritised...And for that, the development of an intercity high-speed railway system must start immediately' (*Today Online* 2015, July 14).

However, after much speculation over whether China or Japan had won the contract, the Government announced its decision to scrap altogether the plans to build a high-speed railway, claiming the short distance between Jakarta and Bandung meant it was unlikely a train would ever reach such high speeds. To the dismay of Beijing and Tokyo, the Government instead called on the two to submit proposals for a medium-speed railway instead. Confusingly, a few weeks later, it was announced that the plans for a high-speed railway was back on and that China had won the contract. In response to the Government's inconsistency, Japan's Chief Cabinet Secretary Yoshihide Suga described the decision as both 'extremely regrettable' and 'difficult to understand' (*The Japan Times* 2015, September 30).

One area where President Widodo has been firm on has been in the Government's hard stance on drugs. Describing Indonesia as facing a 'state of drugs emergency', the President has refused to grant clemency to drug offenders facing the death penalty. This was despite various appeals made by foreign governments such as Australia, Brazil, France, and the Netherlands to save their citizens from death row, and the negative impact their executions had on Indonesia's bilateral relations with the aforementioned country. Justifying his uncompromising position, the President stated '[i]n total about 18,000 die every year due to illegal drug consumption' averaging 40–50 deaths each day (Endi, 2015, January 20). The Government has further defended its decision to execute the drug traffickers, describing it as an 'important shock therapy', and calling on other nations to respect its national laws (*The Guardian* 2014, December 14).

Nevertheless, President Widodo has repeatedly failed to translate his rhetoric on various key foreign policy initiatives into concrete action, having on numerous occasions reversed on earlier decisions. While this is to be expected from a new leader in his first year in office, it nonetheless serves as useful homework for President Widodo's second year.

## 2.5. Challenge No. 5: Ensuring Cooperation with External Parties

The final key initial challenge facing the new president was ensuring cooperation with external parties. Widodo's predecessor, Susilo Bambang Yudhoyono, had previously proposed a number of good initiatives during his two terms to external parties but often found an unwillingness to cooperate from the other side. For example, Jakarta's strong advocacy for a groundbreaking ASEAN Charter incorporating Indonesia's democratic and human rights agenda met with resistance from some ASEAN member-states unwilling to depart radically from the status quo — resulting in a severely watered-down version. As noted earlier, President Widodo had announced a number of innovative ideas of his own that would require the cooperation of external parties to ensure their success. In particular is Widodo's World Maritime Fulcrum initiative, which the President had previously promoted to a global audience at the 25th ASEAN Summit in Naypyidaw on November 12, 2014. While the initiative has yet to be developed further via a blueprint or white paper, there have been some actions taken by the Government. Most notably is Indonesia's high profile sinking of foreign vessels conducting illegal fishing in Indonesian waters. The first sinking of foreign vessels was carried out on December 5, 2015 and saw three Vietnamese boats blown up by the Indonesian Navy off Riau Island. More recently in the run-up to Indonesia's 70th Independence Day celebrations, it was announced that the Government would sink 70 foreign vessels, although on the day itself, only 34 were destroyed. To date, foreign vessels from China, Malaysia, Papua New Guinea, the Philippines, Thailand, and Vietnam have been the target of President Widodo's hard stance on illegal fishing. Claiming that Indonesia loses IDR 300 trillion each year from illegal fishing, President Widodo has put the issue high up on his agenda (Widhiarto, 2014, November 18). As recently as October 2015, President Widodo announced the formation of a special task force to combat illegal fishing via Presidential Decree No 115/2015. Significantly, the new task force will have the authority to sink any foreign vessels caught fishing illegally in Indonesian territory without having to undergo prosecution in a court of law.

However, given the international element of illegal fishing, it could be argued that any effort to address the issue requires the cooperation of neighboring countries. Unfortunately, President Widodo's stance appears to have angered countries in the region. Following the sinking of two Thai fishing vessels on December 28, an editorial in the *Bangkok Post* (2015, January 5) strongly criticized Indonesia's 'outrageous acts' and warned, 'Jakarta should know that such aggressively destructive action is unwelcome, undiplomatic and frankly unfriendly towards its ASEAN partner.' A prominent Malaysian observer, Farish Noor (2014, December 15) criticized President Widodo's hardline stance as 'a demonstration of power in terms that seem harsh, over-the-top, and contrary to the Asean spirit of compromise and dialogue.' Meanwhile, a spokesperson for Vietnam's Foreign Ministry expressed Hanoi's deep concern and added that Vietnam had sent a diplomatic note to Indonesia reminding Jakarta to 'pay attention to the strategic partnership of the two countries while dealing with such Vietnamese fishermen' (*Tuoi Tre News* 2015, August 20).

As such, while addressing illegal fishing is high on the agenda of President Widodo, Indonesia has not been able to find the cooperation of external parties, instead drawing their ire. This is unfortunate, given that Widodo's skills at persuasion and conciliatory approach were well regarded prior to becoming President. As the Governor of Jakarta, Widodo had effectively used his persuasive skills to relocate hawkers off the streets of Tanah Abang or move slum dweller from the banks of the Pluit reservoir. However, from the above, it would appear that President Widodo has been unable to apply his persuasive and conciliatory approach to ensure cooperation with external parties on issues of international politics.

## 3. Summary and Conclusion

Upon the accession of Widodo as the seventh President of the Republic of Indonesia, there were natural question marks about the implications the new leader would have on government policy. These question marks were fuelled not only by the inherent uncertainty that exists during any change in personnel at the highest executive office in the Republic, but more so because of President Widodo's status as a political outsider with no connections to the traditional political, military, and/or big business elites.

This was especially true in the area of foreign policy given that his predecessor, Susilo Bambang Yudhoyono had been widely lauded for his efforts and achievements on the international stage and given Widodo's perceived lack of sufficient foreign policy experience and knowledge. The President's strong stance on illegal fishing, uncompromising position on drug smuggling, and perceived indifference to ASEAN have demonstrated clearly that the new Government would not continue the previous 'a million friends and zero enemies' foreign policy approach. Indeed, it could be argued that the new Government's approach has alienated Indonesia with her neighbors, leaving President Widodo with few friends and many enemies.

President Widodo undoubtedly faced enormous challenges in his first year in office. Based on a previous critical examination of his predecessor, Susilo Bambang Yudhoyono's decade in office, five key initial challenges were identified. Namely: (1) building and maintaining good relations between the Government and Parliament; (2) deciding between maximizing parliamentary support at the expense of an unruly and unwieldy ruling coalition or maintaining a strong command of the ruling coalition at the risk of limited support in the legislature; (3) appointing a foreign minister to carry out Jakarta's foreign policy; (4) translating rhetoric into concrete action; and (5) ensuring the cooperation with external parties to ensure the successful implementation of Jakarta's foreign policy initiatives.

With regards to the first key initial challenge, it was shown that while there were initial fears that President Widodo would face a hostile Parliament controlled by a coalition favoring his rival Prabowo Subianto, in reality, the opposition KMP has largely disintegrated. Two parties within the KMP were split apart by internal rifts and another opted to join the ruling coalition. At the same time, Parliament has mostly made little ventures in the area of Indonesia's foreign policy and for the most part supported President Widodo's assertive stance on issues such as addressing illegal fishing by foreign vessels and the 'state of drugs emergency' brought about by foreign smugglers.

In terms of the second key initial challenge, it was shown that despite promising a Cabinet that would see more technocrats and professionals take up ministerial positions, President Widodo was unable to avoid the transactional politics that had marked the cabinet of his predecessor. The "Working Cabinet" announced by President Widodo drew mixed reactions with nearly half of positions going to political allies. Widodo's inclusion of individuals seen as close to PDI-P's chairwoman, Megawati Sukarnoputri, disappointed many, and saw the President's Cabinet criticized as 'overshadowed by political interests.' Furthermore, the concern that Megawati Sukarnoputri would have a strong say over the

Widodo Government and its policies, appear to be true. Certainly, Megawati Sukarnoputri has done little to dispel the notion that the President is beholden to her and, in many ways, the PDI-P has acted as the main opposition to the President.

The third key initial challenge facing President Widodo was deciding on who to appoint as foreign minister. It was shown that Widodo decided against continuing the service of the highly regarded Marty Natalegawa, instead appointing Retno Marsudi, who was then the Indonesian Ambassador to the Netherlands, as his foreign minister. This move was significant as she became the country's first female foreign minister. By appointing a career diplomat, it was argued that President Widodo was sending a message of continuity in terms of Indonesia's foreign policy. Moreover, while Retno Marsudi does not have the same charisma or profile as Natalegawa, she has nonetheless impressed with her handling of certain foreign policy issues and has managed to navigate Indonesia through a difficult period in its foreign relations with a number of countries angered by Jakarta's strong stance on drug executions, illegal fishing, and so forth.

With regards to the fourth key initial challenge, it was argued that President Widodo has repeatedly failed to translate his rhetoric on various key foreign policy initiatives into concrete action, having on numerous occasions reversed earlier decisions. Demonstrative of this is the fact that President Widodo's World Maritime Fulcrum initiative has yet to been developed further into a blueprint or white paper. At the same time, while President Widodo has often urged foreign investors to invest in Indonesia on his trips abroad, the Government has often introduced policies seen as discouraging foreign investment. Most illustrative of President Widodo's struggle to translate rhetoric into concrete action was with the project to build Indonesia's first high-speed railway, which saw the Government give conflicting messages about whether China or Japan would be granted a contract for the project.

Lastly, in terms of the fifth key initial challenge, President Widodo has not been able to find the cooperation of external parties, and in the case of the Government's efforts to address illegal fishing by foreign vessels in Indonesian waters, Widodo has instead drawn their ire. The President's approach of sinking foreign vessels has attracted criticisms and warnings from abroad, and Widodo has not been able to employ the persuasive skills and conciliatory approach that he used as the Governor of Jakarta to ensure cooperation with external parties on issues of international politics.

Having gone through each initial key challenge one-by-one and assessing the strengths and weaknesses of the President's approach to resolve them, it can be argued that the various incidents and issues raised above have given some indication *vis-à-vis* Indonesia's foreign policy under the new Government. A running theme that appears to be present in each of the key initial challenges is how President Widodo and Indonesia have emerged with few friends and many enemies — a significant departure from Yudhoyono's 'a million friends and zero enemies' outlook.

Domestically, President Widodo initially had few friends in Parliament and whilst his 'enemies' in the KMP have largely disintegrated into ineffectiveness, this was largely not of the President's doing. Curiously, the President's friends in PDI-P have instead emerged as his biggest opponents, acting as obstacles to his policies. Internationally, President Widodo's 'state of drugs emergency' and 'state of illegal fishing emergency' naturally suggest 'enemies' in the form of drug smugglers and illegal fishers. Unfortunately, the President's strong stance has unnecessarily threatened to create 'enemies' with other governments in the region that have taken acts such as withdrawing ambassadors, warning of diplomatic 'consequences', and refusing to accept the credentials of Indonesian representatives. If in 2009, Yudhoyono had argued that 'Indonesia is facing a strategic environment where no country perceives Indonesia as an enemy and there is no country which Indonesia considers an enemy', it could be argued that the present strategic environment today is very much different.

In this regard, President Widodo's first year in office appears to be a step backwards in terms of foreign policy. This view is reinforced if one were to consider the argument that while the Yudhoyono era saw a high point in Indonesia's foreign policy and will be remembered for an assertive and active Indonesia in the field of foreign policy, missing in this equation was 'effective'. It was greatly hoped that in the five (or 10) years that President Widodo leads the country, Indonesians would be able to look back on the Widodo Years, and regard his foreign policy as assertive, active, and *effective*. Based on Widodo's first year in office, it would seem the goal of an assertive, active, and effective foreign policy is a long way from realization.

# References

Almuttaqi, A.I. (2014). 'Indonesia's Foreign Policy: Reflections on the Yudhoyono Years and Prospects for the Next Government' in Salim, Z. (2014). *THC Review — Indonesia Pasca Peta Demokrasi 2014*, Vol. 2/2014 (Jakarta: The Habibie Center).

Aspinall, E. (2014, November 1). 'Close enough not good enough for Jokowi's cabinet picks.' *East Asia Forum.* Retrieved from: http://www.eastasiaforum. org/2014/11/01/close-enough-not-good-enough-for-jokowis-cabinet-picks/

*Bangkok Post* (2015, January 5). 'Indonesia is wrong.' Retrieved from: http://m. bangkokpost.com/opinion/454323

*BBC* (2014, October 27). 'Indonesia's new cabinet sparks mixed reaction.' Retrieved from: http://www.bbc.com/news/world-asia-29782675

Chrisafis, A. (2015, April 29). 'France increases diplomatic efforts to save man from execution in Indonesia.' *The Guardian.* Retrieved from: http://www. theguardian.com/world/2015/apr/29/france-increases-diplomatic-efforts-to-save-man-from-execution-in-indonesia

Connelly, A.L. (2014). 'Indonesian Foreign Policy under President Jokowi.' Retrieved from: http://www.lowyinstitute.org/files/indonesian-foreign-policy-under-president-jokowi_0.pdf

Dahal, L. and Busyra, V.A.D. (2014, August 14). 'For Indonesia's Foreign Minister Post, Best Man May Already Be in the Job.' *Jakarta Globe.* Retrieved from: http://jakartaglobe.beritasatu.com/news/indonesias-foreign-minister-post-best-man-may-already-job/

*The Economist* (2014, September 7). 'Blocking the Winner'. Retrieved from: http://www.economist.com/blogs/banyan/2014/09/indonesian-politics

Endi, S. (2015, January 20). 'Jokowi reminds RI of state emergency regarding drugs.' *The Jakarta Post.* Retrieved from: http://www.thejakartapost.com/news/2015/01/20/jokowi-reminds-ri-state-emergency-regarding-drugs.html

*The Guardian* (2014, December 14). 'Bali Nine: Indonesian president rules out clemency for inmates on death row.' Retrieved from: http://www.theguardian. com/world/2014/dec/10/bali-nine-indonesian-president-rules-out-clemency

Hermawan, B. (2014, October 20). 'Ini Isi Pidato Kenegaraan Pertama Presiden Joko Widodo.' *Republika.* Retrieved from: http://www.republika.co.id/berita/ nasional/politik/14/10/20/ndqafl-ini-isi-pidato-kenegaraan-pertama-presiden-joko-widodo

*Jakarta Globe* (2015, October 22). 'One Year in Power: Foreign Ministry Reports on its Performance.' Retrieved from: http://jakartaglobe.beritasatu.com/ multimedia/one-year-power-foreign-ministry-reports-performance/

*Jakarta Globe* (2014, November 11). 'We are Waiting for you to Invest in Indonesia, Jokowi tells APEC in Speech.' Retrieved from: http://jakartaglobe. beritasatu.com/news/waiting-invest-indonesia-jokowi-tells-apec-speech/

*The Jakarta Post* (2014, June 23). 'Jokowi wins on Prabowo's turf.' Retrieved from http://m.thejakartapost.com/news/2014/06/23/jokowi-wins-prabowo-s-turf.html

*The Jakarta Post* (2015, September 2). 'PAN joins the ruling coalition.' Retrieved from: http://www.thejakartapost.com/news/2015/09/02/pan-joins-ruling-collation.html

*The Jakarta Post* (2014, October 13). 'KMP eyes leadership of all House bodies.' Retrieved from: http://www.thejakartapost.com/news/2014/10/13/kmp-eyes-leadership-all-house-bodies.html

*The Japan Times* (2015, September 30). 'Japan loses Indonesian high-speed railway contract to China.' Retrieved from: http://www.japantimes.co.jp/ news/2015/09/30/business/japan-loses-indonesian-high-speed-railway-contract-china/#.Vix_cfkrLIW

Kandi, R.D. (2015, August 12). 'Hanya Puan Menteri Koordinator yang Selamat dari Reshuffle.' *CNN Indonesia.* Retrieved from: http://www.cnnindonesia. com/politik/20150812163253-32-71699/hanya-puan-menteri-koordinator-yang-selamat-dari-reshuffle/

Kapoor, K. (2014, October 7). 'Indonesian president-elect's principle could derail his reforms.' *Reuters.* Retrieved from: http://www.reuters.com/article/2014/ 10/07/us-indonesia-politics-idUSKCN0HW24N20141007

*Kompas* (2015, April 11). 'Megawati: Kalau Tidak Mau Disebut Petugas Partai, Keluar!' Retrieved from: http://nasional.kompas.com/read/2015/04/11/16335651/ Megawati.Kalau.Tidak.Mau.Disebut.Petugas.Partai.Keluar

Liddle, R.W. and Mujani, S. (2005). 'Indonesia in 2004: The Rise of Susilo Bambang Yudhoyono.' *Asian Survey*, Vol. 45, No. 1 (January/February 2005), pp. 119–126.

MacIntyre, A. and Ramage, D.E. (2008). *Seeing Indonesia as a Normal Country: Implications for Australia* (Barton ACT: Australian Strategic Policy Institute). Retrieved from https://www.aspi.org.au/publications/seeing-indonesia-as-a-normal-country-implications-for-australia/Seeing_Indonesia.pdf

Manggala, P.U. (2015, March 22). 'Rethinking Indonesia's Global Maritime Axis.' *The Jakarta Post.* Retrieved from: http://www.thejakartapost.com/news/2015/03/22/rethinking-indonesia-s-global-maritime-axis.html

Medhora, S. (2015, July 14). 'Indonesia's 80% cut in cattle imports takes Australian industry by surprise.' *The Guardian.* Retrieved from: http://www.theguardian.com/australia-news/2015/jul/14/indonesias-80-cut-in-cattle-imports-takes-australian-industry-by-surprise

Mietzner, M. (2009). 'Indonesia in 2008 — Yudhoyono's Struggle for Reelection.' *Asian Survey*, Vol. 49, Issue 1, pp. 146–155.

Mietzner, M. (2010). 'Indonesia in 2010: Electoral Contestation and Economic Resilience.' *Asian Survey*, Vol. 50, Issue 1, pp. 185–194.

Ministry of Foreign Affairs, Republic of Indonesia (2015, January 8). *Annual Press Statement Minister for Foreign Affairs Republic of Indonesia 2015.* Retrieved from: https://www.kemlu.go.id/Documents/PPTM%202015/PPTM%202015%20ENG%20final%201.pdf#search=annual%20press%20statement%202015

Natahadibrata, N. (2015, March 23). 'Free visas for 30 nations violates law, may not fly.' *The Jakarta Post.* Retrieved from: http://www.thejakartapost.com/news/2015/03/23/free-visas-30-nations-violates-law-may-not-fly.html

Noor, F. (2014, December 15). 'Troubling display of populism.' *New Straits Times.* Retrieved from: http://www.nst.com.my/news/2015/09/troubling-display-populism

Otto, B. and Sentana, I.M. (2015, April 1). 'Indonesia Looks to Erect Language Barrier.' *The Wall Street Journal.* Retrieved from: http://www.wsj.com/articles/indonesia-looks-to-erect-language-barrier-1427923801

Poole, A. (2015, September 7). 'Is Jokowi Turning His Back on ASEAN?' *The Diplomat.* Retrieved from: http://thediplomat.com/2015/09/is-jokowi-turning-his-back-on-asean/

Purba (2015, March 29). 'View Point: When Jokowi is much more trusted than Megawati in leading PDI-P.' *The Jakarta Post.* Retrieved from: http://www.thejakartapost.com/news/2015/03/29/view-point-when-jokowi-much-more-trusted-megawati-leading-pdi-p.html

Rachman, A. and Otto, B. (2015, April 11). 'Mega's Message to Jokowi: I'm the Boss.' *The Wall Street Journal*. Retrieved from: http://blogs.wsj.com/indonesiarealtime/2015/04/11/megas-message-to-jokowi-im-the-boss/

Rahadiana, R. and Purnomo, H. (2015, July 8). 'No more flip flops, Indonesia's Widodo tells under-fire team.' *Bloomberg*. Retrieved from: http://www.bloomberg.com/news/articles/2015-07-07/no-more-flip-flops-indonesia-president-tells-under-fire-cabinet

*Reuters* (2015, February 21). 'Indonesia recalls envoy to Brazil amid row over execution.' Retrieved from: http://www.reuters.com/article/2015/02/21/us-indonesia-brazil-executions-idUSKBN0LP05720150221

Sekretariat Kabinet Republik Indonesia (2014, November 12). *Pidato Presiden RI Joko Widodo Pada KTT ke-25 ASEAN di Nay Pyi Taw, Myanmar, 12 November 2014*. Retrieved from: http://setkab.go.id/pidato-presiden-ri-joko-widodo-pada-ktt-ke-25-asean-dinay-pyi-taw-myanmar-12-november-2014/

Stefanie, C. (2015, September 12). 'PAN Gabung ke Pemerintah Tak Kuatkan KIH dan Lemahkan KMP.' *CNN Indonesia*. Retrieved from: http://www.cnnindonesia.com/politik/20150911180057-32-78166/pan-gabung-ke-pemerintah-tak-kuatkan-kih-dan-lemahkan-kmp/

Susilo, D. (2014, August 19). 'The death of reforms in the foreign ministry.' *The Jakarta Post*. Retrieved from: http://www.thejakartapost.com/news/2014/08/19/the-death-reforms-foreign-ministry.html

*Tempo* (2014, October 3). 'Jokowi to Stick to Non-Transactional Politics.' Retrieved from: http://nasional.tempo.co/read/news/2014/10/03/055611783/jokowi-to-stick-to-non-transactional-politics

*Today Online* (2015, July 14). 'Widodo puts Indonesian rail project on the fast track.' Retrieved from: http://www.todayonline.com/world/asia/widodo-puts-indonesian-rail-project-fast-track?singlepage=true

*Tuoi Tre News* (2015, August 20). 'Hanoi asks Jakarta to humanely treat Vietnamese fishermen violating territorial waters.' Retrieved from: http://tuoitrenews.vn/politics/29956/vietnam-asks-indonesia-to-humanely-treat-vietnamese-fishermen-violating-territorial-waters

Widhiarto, H. (2014, November 18). 'Jokowi declares war on illegal fishing.' *The Jakarta Post*. Retrieved from: http://www.thejakartapost.com/news/2014/11/18/jokowi-declares-war-illegal-fishing.html

# Chapter II

# Jokowi's Second Year in Charge: Consolidating Domestically, Reacting Externally

## 1. Introduction

Two years have passed since Joko "Jokowi" Widodo was sworn in as the seventh President of the Republic of Indonesia. After a rocky and tumultuous start to his presidency, which saw him with few friends and a number of so-called enemies, President Widodo has since grown in confidence, consolidating his position domestically. President Widodo's second year in charge saw him secure a majority in Parliament, enjoy high public ratings, and even receiving early endorsements for a second term despite the next Presidential Elections still far away in 2019.

Yet, for all these achievements, the Joko Widodo–Jusuf Kalla Government continues to face questions over Indonesia's foreign policy. Initial concerns that the President simply lacks interest in world affairs have seemingly borne out, and in many cases, it was only when an issue became unavoidable that Widodo was forced to react. This was especially the case when Jakarta's sovereignty was at stake, such as in response to China's increasing assertiveness to waters surrounding Indonesia's Natuna

Islands or when Indonesian citizens were being kidnapped by militants from the Philippines' restive south. On the occasions that the Government did venture on the world stage, the President's foreign policy disinterest arguably undermined such forays. This was perhaps most apparent during Indonesia's official announcement that it would seek a non-permanent seat at the U.N. Security Council for 2019–2020 — an announcement made by the Vice President and not Widodo himself, who decided to skip the U.N. General Assembly for a second year in a row.

Widodo's second year in charge was thus summed up by domestic consolidation on the one hand, but a reactionary external approach on the other hand. Why was this so? Why was Widodo an active agent domestically, but a passive actor internationally? And where does it leave Indonesia's position on the world stage two years into a Widodo Government? It is in this sense that a reflective review of the second year of Widodo's presidency becomes an appropriate topic to study and serves as the motivation for this chapter, 'Jokowi's Second Year in Charge: Consolidating Domestically, Reacting Externally'.

## 2. The Domestic Scene

### 2.1. *The End of Widodo's Political Honeymoon*

President Widodo's first year was initially marked by an unfavorable domestic scene. Parliament was dominated by the opposition *Koalisi Merah Putih* (KMP, or Red and White Coalition) who had stated their intention to make life difficult for the Government. Moreover, they had made good on that promise, securing for themselves the positions of Speaker of the House of Representatives and the four Deputy Speakers. At the same time, the ruling PDI-P party — to which Widodo belonged to — had curiously emerged as the President's biggest opponent, often acting as obstacles to his policies. Notably, the PDI-P chairperson, Megawati Sukarnoputri, warned the President that he was merely a party cadre who should follow the party's line as determined by her.

Struggling with such unfavorable conditions domestically, President Widodo's approval ratings unsurprisingly fell. While his approval ratings stood at 65.1 percent at the beginning of 2015 — despite the Government's decision to remove the politically-sensitive fuel subsidies — it dropped to 53.8 percent just six months into his presidency (Belarminus, 2017, May 30). Several months later in September, it fell further to 41 percent, 'a level Yudhoyono had not fallen to in his 10 years as president' (Mietzner, 2017). The controversy surrounding his nomination of Budi Gunawan for National Police Chief — a former adjutant to Megawati Sukarnoputri when she was president and who the Corruption Eradication Commission (Komisi Pemberantasan Korupsi, or KPK) named as a suspect — marked the end of Widodo's political honeymoon.

## 2.2. Coercive Interventions in Opposition Parties

There was, though, a silver lining over the horizon. The opposition coalition had largely disintegrated into ineffectiveness when two parties from the KMP — Golkar and PPP — split into rival factions, whilst another, PAN, left to join the ruling *Koalisi Indonesia Hebat* (KIH or Awesome Indonesia Coalition) and support the Widodo Government. PAN's move tipped the legislative balance in favor of Widodo and gave the President a slim majority in the 560-seat House of Representatives with 256 seats (the opposition KMP were left with 243 seats and the neutral Partai Demokrat held 61 seats). Despite some early confusion as to whether PAN was merely supporting the Government or had genuinely left KMP/joined KIH, the party was rewarded with a Cabinet position when PAN's Asman Abnur replaced Hanura's Yuddy Chrisnandi as Minister of Administrative and Bureaucratic Reform during a reshuffle in July 2016 (Stefani, 2015, September 12).

President Widodo's fortunes improved further when pro-government figures took over the two aforementioned KMP parties that had been split by internal rival factions. Abu Rizal Bakrie's chairmanship of Golkar, which held 91 seats in Parliament, was challenged by Agung Laksono who intended to bring the party within the KIH fold. Similarly, PPP, which held 39 seats, was divided between the pro-government Muhammad Romahurmuziy and the pro-opposition Djan Faridz. While the disintegration of the opposition KMP was largely not of the President's doing, Widodo would seize the opportunity to ensure a commanding parliamentary majority. One commentator noted that 'the Jokowi administration intervened aggressively in the internal affairs of [the] two opposition parties' (Mietzner, 2017). In particular, the Widodo Government took full advantage of Law No. 2 Year 2011 on Political Parties, which required any changes to a party's leadership to be registered and recognised by the Ministry for Law and Human Rights.

While publicly, the Widodo Government stated it was up to political parties to resolve their internal disputes on their own, through quiet but 'coercive interventions', it supported pro-government factions within Golkar and PPP, thus forcing the pro-opposition factions to turn to the courts (Mietzner, 2017). However, with the September deadline fast approaching for political parties to register their candidates for next year's regional elections, including the high-profile Jakarta Gubernatorial Elections, the two disputing parties faced the very real possibility that they would not be allowed to participate. A prolonged court battle was effectively a death sentence for the two political parties. It was in this context that Widodo used his prerogative to grant/withhold the Government's recognition of any changes to a party's leadership to consolidate his control. In doing so, the President 'practically coerced both Golkar and PPP into electing new leaders who were amenable to his government' (Tomsa, 2017). Golkar's eventual new chairman was described as 'handpicked by Jokowi' and the President 'applied the same approach to...PPP' (Mietzner, 2017).

## 2.3. *Avoiding the Large Coalition Trap*

If at the start of his presidency, Widodo could only rely on a minority 36.96 percent of the 560-seat House of Representatives, the President could now count on a commanding 386 seats. However, the President's newfound control over Parliament was not without its own challenges. Concerns were expressed that the House of Representatives' oversight function over the Government had been made virtually redundant. One expert noted, '[t]he presence of opposition parties is needed to ensure the system of checks and balances in the current government runs well' (*The Jakarta Post* 2017, September 14). Widodo's interventions, however, meant only Gerindra and PKS remained in the opposition KMP. A large coalition though was not new in Indonesian politics. Widodo's predecessor,

Susilo Bambang Yudhoyono, had also enjoyed a parliamentary majority, especially in his second term (2009–2014). The five political parties — Partai Demokrat, PKS, PAN, PPP, and PKB — that had supported Susilo Bambang Yudhoyono during the Presidential Elections in 2009 held 317 seats in Parliament, and this was increased to 423 when Golkar also joined the Yudhoyono Government.

Yet, despite a 'political contract' supposedly binding the pro-Susilo Bambang Yudhoyono parties together, the then-President struggled to assert his will over his own ruling coalition. As such, the other challenge to Widodo's newfound control over Parliament was whether he could avoid a similar fate as his predecessor. There were, however, crucial differences in the coalition-building approaches employed by Susilo Bambang Yudhoyono and Widodo. If the former had employed the 'carrot' — promising Cabinet positions in return for loyalty to the Government, the latter employed the 'stick' — through coercive interventions in the internal affairs of political parties. For Susilo Bambang Yudhoyono, Cabinet reshuffles were *quid pro quo* arrangements between equals that were dependent on one another. For Widodo, Cabinet reshuffles were a tool to wield the powers of the presidency over weakened political parties whose leaders had depended on the Government to recognize their legitimacy against rival claimants.

Three characteristics defined Cabinet reshuffles under Widodo. First, they were conducted only after a political party's support for him had been secured. PAN, which had switched sides to the Government as early as September 2015, would have to wait almost a year before it received a Cabinet position in July 2016. Golkar, which likewise received a Cabinet position in the same July 2016 reshuffle, was also made to wait several weeks after the pro-government Setya Novanto took over the party's leadership in May.

The second characteristic of Widodo's reshuffles was that 'relatively unimportant' Cabinet positions were given in return for switching to the Government (Tomsa, 2017). Golkar was rewarded with the position of Minister of Industry, whilst PAN, as noted earlier, received the position of Minister of Administrative and Bureaucratic Reform. Meanwhile, there were no additional Cabinet positions for PPP who already had party cadre Lukman Hakim Saifuddin as Religious Affairs Minister in Widodo's

*Kabinet Kerja* (Working Cabinet) since before they made the switch to the Government.

The case of the Religious Affairs Minister pointed to the third characteristic of Widodo's reshuffles — that they often went to party cadres not always favored by their own party's leadership (Mietzner, 2017). At the time of Lukman Hakim Sauifuddin's appointment, PPP was still officially part of the opposition KMP, and the party (especially the pro-opposition faction) made clear that his presence in Widodo's Cabinet was not as their representative (Sholeh, 2014, October 27). In the case of PAN, Taufik Kurniawan who serves as Deputy Speaker in the House of Representatives was strongly rumored to be the preferred candidate over the eventually appointed Asman Abnur who, at the time, was only a Deputy Chair of the House's Commission IX (Firdaus, 2015, December 30). The three characteristics of Widodo's reshuffles meant that the expansion of the pro-government coalition was not done at the expense of any significant concessions to its newest members, thus ensuring that the President maintained control over his Cabinet (Tomsa, 2017).

## 2.4. Redefining the President's Relationship with Megawati

Among the three parties to switch sides to the Government, the most significant was arguably that of Golkar. This was not only because of the 91 seats it held in Parliament, but because of its endorsement for Widodo to run for a second term despite the Presidential Elections still being far away in 2019. The endorsement was officially announced during the closing of Golkar's party conference in July 2016, which the President himself had attended to deliver a speech (Simanjuntak, 2016, July 28). Under Indonesia's electoral system, only candidates nominated by political parties (either individually or collective) that secured 20 percent of parliamentary seats, or 25 percent of the votes in the General Election, could run for the presidency. In 2014, Widodo had received PDI-P's nomination rather late in the process from a reluctant Megawati Sukarnoputri who had her own ambitions to run — ambitions that she arguably still has. This had put Widodo on shaky grounds, with no guarantees that PDI-P would nominate him again in 2019. As the second largest party in Parliament, and with the best vertical and horizontal organisation in the country (Bulkin, 2013, October 24), Golkar's endorsement offered Widodo an alternative option, thus 'redefining' the President's subordinate relationship with Megawati Sukarnoputri (Mietzner, 2017).

In this redefined relationship, Widodo ignored pressures from PDI-P to sack ministers that had fallen out of favor with Megawati Sukarnoputri, in particular, State Enterprises Minister Rini Soemarno who, though a member of PDI-P, had been accused of leading the President astray from the party line (Aritonang, 2015, April 10). Moreover, if in 2015, during the fourth PDI-P national congress, Widodo had suffered the humiliation of being reminded that he was merely a PDI-P cadre — forced to dress like any other party member and denied the opportunity to even speak during that congress — things were much different in 2016. Widodo was now invited to speak as President of the Republic of Indonesia, donning a traditional *batik* shirt rather than the party's red blazer (Kami, 2016, January 11).

By the end of the President's second year in office, his approval ratings had climbed to 65.9 percent (Belarminus, 2017, May 30). Coupled with his newfound majority in Parliament, continued control over his Cabinet, early endorsements for a second term, and a redefined relationship with Megawati Sukarnoputri, there remained no doubt over who was in charge now. Widodo had grown in confidence, aggressively setting out to change his situation, and consolidating his position domestically.

Yet, if there was no doubt over President Widodo domestically, there remained questions about Indonesia's foreign policy. The events of the past year and the Government's responses to them have seemingly failed to allay initial concerns that the President simply lacks interest in world affair. As such, this chapter shall now turn its attention to examining some of the key foreign policy issues faced by the Government during Widodo's second year.

# 3. Key Foreign Policy Issues

## 3.1. *Recurring Concerns about Widodo's Foreign Policy Interests*

From the very outset, President Widodo's interest in foreign policy had been questioned. As the leader of the world's third largest democracy, the most populous Muslim nation, and the *primus inter pares* in ASEAN, this mattered. The preamble to Indonesia's Constitution makes clear of the country's obligations to 'participate toward the establishment of a world order based on freedom, perpetual peace and social justice.' To turn away from world affairs would thus not only mean reversing from decades of proud Indonesian foreign policy achievements, traditions, and norms, but to also arguably violate the Constitution that the President swore to uphold.

As such the Government went to great lengths to show that Indonesia under President Widodo remained as committed to the world order its Constitution mandated it to help establish. Foreign Minister Retno Marsudi, for example, pointed out that the President attended a total of 64 bilateral and international meetings throughout 2015 (Ministry of Foreign Affairs, Republic of Indonesia, 2016, January 7). At the same time, Widodo's second year in office saw Indonesia host the Fifth Extraordinary Summit of the Organization for Islamic Cooperation (OIC), chair the Indian Ocean Rim Association (IORA), and also make plans to organise the 85th General Assembly of INTERPOL later in November 2016.

However, if throughout 2015, the President had participated in 64 bilateral and international meetings, this figure had fallen to 55 in 2016 (Ministry of Foreign Affairs, Republic of Indonesia, 2017, January 10). Beyond the numbers, the quality of Widodo's participation at bilateral and international meetings was questioned. For example, it was noted that while the President attended the opening procession of the 26th ASEAN Summit in Kuala Lumpur, he did not stay for the retreat session. Instead, Vice President Jusuf Kalla was delegated to stay at that crucial session, 'where leaders could talk openly about the region's strategic issues' (Salim, 2016, October 21).

The Vice President was also tasked with attending the U.N. General Assembly in September 2016, marking the second year in a row that Widodo had skipped the international gathering. Under normal circumstances, the President's absence may have raised a few eyebrows. The fact that Indonesia was also officially announcing its bid for a non-permanent seat at the U.N. Security Council left many scratching their heads.

## 3.2. *'Who Do I Call if I Want to Call Jakarta?'*

Perhaps the most perplexing thing to have occurred during Widodo's second year, however, was the appointment of so-called liaison ministers. Announced near the start of his second year in office in November 2015, 12 Cabinet ministers were assigned to be directly responsible for forging investment relationships with a specific country, economic area, or region, as well as be the point of contact for foreign investors from that country or economic region. The countries/economic regions included Australia, China, Europe, Hong Kong, India, Japan, Malaysia, the Middle East, Russia, Singapore, South America, South Korea, Taiwan, the U.S., and other ASEAN countries (Sekretariat Kabinet Republik Indonesia, 2015, November 25a). President Widodo was reportedly unhappy with the level of investment realization, highlighting problems in the implementation of investment deals between Indonesia and other countries, including with permits, licensing, and other bottlenecks. This came at a time when the Government required IDR 5,000 trillion (USD 384 billion) to fund its ambitious infrastructure plans over the next five years (Amindoni & Yosephine, 2015, November 24). The role of the liaison ministers was thus to ensure that overseas investment could be effectively realized. As Cabinet Secretary Pramono Anung explained, '[p]roblems emerge in sectorial issues, which mostly do not get solved. Therefore…the President has appointed these specific individuals' (Amindoni & Yosephine, 2015, November 24).

The initiative was not without its controversy. For example, both the Minister of Marine Affairs and Fisheries, Susi Pudjiastuti, and the Minister of Communication and Information Technology, Rudiantara, were both confusingly assigned to the U.S. However, Cabinet Secretary Pramono Anung explained, '[l]ater for the US in a part would be set the authority to the MCIT (Minister of Communication and Information Technology), Rudiantara, so there is sharing' (Sekretariat Kabinet Republik Indonesia, 2015, November 25). Another controversy was over the additional burden the liaising task would put on the Cabinet ministers who were still expected to focus on their main roles. Again, confusingly, it was explained that since 'their main job is still the same…the President instructed the ministers to visit the country where they are responsible for, only twice a month' (Sekretariat Kabinet Republik Indonesia, 2015, November 25b). How a Cabinet minister would be able to balance carrying out their main job, and yet, at the same time, be expected to travel to a country twice a month was not explained.

The balancing act was made even more daunting given that only 'specific individuals' were appointed by the President (Amindoni & Yosephine, 2015, November 24). It was not explained whether Cabinet ministers would or could be supported by their staff in their respective ministries with their new liaising task. Even if Cabinet ministers were to be supported by their staff, there remained questions over the specific individuals' qualifications to conduct foreign diplomacy. For former Indonesian Ambassador to Switzerland, Djoko Susilo, the liaison initiative was an 'unreasonable' one, and he highlighted the problem of involving Cabinet ministers 'not privy to the nuances of foreign diplomacy' (Salim, 2015, November 26).

If there was one specific individual in Widodo's Working Cabinet that did understand such nuances, it should have been his foreign minister. However, the biggest controversy over the liaison initiative was where it left Foreign Minister Retno Marsudi, raising questions over whether she was being undermined. A member of the House of Representatives' Commission I overseeing foreign affairs speculated, 'If, for instance, the President is not satisfied with the work of the foreign minister, he just needs to replace her' (Salim, 2015, November 26). For her part, Foreign Minister Retno Marsudi attempted to downplay speculations she was being undermined, arguing, '[i]t's a matter of investment realization. So there will be no overlapping' (Sekretariat Kabinet Republik Indonesia, 2015, November 25b). Cabinet Secretary Pramono Anung concurred, stating the liaison ministers 'do not take the domain or authority of the Minister of Foreign Affairs' (Sekretariat Kabinet Republik Indonesia, 2015, November 25b). He further added that Foreign Minister Retno Marsudi would be charged with coordinating the liaison ministers and assured that,

> '[the] Minister of Foreign Affairs retains full responsibility in conducting economic diplomacy, organizing matters relating to foreign relations and responsibly for Indonesia to establish good relations with friendly countries' (Sekretariat Kabinet Republik Indonesia, 2015, November 25c).

Despite such reassurances, if the former U.S. Secretary of State, Henry Kissinger, had famously asked, 'Who do I call if I want to call Europe?', foreign diplomats and investors in Indonesia may well have been left wondering the same thing about Jakarta.

## 3.3. *Economic Diplomacy*

If logic was to be found behind President Widodo's controversial liaison initiative, it was perhaps in the importance the Government now places on trade in its foreign policy. One expert noted that 'the primary function of Indonesia's external affairs is to support the domestic development agenda' (Mietzner, 2017). It was further noted, 'geopolitical considerations — which dominated the Yudhoyono presidency's international agenda — are now subordinated to trade and investment targets' (Mietzner, 2017).

In her first Annual Press Statement in January 2015, Foreign Minister Retno Marsudi announced that over the next five years, Indonesia's foreign policy would be based on three priorities, namely: (1) maintaining Indonesia's sovereignty; (2) enhancing the protection of Indonesian citizens and legal entities; and (3) intensifying economic diplomacy (Ministry of Foreign Affairs, Republic of Indonesia, 2015, January 8). Interestingly, in her next Annual Press Statement, delivered during Widodo's second year in office, a fourth priority was added — advancing Indonesia's regional and international role (Ministry of Foreign Affairs, Republic of Indonesia, 2016, January 7).

Nevertheless, Foreign Minister Retno Marsudi went on to outline some of the Government's achievement in the area of economic diplomacy. In particular, the Government had revived and intensified negotiations on comprehensive economic partnership agreements (CEPA) with a number of countries. Foreign Minister Retno Marsudi noted,

'Throughout 2015, we have carried out at least 37 economic partnership agreement negotiations, among others: the Indonesia-Japan Economic Partnership Agreement (IJEPA), the ASEAN–Japan Comprehensive Economic Partnership (AJCEP), the ASEAN–Hong Kong Free Trade Agreement (AHKFTA), the ASEAN–Korea Free Trade Agreement

(AKFTA) and the Regional Comprehensive Economic Partnership (RCEP)' (Ministry of Foreign Affairs, Republic of Indonesia, 2016, January 7).

It is worth noting that apart from the IJEPA, the negotiations cited by the Foreign Minister referred to those under the umbrella of ASEAN. Further, the ASEAN-led RCEP involving the 10 ASEAN member-states and the six countries it has free trade agreements with (i.e., Australia, China, India, Japan, Korea, and New Zealand) missed its deadline for conclusion by the end of 2015. In August 2016, it was reported that the RCEP would again likely miss its new deadline which had been slated for end of 2016 (*The Hindu* 2016, August 24).

Interestingly, there was no mention of the Trans-Pacific Partnership (TPP) in Foreign Minister Retno Marsudi's second Annual Press Statement. Often held up (incorrectly) as a rival to the ASEAN-led RCEP, the TPP initiative is currently being negotiated by the U.S., Australia, Brunei Darussalam, Canada, Chile, Japan, Malaysia, Mexico, New Zealand, Peru, Singapore, and Vietnam. President Widodo had surprised many during a state visit to the U.S. in October 2015 when he told U.S. President Barack Obama, 'Indonesia intends to join the Trans-Pacific Partnership' (*The Guardian* 2015, October 27). Although Widodo believed that Indonesia risked losing out to its regional neighbors if it failed to join the TPP, his announcement was remarkable, 'given that Indonesia has long refrained from committing to the Trans-Pacific Partnership' (Williamson, 2015, December 5).

Surprise at the announcement was quickly followed by criticism back home, especially by economic nationalists. One expert noted, '[o]ur state-owned enterprises (SOEs) will be in under serious threat' (Hermansyah, 2015, November 29) whilst another questioned the country's readiness arguing, '[w]e can't narrow the question to only joining or not joining and when to join. We must also prepare ourselves' (Wirayani, 2015, November 12). Former Coordinating Finance and Industry Minister, Ginandjar Kartasasmita, added 'that rather than joining the TPP, it would be better if Indonesia focused on RCEP, in which Indonesia had a bigger role' (Hermansyah, 2015, November 29). This point was important. Unlike the RCEP negotiations which Indonesia has been involved in since the very beginning, Jakarta would be unable to shape the TPP negotiations, instead having to accept whatever terms were eventually agreed by the 12 current members.

The Widodo Government also sought to increase trade with non-traditional markets. Foreign Minister Retno Marsudi noted that Indonesia's trade in a number of non-traditional markets 'experienced a significant increase', citing Papua New Guinea (32 percent increase in trade), Palestine (266 percent increase), Angola (57 percent increase), El Salvador (53 percent increase), and Serbia (31 percent) as examples (Ministry of Foreign Affairs, Republic of Indonesia, 2016, January 7).

When Sri Lankan Prime Minister Ranil Wickremesinghe visited Widodo in August 2016, the President made a pitch to export Indonesian-made train wagons, noting, '[w]e are sending train wagons from INKA (*Industri Kereta Api*) to Bangladesh. Now we have pitched the idea to Sri Lanka' (Prasetyo, 2016, August 3). By the end of 2016, Indonesia was recorded to have exported a total of 150 train carriages worth USD 72.3 billion (Ministry of Foreign Affairs, Republic of Indonesia, 2017, January 10).

Indonesia's traditional markets were not neglected. Apart from the aforementioned state visit to the U.S. in October 2015, President Widodo also travelled to Europe, including Belgium, Germany, the Netherlands, and the United Kingdom (April 2016), China (September 2016), Russia (May 2016), and South Korea (May 2016). The visit to China was notable as it was his fifth meeting with Chinese Premier Xi Jinping in less than two years.

The Government also expanded its visa exemption facilities, which had first been announced in June 2015, in an effort to further increase the number of foreign visitors to Indonesia. During her second Annual Press Statement in January 2016, Foreign Minister Retno Marsudi noted that 75 countries could now enjoy such facilities. However, she omitted the controversy from a few weeks earlier when Israel was initially included in the list of expanded countries to enjoy visa exemptions (*The Jakarta Post* 2015, December 21). The announcement was surprising, given the lack of diplomatic relations between Jakarta and Tel Aviv, as well as the Indonesian public's traditionally pro-Palestine sentiments. The predictable backlash would see the Government reverse the decision within 24 hours (Nursyamsyi, 2015, December 22).

Embarrassingly, the 'flip-flop' exposed a worryingly lack of coordination within the Government. It should be noted that the initial announcement was not made by the Foreign Ministry or the Ministry of Law and Human Rights (which usually handles immigration issues), but by the Coordinating Minister for Maritime Affairs, Rizal Ramli (who did admittedly oversee the Ministry for Tourism). Interestingly, when Minister Retno Marsudi was questioned about the announcement, she was reported to have simply replied, '*Mohon ditanyakan ke Pak Menko Maritim. Saya masih di Sydney'* ("Please ask the Coordinating Minister for Maritime Affairs. I am still in Sydney") (Amanda, 2015, December 21).

Like the liaison initiative, the controversy over granting Israel visa-free facilities suggested that on a matter that involved Indonesia's foreign policy, Minister Retno Marsudi had not been initially involved. However, the quick retraction by the Government may also suggest that the Foreign Ministry was able to quickly assert its authority, ensuring that Jakarta's principled stance with regards to the Palestine issue was non-negotiable and trumped any effort for greater economic diplomacy.

## 3.4. *The Question of Palestine*

President Widodo had campaigned on a pledge to advance the Palestinian cause, publicly stating his position during a televised presidential candidate debate back in June 22, 2014. Seen as an attempt to win over the Muslim vote, Widodo had promised to open an Indonesian embassy in Palestine if elected, and to support their effort for full membership in the United Nations. It was in this sense that in March 2016, Indonesia opened an honorary consulate in Ramallah, appointing Palestinian businesswoman, Ms. Maha Abou Susheh, as honorary consul. Attending the inauguration of the new honorary consulate, Foreign Minister Retno Marsudi stated the move was a manifestation of Indonesia's support for the freedom of Palestine (*The Jakarta Post* 2016, March 21).

Despite this, the aforementioned lack of diplomatic relations between Indonesia and Israel meant that the inauguration ceremony could not take place in Ramallah itself but instead, had to be moved to Amman, in neighboring Jordan. Israeli authorities refused to permit the high level Indonesian delegation from entering Ramallah, thus demonstrating some of the challenges Indonesia must face as it tries to support the Palestinian cause.

It should also be noted that an honorary consul lacks the same authority and status as a fully-fledged ambassador. As honorary consul, Ms. Maha Abou Susheh will not be able to conduct any diplomatic activities and her role is limited to providing assistance to Indonesian citizens in the Holy Lands, and advancing economic and sociocultural cooperation between Indonesia and Palestine (*The Jakarta Post* 2016, March 21). In this sense, the opening of an honorary consulate is a far cry from the embassy that President Widodo had campaigned on.

Indonesia's support for the Palestinian cause was manifested in other ways too. In the same month that Indonesia opened an honorary consul, Jakarta would also rebuff calls from Israeli Prime Minister Benjamin Netanyahu to establish official bilateral relations (*The Times of Israel* 2016, April 1). The Israeli Prime Minister stated, 'It's time to change our relationship, because the reasons preventing it are no longer relevant' (Pileggi, 2016, March 28). Despite Jakarta's refusal, it was worth noting that the two sides did conduct covert trade, totaling USD 180 million in 2015 (*The Times of Israel* 2016, April 1).

The other major manifestation of Indonesia's support for the Palestinian cause was the holding of the Fifth Organization of Islamic Cooperation (OIC) Extraordinary Summit on Palestine and Al-Quds Al-Sharif in Jakarta, also in March 2016. Over 500 delegates from the 49 OIC member-states took part, including Palestinian President Mahmoud Abbas. In addition, representatives from the five permanent members of the U.N. Security Council as well as from the United Nations and the European Union (who, together with the United States and Russia, make up the 'Quartet on the Middle East') were also invited (Ministry of Foreign Affairs, Republic of Indonesia, 2016, March 5). Closing the Fifth OIC Extraordinary Summit, President Widodo stated, '[t]his extraordinary summit is proof of the tangible support for Palestine' before adding, '[t]he Islamic world still owes the Palestinian people their independence. The Palestinian struggle is our struggle' (Ministry of Foreign Affairs, Republic of Indonesia, 2016, March 7).

The Fifth OIC Extraordinary Summit produced two key outcome documents. The first was the Jakarta Declaration on Palestine and Al-Quds

Al-Sharif which, according to the Indonesian Foreign Ministry's (2016, March 7) website, 'contains a tangible action plan for OIC leaders for the resolution of the Palestinian and Al-Quds Al-Sharif issues.' Meanwhile, the second outcome document was the Resolution on Palestine and Al-Quds Al-Sharif, which 'reaffirms the principle position and commitment of the OIC to Palestine and Al-Quds Al-Sharif' (Ministry of Foreign Affairs, Republic of Indonesia, 2016, March 7). Despite the wide news coverage, the Fifth OIC Extraordinary Summit received in the Indonesian media, it did not appear to attract much attention in the West. This was perhaps unsurprising, given that none of the permanent members of the U.N. Security Council or members of the Quartet sent their foreign ministers to the Summit, with countries such as the U.S. being represented by a junior acting envoy, and Russia and the European Union by their Jakarta-based ambassadors (U.S. Department of State, 2016, March 7; *Republika* 2016, March 6; and European Union External Action, 2016, March 7).

Nevertheless, the Fifth OIC Extraordinary Summit can be a considered a success for the Widodo Government, as it achieved its aim to demonstrate Jakarta's commitment to the Palestinian cause and to unite the Islamic world in adopting a common position through the Jakarta Declaration and the Resolution. It was also one of the few examples whereby Widodo's Indonesia was shaping the foreign discourse, rather than reacting to it.

### 3.5. The Region's Two Elephants — The United States and China

One area where Indonesia had less success in shaping the foreign discourse was perhaps in its relationships with the region's two major powers. The ongoing contestation between Beijing and Washington D.C. and its implications for Jakarta are perhaps aptly described by the following idiom — 'When two elephants fight, it is the grass that suffers.' The challenge for Indonesia, therefore, was to ensure it would not be trampled by the two contesting 'elephants'.

The U.S. attempted to steal a march on its rival by hosting the Special U.S.–ASEAN Leaders Summit in Sunnylands, California, in February 2016. The Summit was notable as it was the first time such a gathering had taken place on American soil. It was also the first major ASEAN gathering since the establishment of the ASEAN Community on December 31, 2015. In his remarks, U.S. President Barack Obama stated that the gathering,

> 'reflects my personal commitment, and the national commitment of the United States, to a strong and enduring partnership with your ten nations individually and to Southeast Asia as one region, as one community — ASEAN' (The White House, 2016, February 15).

That commitment was made not only for the benefit of his ASEAN counterparts, but also to whoever would succeed him following the U.S. Presidential Elections later this year in November. As one expert noted, '[s]ending that message is vital because...there is no guarantee that any of the other U.S. presidential candidates would necessarily demonstrate the same regard for the [ASEAN] subregion' (Parameswaran, 2016, February 11). Indeed, with the exception of Hilary Clinton, there are serious concerns in the region — including in Jakarta — that no other presidential candidate has committed to continuing the U.S. 'pivot' to Asia if elected to the White House. In May 2016, Donald Trump became the presumptive nominee for the Republican Party, whilst Hilary Clinton became the presumptive nominee for the Democrat Party a month later in June — thus setting the stage for an interesting U.S. presidential election later this year. In this sense, one of the major challenges for President Widodo is to ensure that the next U.S. Administration remains as engaged with ASEAN and the region, of which Indonesia is the largest member. This had been easier with Barack Obama, given his special connection to the region, having spent part of his childhood in Jakarta. Whether President Widodo could do the same with a future U.S. President with little links to the region remains to be seen.

President Widodo, for his part, was considered to have a successful Summit, with his positions on the importance of a tech-based creative economy and the role of small- and medium-sized enterprises (SMEs) being incorporated into the Sunnylands Declaration. The President was also invited to lead a discussion on counter-terrorism on the second day of the Summit (Fitriyanti, 2016, February 11). The invitation to lead the meeting was significant, given that a month earlier in January 2016, Jakarta had suffered from the Sarinah terrorist attack. In that incident, Indonesia won plaudits for its swift and proportionate response (*The Jakarta Post* 2016, January 16). It was noted, for example, that the Government did not feel the need to declare a state of emergency like in France following the Paris attacks in November 2015 and which remained in place for several months after the incident.

There was some controversy though when reports emerged that Beijing had deployed missile launchers in the South China Sea on the same day the U.S. and ASEAN leaders were drafting a joint statement on their stance on the dispute area. The failure of the final joint statement to specifically mention China and its counter-productive behavior in the South China Sea coupled with the revelations of missile launchers was considered an embarrassment for President Barack Obama and his ASEAN guests (Mason & Wallace, 2016, February 16).

President Widodo, too, was embarrassed by Chinese action in the South China Sea in his second year in office. Whilst Jakarta does not consider itself a claimant to the South China Sea, Beijing's 'Nine-Dashed Line' does appear to overlap with Indonesian waters surrounding Indonesia's Natuna Islands. Jakarta has traditionally adopted a policy of strategic ambivalence to deliberately avoid any direct confrontation with China but made a departure in March 2016. Maritime and Fisheries Minister Susi Pudjiastuti made public an incident involving a Chinese Coast Guard ship that had prevented Indonesian maritime law enforcement vessels from towing a Chinese illegal fishing ship back to land for legal processing.

Describing the acts of China's coast guard as 'interrupts and sabotages our efforts' Maritime and Fisheries Minister Susi Pudjiastuti threatened to take China to the International Tribunal for the Law of the Sea and demanded Beijing return the offending fishing vessel (*The Straits Times* 2016, March 22). While Foreign Minister Retno Marsudi followed up by issuing a diplomatic protest to Beijing, it was interesting to note that the Indonesian Navy Chief of Staff, Admiral Ade Supandi sought to downplay the incident by describing it as 'a fishing dispute' and not a defence/security issue (*Kontan* 2016, March 23).

Three weeks later, it appeared that the incident had been brushed over with the Cabinet Secretary Pramono Anung declaring the incident was a 'misunderstanding' and that Indonesia and China had reached closure (Setuningsih & Prasetyo, 2016, April 14). This was despite the fact that the offending fishing vessel was never returned to Indonesia as initially demanded by the Maritime and Fisheries Minister. Unfortunately, for President Widodo, there was to be further 'misunderstandings' in the months to come. In May, it was reported that an Indonesian Navy frigate had opened fire and seized a Chinese fishing vessel, arresting all eight crew that had been caught in Indonesia's exclusive economic zone (EEZ) (Panda, 2016, May 31). A month later in June, there was another incident whereby an Indonesian Navy warship fired on a group of Chinese trawlers fishing in Indonesia's EEZ, this time injuring a Chinese sailor (Panda, 2016, June 21). It is worth observing the involvement of the Indonesian Navy in these two latter incidents. Despite the earlier March incident being downplayed as a 'fishing dispute', it was clear that the Navy — not maritime law enforcement agencies — was now taking the lead role of patrolling Indonesia's EEZ.

In response to these incidents, President Widodo decided to make a very public show of force. On June 23, 2016, the President held a Cabinet meeting onboard an Indonesian Navy warship as it patrolled Indonesia's EEZ. Symbolically, the warship was the KRI Iman Bonjol, the same one involved in the June incident with a group of Chinese trawlers. The Cabinet meeting, which included the Cabinet Secretary, Coordinating Minister for Political, Legal and Security Affairs, the Foreign Minister, the Minister of Marine Affairs and Fisheries, and Indonesian Military Commander among others was described as 'sending a bold message to assert Indonesia's sovereignty' (Paath, 2016, June 23). Coordinating Minister for Political, Legal and Security Affairs Luhut Pandjaitan later explained to the press, '[i]n the course of our history, we've never been this stern (with China). This is also to demonstrate that the president is not taking the issue lightly' (Kapoor & Jensen, 2016, June 23).

With Jakarta's sovereignty at stake, President Widodo was forced to react, abandoning his usual lack of interest in world affairs to go on the offensive and send a bold message to Beijing. Interestingly, a month later on July 12, 2016, when The Hague-based Permanent Court of Arbitration (PCA) delivered its ruling on the case of the Philippines versus China concerning the dispute over maritime jurisdiction in the South China Sea, Widodo resorted to his usual lack of interest. With expectations high that, on the one hand, the PCA would rule overwhelmingly in favor of the Philippines, and that on the other hand, China would totally reject the court's ruling, much attention had focused on how ASEAN, of which Indonesia was a member of, would respond. Given its self-proclaimed 'ASEAN centrality' role at the heart of the region's security architecture, in addition to the fact that four of its member-states are claimants to the South China Sea, a multilateral response from ASEAN was hoped for (*The Straits Times* 2016, July 14). Unfortunately, ASEAN was unable to issue a joint statement following the PCA's ruling. This was despite the fact ASEAN member-states, including Indonesia, had been discussing the possibility of issuing such a joint statement for some time, with experts expecting at worst a watered-down and generic output. Significantly, President Widodo did not feel the need to expend any diplomatic effort in uniting ASEAN behind a common position, contrasting sharply with the actions of the previous Susilo Bambang Yudhoyono Government, when ASEAN failed to issue a joint communique following an ASEAN Foreign Ministers Meeting in 2012.

The above reinforced the view that President Widodo would only get involved when Indonesia's sovereignty was directly threatened. Otherwise, he was happy to withdraw himself.

### 3.6. *Indonesia's Own Backyard — Kidnappings in the Sulu Seas*

Another major sovereignty issue that President Widodo was forced to react to during his second year in office was the issue of Indonesian citizens being kidnapped by militants from the Philippines' restive south. Estimated to accommodate more than 100,000 ships, 18 million people and 55 million metric tons of cargo passing through its waters every year, the Sulu Sea has witnessed a host of non-traditional security threats, including a spate of piracy and kidnapping incidents (Anggianto & Muhamad, 2016, June 6). Indonesian fishermen have borne the brunt of such kidnappings, and in the first six months of 2016, 24 Indonesians were kidnapped — whilst nationals from Canada, Norway, and other countries have also been victims, with some killed after ransom demands went ignored. Intense negotiations have resulted in 17 kidnapped Indonesians being released, although there have been some speculations as to whether Jakarta paid ransoms in order to secure the release of its hostages.

The Widodo Government has strongly denied making any payments, with lead negotiator General (Ret.) Kivlan Zein stating, '[t]he release was conducted without paying a ransom, based on negotiations and cooperation between the TNI [Tentara Nasional Indonesia or the Indonesian Military] and the Philippine military' (*The Jakarta Post* 2016, May 2). However, Philippine media later reported that millions of dollars had indeed been paid to secure the release of the kidnapped Indonesians, forcing Defence Minister Ryamizard Ryacudu to suggest that the money perhaps came from the families or employers of the victims (Gutierrez, 2016, September 21). In an effort to address the spate of kidnappings in a more comprehensive manner, Jakarta has been in talks with the Philippines as well as Malaysia on the possibility of establishing trilateral naval cooperation. The idea was first mooted on the sidelines of the ASEAN Defense Ministers Meeting (ADMM) in May 2016 and by July 2016, a Trilateral Cooperation Agreement was signed by the defense ministers from the three countries (Arshad, 2016, August 5).

It remains to be seen whether the initiative will be able to successfully end kidnapping incidents once the naval cooperation is finally operationalized. However, the incidents arguably reinforced the importance of paying attention to Indonesia's own backyard, illustrating how developments in neighbouring Southeast Asian countries impacted Indonesia.

## 3.7. ASEAN: Just a Cornerstone?

In his first year in office, President Widodo appeared to have abandoned ASEAN as the singular priority of Indonesia's foreign policy. Yet, events in Southeast Asia during the President's second year meant that as much as Widodo wished to ignore developments in the region, this was not a possible choice. The Rohingya migrant boat crisis in 2015, for example, forced Jakarta — together with Bangkok and Kuala Lumpur — to take in as much as 7,000 Rohingya refugees (*The Guardian* 2015, May 20). The move was meant to be temporary, lasting no more than one year, at which point the international community would resettle and repatriate them. A year on, however, many remain 'languish[ing] in refugee camps or detentions centers, praying that a Western country will take them in' (Cochrane, 2016, June 18). According to one report, only 46 Rohingya had been resettled to a third country, whilst out of the 999 Rohingya that Indonesia took in, 723 had managed to smuggle themselves into Malaysia (Cochrane, 2016, June 18).

There is some hope, though, following historic elections in Myanmar in November 2015 that saw Aung San Suu Kyi's National League for Democracy (NLD) sweep to power, becoming the first truly civilian government in decades. Indonesia has been one of the strongest supporters of Myanmar's democratization process, and Jakarta's efforts was even acknowledged by Aung San Suu Kyi who expressed her appreciation and admiration of Indonesia's role in helping the development of democracy in Myanmar. Surprisingly, the Widodo Government took almost two weeks to congratulate Myanmar's historic elections, leading to some criticisms in the Indonesian media (Almuttaqi, 2016, March 31). Given concerns that Indonesia's previous efforts to integrate Myanmar with the international community have not reaped any significant economic benefits for Jakarta, the two-week delay seems highly questionable. Seen as the last frontier in Southeast Asia, Myanmar promises to be the next economic 'tiger' with above-8 percent annual growth predicted for the years to come. This boom will be driven by rapid expansion in the oil and gas sector, tourism, textiles, and telecommunications — areas where Indonesia could do business. While concerns over President Joko Widodo's interest in foreign policy remain, the economic argument should be apparent to him and the Government. Indonesia should thus not miss out on seizing the opportunity of Myanmar's first civilian government to lift Jakarta–Naypyidaw relations to new heights and to ensure that Indonesia benefits from Myanmar's opening up.

Elsewhere, Indonesia appears to have given up on its regional democracy and human rights agenda. Jakarta was silent as Thailand's ruling junta forced through a military-drafted constitution without any public debate and a low referendum turnout of only 59 percent (Almuttaqi, 2016, August 19). The referendum marks an important step in the military junta's repeatedly-postponed roadmap towards a 'fully functioning democracy' and opens the way for a general election to be held next year. Among the contentious provisions in the new constitution is one that sets forth an upper Senate entirely appointed by the military junta. This is significant as the Senate will play a role in appointing the next prime minister — leading to fears that the military junta will be able to ensure its preferred candidate occupies Government House.

Jakarta has also been silent with regards to Philippine President Rodrigo Duterte and his 'War on Drugs' that has left some 3,600 people dead. President Rodrigo Duterte has gone on to insult U.S. President Barack Obama while announcing his country's 'separation' from its long-time treaty ally, as well as pledging to realign Manila's 'ideological flow' with that of China, adding, '[t]here are three of us against the world: China, Philippines and Russia' (Blanchard, 2016, October 20). In a hard-hitting editorial from the *Bangkok Post* (2016, October 26), Duterte was described as causing 'massive and unnecessary diplomatic upheaval', leaving the region 'in complete confusion', and 'doing a disservice' to ASEAN. The editorial went on to say that with regards to the South China Sea, 'ASEAN policy now means nothing' as a result of Duterte's statements (*Bangkok Post* 2016, October 26). Worryingly, the Philippines is set to take up the chairmanship of ASEAN in 2017 and the region will perhaps never before have seen an ASEAN Chair so openly siding with one major power over the others in the way it will when the Philippines takes over. It should be noted that even when Cambodia — often accused as Beijing's 'puppet' — chaired the regional organisation in 2012, it at least attempted to maintain an outwardly image of neutrality. At a time when Indonesia no longer sees ASEAN as '*the*' cornerstone of its foreign policy, there are question marks over whether Jakarta is still prepared to step in and expend diplomatic capital in order to maintain ASEAN unity like it did in 2012.

Meanwhile, the ambitious regional integration project known as the ASEAN Community was officially launched on December 31, 2015. However, many, including in Indonesia, were arguably more occupied about celebrating the New Year rather than marking this important milestone. Perhaps, in recognition of the lack of public engagement with the ASEAN Community, the 2015 goalpost has been cleverly moved with the adoption of the ASEAN Community Vision 2025. While the new ASEAN Community Vision 2025 is officially described as 'charting the path for ASEAN Community building over the next ten years', critics have described it as an admission of the failure of ASEAN, including Indonesia, to achieve the 'people-centered' ASEAN by the end of 2015.

## 4. Summary and Conclusion

At the end of his second year in office, President Widodo has seen his fortunes dramatically change. Recovering from his rocky and tumultuous start, Widodo presents a more confident and assertive style of leadership. This was largely aided by the advantageous situation he found himself domestically — demonstrated by finally securing a majority in Parliament, enjoying high public ratings, and even already receiving early endorsements for a second term.

As noted, while the disintegration of the opposition KMP was largely not of the President's doing, Widodo did seize the opportunity to ensure a commanding parliamentary majority. The President took full advantage of the laws surrounding political parties to quietly but coercively ensure that pro-government factions would take over the leadership of the divided Golkar and PPP. Crucially, Widodo gave little in return for their support, thus avoiding the large coalition trap that had befallen his predecessor. For Widodo, Cabinet reshuffles were a tool to wield the powers of the presidency over weakened political parties whose leaders depended on the Government to recognize their legitimacy against rival claimants. Moreover, Widodo's reshuffles were: (1) conducted only after a political party's support for him had been secured; (2) offered 'relatively unimportant' Cabinet positions in return for switching to the Government; and (3) often went to party cadres not always favoured by their own party's leadership. In doing so, Widodo ensured that the expansion of the pro-government coalition was not done at the expense of any significant concessions to its newest members, thus ensuring that the President maintained control over his Cabinet.

Widodo's second year in office also saw him redefine his relationship with his party chairwoman, Megawati Sukarnoputri. Golkar's switch to the pro-government camp and their early endorsement for Widodo to run for another term meant the President could emerge from his previously subordinate position *vis-à-vis* Megawati Sukarnoputri. Safe in the knowledge that he had Golkar's backing, Widodo ignored pressures from Megawati Sukarnoputri's PDI-P to sack ministers that had fallen out of favor with the chairwoman, and even symbolically attended PDI-P's national congress as the Head of State/Government rather than merely a party cadre.

Widodo thus ended his second year in office with a newfound majority in Parliament, continued control over his Cabinet, early endorsements for a second term, and a redefined relationship with Megawati Sukarnoputri. As a result, his approval ratings climbed to an impressive 65.9 percent and there remained no doubt over who was now in charge.

Yet, for all these achievements, it has also been shown that the Joko Widodo–Jusuf Kalla Government was unable to give a satisfying answer to those that continued to question its interest in Indonesia's foreign policy. The President seemed to only intervene when an issue became unavoidable and he was forced into a reaction. This was especially the case when Jakarta's sovereignty was at stake, such as in response to China's increasing assertiveness to waters surrounding Indonesia's Natuna Islands, or when Indonesian citizens were being kidnapped by militants from the Philippines' restive south. On the occasions that the Government did venture on the world stage, the President's foreign policy disinterest arguably undermined such forays. For example, Widodo decided to skip the U.N. General Assembly for the second year in a row, even though Indonesia was officially announcing that it would seek a non-permanent seat at the U.N. Security Council for 2019–2020. Widodo also had mixed results in his ambitions to advance the Palestinian cause. The opening of an Honorary Consulate fell short of the embassy that Widodo had campaigned for, whilst the hosting of the Fifth Extraordinary Summit of the OIC did produce two key documents but attracted very little attention in the West, including among major powers that have key roles in the Holy Lands issue.

On other occasions, the Government's ventures on the world stage were confusing. Widodo's surprise announcement that Indonesia intended to join the TPP was at odds with the country's long refrain from committing to the mega free trade agreement, and was quickly followed by criticism back home. Meanwhile, the announcement of so-called liaison ministers appeared to undermine the position of Widodo's own foreign minister, despite reassurances that she remained in charge. The Government's 'flip-flop' over visa exemption facilities for Israel was another example of confusion at the heart of the Widodo Government, with ministers refusing to take responsibility for the fiasco. Perhaps more worrying was the apparent division between the Government and the Indonesian Navy over whether Chinese actions in Indonesian waters constituted a defence/security issue or was merely a 'fishing dispute.' Having said that, Widodo's decision to hold a Cabinet meeting onboard an Indonesian Navy warship as it patrolled Indonesia's EEZ not far from where the standoff with China took place was a bold, and arguably successful, assertion of Indonesia's sovereignty.

President Widodo also found success at the Special U.S.–ASEAN Leaders Summit with his positions on the importance of a tech-based creative economy and the role of small- and medium-sized enterprises (SMEs) being incorporated into the Sunnylands Declaration. Closer to home, the Government was able to secure the release of 17 kidnapped Indonesians in the Philippines' restive south, following intense negotiations. However, the Government had to deny suggestions it had paid ransoms in order to secure the release of its hostages, with the defense minister claiming that any payments made perhaps came from the families or employers of the victims. Meanwhile, Widodo's abandonment of ASEAN as the singular priority of Indonesia's foreign policy was evident in Jakarta's silence over democracy and human rights issues in the Philippines and Thailand, as well as its delayed congratulations for Myanmar's historic elections. With the Philippine President Duterte set to take over the chairmanship of ASEAN, there are major concerns over how the region will look next year. Further, it would seem that ASEAN will not be able to rely on Jakarta to take up its *primus inter pares* role and give the region a clear sense of direction and leadership in the post-ASEAN Community 2015 era.

Widodo's second year in charge was thus summed up by domestic consolidation on the one hand, but a reactionary external approach on the other hand. In some cases, Jakarta achieved some notable successes in its foreign policy efforts, but in other cases, it came up short. The Government should reflect on these successes and failures in order to improve its performance for the next year. An improved performance is all the more important given that next year will mark the halfway stage in Widodo's presidency. One area the Government should certainly work on is ensuring all components of the State are working on the same page. Too often, Indonesia's foreign policy has been marked by a lack of coordination, conflicting statements, and embarrassing reversals. In this sense, if Widodo's second year was one of domestic consolidation, his third year should be that of foreign policy consolidation. If the original goal was that of an assertive, active, and effective foreign policy, perhaps a more pressing goal heading into the third year is a coordinated, united, and sustainable one.

# References

Almuttaqi, A.I. (2016, March 31). 'Seizing the opportunity to lift Jakarta-Naypyitaw relations.' *The Jakarta Post*. Retrieved from: http://www. thejakartapost.com/news/2016/03/31/seizing-opportunity-lift-jakarta-naypyitaw-relations.html

Almuttaqi, A.I. (2016, August 19). 'Post-Thai referendum: ASEAN turning a blind eye?' *The Jakarta Post*. Retrieved from: http://www.thejakartapost. com/academia/2016/08/19/post-thai-referendum-asean-turning-a-blind-eye. html

Amanda, G. (2015, December 21). 'Soal Israel Bebas Visa, Menlu: Silakan Tanya ke Pak Menko.' *Republika*. Retrieved from: https://www.republika.co.id/ berita/nasional/umum/15/12/21/nzpl2w328-soal-israel-bebas-visa-menlu-silakan-tanya-ke-pak-menko?fb_comment_id=1086172238114249_108625 4824772657#f33a282afc0d2a8

Amindoni, A. and Yosephine, L. (2015, November 24). 'Jokowi appoints 12 top officials to seek foreign funds.' *The Jakarta Post*. Retrieved from: http:// www.thejakartapost.com/news/2015/11/24/jokowi-appoints-12-top-officials-seek-foreign-funds.html

Anggianto, W.K. and Muhamad, D. (2016, June 6). 'Taking the wind out of Abu Sayyaf's sails.' *The Jakarta Post*. Retrieved from: http://www.thejakartapost. com/academia/2016/06/06/taking-the-wind-out-of-abu-sayyafs-sails.html

Aritonang, M.S. (2015, April 10). 'Mega bares her teeth.' *The Jakarta Post.* Retrieved from: http://www.thejakartapost.com/news/2015/04/10/mega-bares-her-teeth.html

Arshad, A. (2016, August 5). 'Jakarta, KL and Manila to start joint patrols in Sulu Sea.' *The Straits Times.* Retrieved from: http://www.straitstimes.com/asia/se-asia/jakarta-kl-and-manila-to-start-joint-patrols-in-sulu-sea

*Bangkok Post* (2016, October 26). 'Duterte fails credibility test.' Retrieved from: https://www.bangkokpost.com/opinion/opinion/1119341/duterte-fails-credibility-test

Belarminus, R (2017, May 30). 'Survei "Kompas": Kepuasan terhadap Pemerintahan Jokowi-JK Menurun.' *Kompas.* Retrieved from: https://nasional.kompas.com/read/2017/05/30/11321561/survei.kompas.kepuasan.terhadap.pemerintahan.jokowi-jk.menurun.

Blanchard, B. (2016, October 20). Duterte aligns Philippines with China, says U.S. has lost.' *Reuters.* Retrieved from: https://www.reuters.com/article/us-china-philippines-idUSKCN12K0AS?

Bulkin, N. (2013, October 24). 'Indonesia's Political Parties.' *Carnegie Endowment for International Peace.* Retrieved from: http://carnegieendowment.org/2013/10/24/indonesia-s-political-parties-pub-53414

Cochrane, J. (2016, June 18). 'Lives still in Limbo, one year after Southeast Asia migrant crisis.' *The New York Times.* Retrieved from: https://www.nytimes.com/2016/06/19/world/asia/myanmar-indonesia-refugees.html

*The Daily Mail* (2016, July 11). '3 Indonesians kidnapped by suspected Abu Sayyaf militants.' Retrieved from: http://www.dailymail.co.uk/wires/ap/article-3683864/3-Indonesians-kidnapped-suspected-Abu-Sayyaf-militants.html

European Union External Action (2016, March 7). 'EU Ambassador Vincent Guérend's intervention at the 5th Extraordinary OIC Summit on Palestine and Al-Quds Al-Sharif.' Retrieved from: https://eeas.europa.eu/headquarters/headQuarters-homepage/4386/eu-ambassador-vincent-guerends-intervention-5th-extraordinary-oic-summit-palestine-and-al-quds_en

Firdaus, R.F. (2015, December 30). 'Isu reshuffle, Taufik Kurniawan sudah pamit dari DPR.' *Merdeka.com.* Retrieved from: https://www.merdeka.com/politik/isu-reshuffle-taufik-kurniawan-sudah-pamit-dari-dpr.html

Fitriyanti, A. (2016, February 11). President Jokowi to lead counter terrorism meeting on US-ASEAN Summit.' *Antara News.* Retrieved from: https://en.

antaranews.com/news/103063/president-jokowi-to-lead-counter-terrorism-meeting-on-us-asean-summit

*The Guardian* (2015, May 20). 'Indonesia and Malaysia agree to offer 7,000 migrants temporary shelter.' Retrieved from: https://www.theguardian.com/world/2015/may/20/hundreds-more-migrants-rescued-off-indonesia-as-pope-calls-for-help

*The Guardian* (2015, October 27). 'Indonesia will join Trans-Pacific Partnership, Jokowi tells Obama.' Retrieved from: https://www.theguardian.com/world/2015/oct/27/indonesia-will-join-trans-pacific-partnership-jokowi-tells-obama

Gutierrez, N. (2016, September 21). 'Millions of dollars paid to free Indonesian hostages.' *Rappler.* Retrieved from: https://www.rappler.com/world/regions/asia-pacific/indonesia/bahasa/englishedition/146840-abu-sayyaf-ransom-indonesian-hostages

Hermansyah, A. (2015, November 29). 'State-enterprises under threat if Indonesia joins TPP: Experts.' *The Jakarta Post.* Retrieved from: http://www.thejakartapost.com/news/2015/11/29/state-enterprises-under-threat-if-indonesia-joins-tpp-experts.html

*The Hindu* (2016, August 24). 'RCEP negotiations may miss December deadline.' Retrieved from: http://www.thehindu.com/business/Economy/RCEP-negotiations-may-miss-December-deadline/article14587100.ece

*The Jakarta Post* (2015, December 21). 'Govt to include 84 more countries in free-entry policy.' Retrieved from: http://www.thejakartapost.com/news/2015/12/21/govt-include-84-more-countries-free-entry-policy.html

*The Jakarta Post* (2016, January 16). 'World praises Indonesian response to terrorist attack.' Retrieved from: http://www.thejakartapost.com/news/2016/01/16/world-praises-indonesian-response-terrorist-attack.html

*The Jakarta Post* (2016, March 21). 'Indonesia opens honorary consulate for Palestine in Ramallah.' Retrieved from: http://www.thejakartapost.com/news/2016/03/14/indonesia-opens-honorary-consulate-for-palestine-in-ramallah.html

*The Jakarta Post* (2016, May 2). 'No ransom paid for release of 10 Indonesians, negotiator claims.' Retrieved from: http://www.thejakartapost.com/news/2016/05/02/no-ransom-paid-for-release-of-10-indonesians-negotiator-claims.html

*The Jakarta Post* (2017, September 14). 'Large coalition weakens checks and balances: Expert.' Retrieved from: http://www.thejakartapost.com/ news/2016/09/14/large-coalition-weakens-checks-and-balances-expert. html?fb_comment_id=1308445822529735_1308617379179246#f19b9f1ee 1b6a3c

Kami, I.M. (2016, January 11). 'Jokowi Pidato di Rakernas PDIP Sebagai Presiden, PDIP: ini Sinergi.' *DetikNews*. Retrieved from: https://news.detik. com/berita/d-3114877/jokowi-pidato-di-rakernas-pdip-sebagai-presiden-pdip-ini-sinergi

Kapoor, K. and Jensen, F. (2016, June 23). 'Indonesia president visits islands on warship, makes point to China.' *Reuters*. Retrieved from: https://www. reuters.com/article/us-southchinasea-indonesia/indonesia-president-visits-islands-on-warship-makes-point-to-china-idUSKCN0Z909D

*Kompas* (2017). 'Rapor 2 Tahun JOKOWI-JK.' Retrieved from: https://vik. kompas.com/dua-tahun-jokowi-jk/

*Kontan* (2016, March 23). 'Natuna Sea dispute a fishing issue: RI Navy.' Retrieved from: http://english.kontan.co.id/news/natuna-sea-dispute-a-fishing-issue-ri-navy

Mason, J. and Wallace, B. (2016, February 16). 'Obama, ASEAN discuss South China Sea tensions, but no joint mention of China.' *Reuters*. Retrieved from: https://www.reuters.com/article/us-usa-asean/obama-asean-discuss-south-china-sea-tensions-but-no-joint-mention-of-china-idUSKCN0VP1F7

Mietzner, M. (2017). 'Indonesia in 2016 — Jokowi's Presidency between Elite Consolidation and Extra-Parliamentary Opposition.' *Asian Survey* Vol. 57, No. 1, January/February, pp. 165–172. Retrieved from: http://as.ucpress.edu/ content/57/1/165

Ministry of Foreign Affairs, Republic of Indonesia (2015, January 8). *Annual Press Statement Minister for Foreign Affairs Republic of Indonesia 2015*. Retrieved from: www.kemlu.go.id/.../PPTM%202015/PPTM%202015%20 ENG%20FINAL%20DF.pdf

Ministry of Foreign Affairs, Republic of Indonesia (2016, January 7). *The Annual Press Statement of the Indonesian Minister for Foreign Affairs 2016*. Retrieved from: https://www.kemlu.go.id/en/pidato/menlu/Pages/The-Annual-Press-Statement-of-the-Indonesian-Minister-for-Foreign-Affairs-2016.aspx

Ministry of Foreign Affairs, Republic of Indonesia (2016, March 5). 'The 5th Extraordinary OIC Summit on Palestine and Al-Quds Al-Sharif: Indonesia's

Contribution for Palestine.' Retrieved from: https://www.kemlu.go.id/en/berita/Pages/oic-summit-contribution.aspx

Ministry of Foreign Affairs, Republic of Indonesia (2016, March 7). 'Fifth OIC Extraordinary Summit Tangible Proof of Support for Palestinian People.' Retrieved from: https://www.kemlu.go.id/en/berita/pages/oic-palestine-support.aspx

Ministry of Foreign Affairs, Republic of Indonesia (2017, January 10). *Annual Press Statement Minister for Foreign Affairs of the Republic of Indonesia Retno L.P. Marsudi 2017.* Retrieved from: https://www.kemlu.go.id/id/pidato/menlu/Documents/PPTM-2017-EN.pdf

Nursyamsyi, M. (2015, December 22). 'Selain Israel, Indonesia Juga Coret 10 Negara Ini dari Daftar Bebas Visa Kunjungan.' *Republika.* Retrieved from: https://www.republika.co.id/berita/nasional/umum/15/12/22/nzqzox383-selain-israel-indonesia-juga-coret-10-negara-ini-dari-daftar-bebas-visa-kunjungan

Paath, C.Y. (2016, June 23). 'Jokowi Holds Cabinet Meeting on Board Warship at Natuna.' *Jakarta Globe.* Retrieved from: http://jakartaglobe.id/news/jokowi-holds-cabinet-meeting-board-warship-natuna/

Panda, A. (2016, May 31). 'South China Sea: Indonesian Navy Fires at and Arrests Chinese Fishermen.' *The Diplomat.* Retrieved from: https://thediplomat.com/2016/05/south-china-sea-indonesian-navy-fires-at-and-arrests-chinese-fishermen/

Panda, A. (2016, June 21). 'A Third 2016 Natuna Stand-Off Highlights Growing Indonesia-China Tensions.' *The Diplomat.* Retrieved from: https://thediplomat.com/2016/06/a-third-2016-natuna-stand-off-highlights-growing-indonesia-china-tensions/

Parameswaran, P. (2016, February 11). 'Why the US-ASEAN Sunnylands Summit Matters.' *The Diplomat.* Retrieved from: https://thediplomat.com/2016/02/why-the-us-asean-sunnylands-summit-matters/

Pileggi, T. (2016, March 28). 'Netanyahu calls for normalizing ties with Indonesia.' *The Times of Israel.* Retrieved from: https://www.timesofisrael.com/netanyahu-calls-for-normalizing-ties-with-indonesia/

Prasetyo, E. (2016, August 3). 'Jokowi and Sri Lankan PM Discusses Procuring Indonesian Goods.' *Jakarta Globe.* Retrieved from: http://jakartaglobe.id/news/jokowi-sri-lankan-pm-discuss-anti-terrorism-procuring-indonesian-goods/

*Republika* (2016, March 6). 'Russia says Indonesia has influence for two-state Palestinian solution.' Retrieved from: https://www.republika.co.id/amp_version/o3m0ab317

Salim, T. (2016, October 21). 'Indonesia's foreign policy: Lack of interest or mere prioritizing?' *The Jakarta Post*. Retrieved from: http://www.thejakartapost.com/news/2016/10/21/indonesia-s-foreign-policy-lack-interest-or-mere-prioritizing.html

Salim, T. (2015, November 26). 'Jokowi criticized for assigning ministers for specific countries.' *The Jakarta Post*. Retrieved from: http://www.thejakartapost.com/news/2015/11/26/jokowi-criticized-assigning-ministers-specific-countries.html

Sekretariat Kabinet Republik Indonesia (2015, November 25a). 'Related with Investments, President Jokowi Appoints a Number of Ministers as the Liaison.' Retrieved from: http://setkab.go.id/en/related-with-investments-president-jokowi-appoints-a-number-of-ministers-as-the-liaison/

Sekretariat Kabinet Republik Indonesia (2015, November 25b). 'Cabinet Secretary: Liaison Minister Shall Not Overlap with Foreign Affairs Minister.' Retrieved from: http://setkab.go.id/en/cabinet-secretary-liaison-minister-shall-not-overlap-with-foreign-affairs-minister/

Sekretariat Kabinet Republik Indonesia (2015, November 25c). 'Minister of Foreign Affairs will Coordinate the Liaison Ministers.' Retrieved from: http://setkab.go.id/en/minister-of-foreign-affairs-will-coordinate-the-liaison-ministers/

Setuningsih, N. and Prasetyo, E. (2016, April 14). 'Govt Calls Natuna Incident 'Misunderstanding,' Claims Resolution.' *Jakarta Globe*. Retrieved from: http://jakartaglobe.id/news/govt-calls-natuna-incident-misunderstanding-claims-resolution/

Sholeh, M. (2014, October 27). 'Kubu SDA: Jadi Menteri Agama, Lukman Hakim tidak mewakili PPP.' *Merdeka.com*. Retrieved from: https://www.merdeka.com/politik/kubu-sda-jadi-menteri-agama-lukman-hakim-tidak-mewakili-ppp.html

Simanjuntak, R.A. (2016, July 28). 'Rapimnas Golkar Resmi Dukung Jokowi untuk Pilpres 2019.' *SindoNews.com*. Retrieved from: https://nasional.sindonews.com/read/1127061/12/rapimnas-golkar-resmi-dukung-jokowi-untuk-pilpres-2019-1469715759

Stefanie, C. (2015, September 12), 'PAN Gabung ke Pemerintah Tak Kuatkan KIH dan Lemahkan KMP.' *CNN Indonesia*. Retrieved from: http://www.cnnindonesia.com/politik/20150911180057-32-78166/pan-gabung-ke-pemerintah-tak-kuatkan-kih-dan-lemahkan-kmp/

*The Straits Times* (2016, March 22). 'Chinese coast guard 'prevented Indonesia from detaining boat.' Retrieved from: https://www.straitstimes.com/asia/se-asia/chinese-coast-guard-prevented-indonesia-from-detaining-boat

*The Straits Times* (2016, July 14). 'Asean will not make statement on South China Sea ruling: Diplomats.' Retrieved from: https://www.straitstimes.com/asia/se-asia/asean-to-keep-mum-on-south-china-sea-ruling-diplomats

*The Times of Israel* (2016, April 1). 'Indonesia rebuffs Netanyahu call for normalized ties.' Retrieved from: https://www.timesofisrael.com/indonesia-rebuffs-netanyahu-call-for-normalized-ties/

Tomsa, D. (2017). 'Indonesia in 2016: Jokowi consolidates power.' *Southeast Asian Affairs* Vol. 2017, pp. 149–162. Retrieved from: https://muse.jhu.edu/article/658018

U.S. Department of State (2016, March 7). 'The Fifth Extraordinary OIC Summit on Palestine and Al-Quds Al-Sharif.' Retrieved from: https://2009-2017.state.gov/s/rga/rls/remarks/254030.htm

The White House (2016, February 15). Remarks by President Obama at Opening Session of the U.S.-ASEAN Summit. Retrieved from: https://obamawhitehouse.archives.gov/the-press-office/2016/02/15/remarks-president-obama-opening-session-us-asean-summit

Williamson, T. (2015, December 5). 'Why Indonesia joining the TPP would be a good thing.' *The Diplomat*. Retrieved from: https://thediplomat.com/2015/12/why-indonesia-joining-the-tpp-would-be-a-good-thing/

Wirayani, P. (2015, November 12). 'Joining TPP or not, Indonesia's readiness is the real question.' *The Jakarta Post*. Retrieved from: http://www.thejakartapost.com/news/2015/11/12/joining-tpp-or-not-indonesia-s-readiness-real-question.html

# Chapter III

# Jokowi at the Halfway Stage: Mid-Term Wobbles

## 1. Introduction

The period October 2016 to September 2017 marked the halfway stage in Joko 'Jokowi' Widodo's presidency, with minds starting to turn towards the Presidential Elections scheduled to be held in 2019. Crucial regional elections, including for the prized position of Governor of Jakarta — which the President previously held and used as a launchpad for the highest position in the Republic — were up for grabs during Widodo's third year, and were widely seen as an early test case for how the 2019 elections may pan out.

The failure of Widodo's ally, Basuki Tjahaja Purnama — popularly known as 'Ahok' — to win the Jakarta Governorship, the scandal surrounding the pro-government Golkar chairman, Setya Novanto, as well as the emergence of a conservative Islamic movement opposed to the President, were major domestic setbacks for Widodo. Indeed, mass demonstrations by the conservative movement would force President Widodo to postpone a planned visit to Australia after it turned violent. Added to this were rumors of a coup plot, which saw the President respond by embarking on a month-long 'safari' to various military and police bases, reminding troops and officers of their loyalty to the 'legitimate government', arresting several individuals on treason charges, and disbanding conservative Muslim groups that wanted to replace the Republic with a caliphate. In this sense, if Widodo had been successful in consolidating power domestically during his second term in office, the gains made were put under enormous strains in this third year, as the President seemingly struggled to keep a grip on power.

Externally, President Widodo's foreign policy was also met by several challenges. The unexpected victory of Donald J. Trump as the U.S. President has turned the world upside down, plunging the region and the wider world into uncertainty. The decision by the 45th President of the United States to pull his country out of the Trans-Pacific Partnership (TPP) negotiations, the imposition of a so-called 'Muslim ban', and his promise to recognise Jerusalem as the capital of Israel have left Indonesian policymakers in a difficult and confusing situation. Jakarta seemingly has yet to devise a strategy on how to deal with the new U.S. President and the consequences of his controversial actions. Much closer to home, Indonesia's relationship with its large neighbor, Australia, proved difficult. Beyond the President's postponed state visit to Australia, the Indonesian Military (Tentara Nasional Indonesia, or TNI) would also suspend ties, following perceived insults to the country's state ideology by their counterparts.

The plight of the Rohingya also became an issue following a heavy-handed response by the Myanmar military that supposedly targeted the terrorist Arakan Rohingya Salvation Army (ARSA) but forced millions of civilians to flee their homes. The issue caused deep splits in ASEAN, with Malaysia in particular describing Myanmar's actions as 'genocide', and Indonesia pressed to deploy diplomatic efforts in order to find a peaceful solution and prevent it from escalating into a regional crisis.

Another potential regional crisis was the siege of Marawi in the southern part of the Philippines that left an estimated 1,100 dead and 350,000 displaced. The siege would be a wakeup call for Jakarta, Kuala Lumpur, and Manila, exposing the weak level of maritime security cooperation that had allowed militants affiliated to the Maute and Abu Sayyaf groups as well foreign fighters from Indonesia and Malaysia to temporarily establish an Islamist foothold in the region.

There were some plus points for President Widodo during his third year in office. The high-profile visit by the King of Saudi Arabia saw significant economic deals signed, while Jakarta would press home its ownership of waters surrounding Natuna Islands by renaming it the North Natuna Sea, much to the annoyance of China and its own claims to the South China Sea.

Entering the halfway point in his presidency, Widodo was thus faced with a deteriorating domestic situation and an uncertain external environment. How was it that the President's domestic consolidation during his second year seemed to have fallen apart? What impact would this have on his international standing? And how did Widodo cope with an uncertain and unpredictable global environment? It is in this sense that this chapter takes the topic of 'Jokowi at the Halfway Stage: Mid-Term Wobbles.'

## 2. The Domestic Scene: One-Step Forward, Two-Steps Back?

### 2.1. *Jakarta Gubernatorial Elections*

At the end of Widodo's second year in office, the President's position had appeared seemingly secure. His newfound majority in Parliament, continued control over his Cabinet, early endorsements for a second term, and a redefined relationship with Megawati Sukarnoputri had left no doubt over who was in charge. Yet, those fortunes were to quickly change in the early months of his third year in office, most demonstrated by the failure of his ally, Basuki Tjahaja Purnama, to win the Gubernatorial Elections for the capital city in February 2017.

Basuki Tjahaja Purnama had served as Widodo's deputy when the latter held the position of Governor, taking over the role when Widodo moved to Merdeka Palace. While the President was 'above politics', his preference for his former deputy was no secret. While the Jakarta Gubernatorial Elections was just one of the many that formed the simultaneous regional elections in 2017, it unsurprisingly drew most of the country's attention as the Republic's capital and center of politics, business, and trade. As noted earlier, Widodo had used the 2012 version as a stepping-stone towards the presidency, and there was much speculation as to whether 2017 would thrust a potential new face into the mix for the

Presidential Elections in 2019. At the same time, the Jakarta Gubernatorial Elections offered an opportunity for political parties to try out different tactics and strategies that, if successful, might be worth replicating for 2019. As an incumbent, free from any corruption scandals, and with high approval ratings, Basuki Tjahaja Purnama's situation was not too dissimilar with the President, and would be the perfect test-case for the Opposition as they prepared for 2019.

Interestingly enough, three major political groupings emerged for the Jakarta Gubernatorial Elections. The ruling PDI-P, together with Hanura, Golkar and NasDem, backed Basuki Tjahaja Purnama. Meanwhile, the opposition Gerindra together with PKS backed Anies Baswedan, a former Education Minister in Widodo's Cabinet who was fired in July 2016. Lastly, Partai Demokrat together with PPP, PKB and PAN, backed the eldest son of former President Susilo Bambang Yudhoyono, Agus Harimurti Yudhoyono, who had to hand in his retirement with the Indonesian Military in order to contest. Most political observers predicted that for the Presidential Elections 2019, the major political groupings will be more or less similar, with a Megawati Sukarnoputri-backed Widodo contesting against Prabowo Subianto and a Susilo Bambang Yudhoyono-backed candidate.

Despite being far ahead in the polls initially, the ethnic Chinese and Christian Basuki Tjahaja Purnama controversially referenced a verse from the *Qur'an,* telling voters not to be duped by religious leaders who quoted the verse to argue they should not vote for a non-Muslim leader. An edited version of the speech was later uploaded on the Internet and sparked anger among Muslim conservatives who later filed blasphemy charges against the Governor. The ensuing court case would hurt Basuki Tjahaja Purnama's standing in the polls, and although it was argued that the Governor was only suggesting that it was religious leaders and not the *Qur'an* itself that misled the public, the damage had already been done. Basuki Tjahaja Purnama's opponents would seize on the issue, with the campaign descending into one of the most 'polarising and fraught campaign that exposed religious and ethnic divisions in Indonesia's capital' (Lamb, April 19, 2017).

The first round of results saw Basuki Tjahaja Purnama narrowly come first place with 42.99 percent of the votes, followed by Anies Baswedan who secured 39.95 percent, and Agus Harimurti Yudhoyono far behind with 17.05 percent (KPU Provinsi DKI Jakarta, 2017, February 26). With no candidate securing a majority, a second round was held between the top two, with most of the previous votes for Agus Harimurti Yudhoyono shifting towards Anies Baswedan. After the votes for the second round were tallied up, the former education minister secured a convincing 57.96 percent, while Widodo's ally could only command 42.04 percent (KPU Provinsi DKI Jakarta, 2017, April 29). The results left 'the president damaged', emboldening the Opposition who were now 'well positioned to mount a challenge in the 2019 presidential election' (Gunn, 2018). In this sense, the fallout from the Jakarta Gubernatorial Elections went beyond the mere loss of an ally for the President but potentially had far-reaching the consequences.

## 2.2. The '212' Movement

Perhaps the most far-reaching consequences of the Jakarta Gubernatorial Elections was the birth of the '212' movement. Named after the date (i.e., December 2) of what would become the largest rally in Indonesian history, more than 200,000 Indonesians marched on the capital calling for Basuki Tjahaja Purnama to be jailed over the aforementioned blasphemy issue (Quiano & Griffiths, 2016, December 2). The protest was not the first calling for action to be taken against the then-Governor. Several had taken place in the weeks running up to the 212 demonstration, most notably on November 4, 2016 which though peaceful during the day, 'erupted into violence on Friday night leaving one dead and multiple people injured as police clashed with demonstrators' (Topsfield, 2016, November 5). So serious was the November 4 violence that the President held an impromptu press conference in the early hours immediately after, calling on protestors to return to their homes and to allow the police to handle Basuki Tjahaja Purnama's case in accordance with the law. A visibly shocked Widodo went on to blame 'political actors [that] had ride on (the incident) to take advantage of the situation' and was forced to cancel a planned trip to Australia (Soeriaatmadja & Arshad, 2016, November 4).

Arguably, the President had underestimated the November 4 demonstration, attempting to portray a 'business-as-usual' image by leaving the Merdeka Palace during the day to visit a construction site of an airport train project. That move would backfire as demonstrators demanded to have an audience with President Widodo before dispersing, and were infuriated to find out he was not at the Palace.

It was in this sense that Widodo made the surprising decision to join the demonstrators on December 2 as they held Friday prayers at the site of the National Monument, not far from the Merdeka Palace (*Republika* 2016, December 2). The President would not only join them as they prayed but would listen to a sermon delivered by the firebrand leader of *Front Pembela Islam* (FPI, or Islamic Defenders Front), Rizieq Syihab, before giving a small speech of his own. In doing so, Widodo gave a sense of legitimacy to the '212' movement and their cause. The December 2 protest was widely interpreted as a watershed moment in Indonesian history, not only because of the size of the crowd but also because of its composition. Unlike previous demonstrations, this was not merely a hardcore group of religious conservatives, but instead it drew Muslims from all walks of life, determined to be part of this show of force of Muslim unity that has long been absent in Indonesia's political scene. That unity would go on to help bring about the unexpected defeat of Basuki Tjahaja Purnama in the Gubernatorial Elections, with the '212' movement's leaders promising to do the same in 2019 when the President runs for reelection.

At the same time, the public show of Muslim unity arguably pressured the court into finding Basuki Tjahaja Purnama guilty of committing blasphemy and saw the former Governor sentenced to two years imprisonment starting in May 2017. Curiously, prosecutors had dropped the blasphemy charge, claiming there was not enough evidence, and had thus only demanded a two-year probationary sentence for the lesser charge of defaming clergymen under article 156 of the Criminal Code (Wijaya, 2017, May 9). The judges' decision to nonetheless find Basuki Tjahaja Purnama guilty of blasphemy and impose a harsher punishment than that requested by prosecutors was seen by some as 'a sad day for Indonesia' (Lamb, 2017, May 9).

The '212' movement thus appeared to confirm the country's general shift towards religious conservatism, with officials and public figures frequently claiming Indonesia was in the midst of various state of emergencies over issues such as LGBT, alcohol, pornography, and communism, among others. Rather than push back against such alarmist sentiments, the Government seemed to appease the religious conservatives, with authorities clamping down on such affronts to the Islamic faith. For example, in May 2017, the police raided a fitness center in Jakarta suspected of providing sexual services for homosexuals. Those caught in the raid were paraded on national television, some in a state of undress. As one news media noted, 'an unprecedented wave of police raids, vigilante attacks, and calls for the criminalization of homosexual sex have left many in the country's LGBT community fearing for their safety' (Westcott, 2017, June 1). Indeed, the Constitutional Court is currently considering a lawsuit brought by religious conservatives to review the Criminal Code and its definition of adultery to make illegal all non-heterosexual relations, even if it involves consenting adults.

The above developments make religious issues likely to feature heavily in the upcoming Presidential Elections with Widodo and his rivals attempting to appeal to the '212' movement and its supporters by campaigning on a more conservative agenda — consequently putting Indonesia's global reputation as a modern and pluralistic nation at stake.

## 2.3. Coup Attempts and Political Intrigues

In connection with the heightened tensions following the violence of the November 4 demonstration and in the run-up to the December 2 rally, President Widodo embarked on a series of visits or 'safari' to key military and police bases in the capital. These included visits to the headquarters of the Indonesian Military's Special Forces (Komando Pasukan Khusus, or Kopassus) on November 10, and the police's paramilitary Mobile Brigade (Brimob), as well as the Indonesian Navy's Marines the following day on November 11. That same week, the President gathered thousands of soldiers at the Army Headquarters as well as hundreds of senior- and middle-ranking police officers at the police academy (*Perguruan Tinggi Ilmu Kepolisian*, or PTIK).

In each of his 'safari' visits, the President referred to himself as the highest military commander, or '*Panglima Tertinggi*', demanding loyalty from the troops in attendance (Parlina & Aritonang, 2016, November 11).

For example, during his visit to the Marines, Widodo stated, 'I want to make sure that all are loyal to the state, to the *Pancasila* (state philosophy), to the Constitution (UUD 1945), to the Unitary State of the Republic of Indonesia, and to our diversity' (*Antara News* 2016, November 11). For some, the statement was interpreted as a coded message to the religious conservatives who wanted to see a more Islamic Indonesia.

Moreover, during his 'safari' visit to the Special Forces, the President warned, '[t]his [Special Forces] is a reserve unit that I can deploy as the highest military commander...for special needs' (Lumbanrau, 2016, November 13). The statement was similarly seen as a coded message, warning any potential opponents of the military strength at the President's disposal should anyone dare to dispose the Government. Significantly, the Indonesian Military Commander, General Gatot Nurmantyo and National Police Chief, Pol-Gen Tito Karnavian, accompanied the President during his visits, demonstrating their solidarity with Widodo.

Certainly, there were concerns of a possible coup during the month of November. Banners appeared over the capital reminding the public to safeguard the country's unity and diversity. References were also made to '*Pemerintah yang sah*', or the legitimate Government, suggesting the possibility of unknown actors attempting to establish a rival government. And whilst Vice President Jusuf Kalla dismissed fears of a *coup d'etat*, the fact that he even needed to address the concern was telling (Taufiqqurahman, 2016, November 11).

Indeed, two weeks after the Vice President's denials, the police revealed it had intelligence on unknown actors planning to hijack a planned demonstration on November 25 and December 2 (*BBC Indonesia* 2016, November 21). Pol-Gen Tito Karnavian stated there was a plot to encourage demonstrators to occupy Parliament with the intention of overthrowing the Government. The National Police Chief further added that the demonstrations were no longer a simple protest calling for Basuki Tjahaja Purnama to be legally processed but that there was a hidden political agenda (Faizal, 2016, November 19).

President Widodo similarly made repeated claims that 'political actors' were exploiting the demonstrations and were taking advantage of the situation (*Tempo* 2016, November 5). Whilst the 'political actors' referred to were never specified, speculation fell on Susilo Bambang Yudhoyono.

Indeed, his wife, former First Lady Kristiani Herrawati, issued a vehement statement on social media calling speculations that Susilo Bambang Yudhoyono had initiated and funded the November 4 demonstrations as an 'evil slander' and 'extraordinary insult' (*The Jakarta Post* 2016, November 7). The former president himself held a press conference a few days before the November 4 demonstrations, criticizing the Government for its unclear intelligence and suggesting he himself was being unfairly accused (*BBC Indonesia* 2016, November 7). Notably, whilst President Widodo met with a number of opposition leaders, including Prabowo Subianto, in order to calm tensions during that month, no meetings were made with his predecessor. The lack of a meeting between the sixth and seventh Presidents of the Republic of Indonesia at a time when the country was on edge certainly raised eyebrows, only adding to the rumor mill.

The cold relationship between Widodo and Susilo Bambang Yudhoyono stood in stark contrast to the meetings between the President and his former rival in the Presidential Elections of 2014, Prabowo Subianto. The first meeting took place in the latter's residence in Hambalang, West Java, on October 31, where the two rode horses as part of a photo opportunity in front of the media. The President told reporters that, 'religious and political leaders should join forces to cool down the situation', whilst Prabowo Subianto agreed, adding he had used the meeting to give constructive inputs to the Government out of concern about the state of the nation (Halim & Ramadhani, 2016, November 1).

A second meeting was held at the Merdeka Palace on November 17 amid heightened tensions following the fallout of the November 4 demonstrations. The President again called for national unity, stating, '[w]e do not want to see us divided due to political differences, because the cost will be too high for the Unitary State of the Republic of Indonesia' (*BBC Indonesia* 2016, November 17). Meanwhile, Prabowo Subianto stated that political differences were normal and should not be made into a problem. He went on to praise Widodo for not being afraid of criticism, pledging he would continue to provide constructive criticisms to the Government, stating it as 'good as long as it is not destructive and doesn't lean towards violence' (*BBC Indonesia* 2016, November 17).

As one observer noted, '[w]hen the two leaders [Widodo and Prabowo Subianto] meet, it usually takes place in situations where political tension is at its highest' (Halim & Ramadhani, 2016, November 1). A few weeks after their second meeting and in the morning of the December 2 demonstrations, police conducted a number of arrests against leading opponents of the President, charging them with treason (Ompusunggu & Ramadhani, 2016, December 3). These included Rachmawati Soekarnoputri, the daughter of Indonesia's founding father Soekarno and younger sister of PDI-P chairwoman, Megawati Soekarnoputri, a retired two-star army General (Ret.) Kivlan Zen, and political activist Sri Bintang Pamungkas. The police stated that a total of seven people had been detained, and that these were the same individuals that the police had earlier stated were plotting to encourage demonstrators to occupy Parliament in the hope that a special session of the People's Consultative Assembly (Majelis Permusyawaratan Rakyat, or MPR) would be called to dismiss the Government — despite the fact the MPR no longer had such powers (*The Jakarta Post* 2016, December 3). Whilst fortunately no coup did take place during the tense months of November and December 2016, it was certainly a worrying time for the President, and the gains made by Widodo during his second year in office were put under enormous strains in the early months of his third year.

Things were made worst for the President when the pro-government Golkar chairman, Setya Novanto, was implicated in an IDR 2.3 trillion graft case involving the e-KTP, or electronic identity card project (*The Jakarta Post* 2017, July 17). The Corruption Eradication Commission (Komisi Pemberantasan Korupsi, or KPK) officially named Setya Novanto, who also serves as Speaker of the House of Representatives, a suspect on July 17, 2017, having earlier banned him from leaving the country a few months earlier in April. Given that it was Setya Novanto's decision as party chair to switch Golkar's allegiance to Widodo's camp — thus giving the President a majority in Parliament — the former's alleged involvement in the corruption scandals threatens the President's position *vis-à-vis* the nation's legislature. Whilst maintaining his innocence and launching a counter pre-trial motion, there have been strong calls for Setya Novanto to step down in his roles as party chair as well as Speaker of House of Representatives. If he does indeed step down or is found guilty, there are no guarantees that his replacement would be similarly pro-government, thus providing another major step back for President Widodo.

## 2.4. The President Clobbers Back

In response to being forced onto the back foot domestically, the President hit back in an effort to retake the initiative. Efforts included the aforementioned 'safari' visits to key military and police bases, as well as the treason charges laid on several anti-government figures. However, on July 10, 2017, the President went further by introducing a regulation in lieu of law (*Peraturan Pemerintah Pengganti Undang-Undang*, or Perppu), which gave the Government 'sweeping powers' to disband any mass organizations seen as challenging *Pancasila*, or the 1945 Constitution (*The Jakarta Post* 2017, July 14). Significantly, the new regulation did away with the requirement of Law No. 17 Year 2013 on Mass Organizations that had stipulated a court ruling was first needed before a mass organization could be banned. The new regulation only required the Government to issue a single warning letter, and if the mass organization in question did not respond adequately, it would see itself disbanded within a week of that sole warning.

The Government's rationale behind the regulation was that Law No 13. Year 2013 was 'no longer sufficient', and its definition of threats to *Pancasila* and the 1945 Constitution were 'narrowly formulated' (Hamid & Gammon, 2017, July 13). Whilst it was emphasized that the new Perppu is 'not meant to discredit Islamic organisations, let alone the Muslim community', it was notable that the first target was *Hizbut-Tahrir Indonesia* (HTI) (Topsfield & Rompies, 2017, July 12). Disbanded a few days after the new regulation came into force, HTI had long campaigned for Indonesia to become part of a global Islamic caliphate and was, prior to the ban, a legally registered entity with tens of thousands of followers in the country. Interestingly, HTI had helped organize the series of anti-Basuki Tjahaja Purnama demonstrations in 2016, and it has been suggested that 'the banning of HTI was politically motivated, a retaliation against or a way to crack down on the supporters' of those demonstrations (Burhani, 2017, September 19).

In response, HTI filed for a judicial review at the Constitutional Court to examine the legal standing of the new regulation, arguing the Government's move was an 'arbitrary action' and moreover, that HTI was a 'legal religious organisation and has been spreading its messages peacefully, in an orderly manner, in accordance with the law' (*Al Jazeera* 2017, July 19). Meanwhile, the Government is pushing for the new regulation to be passed into law by the House of Representatives during its next sitting, thus making permanent the Government's temporary sweeping powers. The Government's push is not yet certain to succeed in the House, with the pro-Government PAN siding with opposition parties in threatening to reject the move (*Tempo* 2017, July 18). Indeed, the regulation has received plenty of criticisms ranging from religious conservatives who feel they are being especially targeted, to pro-democracy and human rights activists who decry it as a return to the dark days of the New Order regime. An editorial by *The Jakarta Post* (2017, July 14), for example, described the regulation as 'draconian' and 'a holdover from the New Order regime' warning, '[i]t's a slippery slope from here.' Observers added the new regulation was a 'formidable tool of political repression' and that by signing it, 'the president has mounted a serious attack on legal protections of freedom of association in Indonesia' (Hamid & Gammon, 2017, July 13).

This was not the first time the President was accused of trying to turn back the clocks to the New Order regime. A few months earlier in May 2016, Widodo threatened to '*gebuk*', or 'clobber' anyone who wanted to demonstrate in expressing their opinions or to assemble outside the legal corridors (Patria & Halim, 2017, May 18). He also threatened to 'clobber' anyone that tried to revive the defunct Indonesian Communist Party (*Partai Komunis Indonesia* or PKI) (Nugroho, 2017, May 17). Observers noted that the only other time a leader had used the word to 'clobber' was when Soeharto warned, in September 1989, '[i]f they want to replace me in an unconstitutional way, I'll clobber them whether they are politicians or generals' (Patria & Halim, 2017, May 18). The similarities earned President Widodo the moniker of 'little Soeharto', and one observer noted that the term 'clobber' was deliberately used to convey Widodo's sense of anger, adding, '[w]hen someone uses the word, they are aware of the consequences and risks they might face' (Patria & Halim, 2017, May 18). Indeed, when the President was challenged that the term brought back memories of the New Order regime, Widodo was reported to have said there was no other term that could describe his feeling (*The Straits Times* 2017, May 26).

The President's seemingly transformation into a 'little Soeharto' may on the one hand be interpreted as a sign of Widodo's growing strength domestically, building on the gains he made in his second year in office. More likely, however, it perhaps demonstrated Widodo's increased frustrations with the enormous strains faced by the Government as its domestic consolidation during the second year appeared to fell apart. The question was how would the domestic wobble impact President Widodo's international standing, and how did he cope with the uncertain and unpredictable global environment he was confronted with?

## 3. Coping with an Uncertain and Unpredictable Global Environment

### 3.1. *Frosty Relations Down Under*

As referred to earlier, one of the immediate impacts of President Widodo's domestic struggles was the cancellation of his planned visit to Australia. Scheduled to fly out of Jakarta on November 6, 2016, for a three-day trip, the President instead found himself having to deal with the aftermath of the November 4 demonstration that turned violent. A statement by the Indonesian Foreign Ministry (2016, November 5) announced that 'current development has required the President to stay in Indonesia', explaining Widodo had called Australian Prime Minister Malcolm Turnbull to convey the news as well as tasked Foreign Minister Retno Marsudi to find a new date for the postponed trip to Australia. On the part of the Australians, Prime Minister Malcolm Turnbull responded that he 'entirely understood' Widodo's decision and that while disappointing, the postponement 'would not affect the bilateral relationship' (Topsfield, 2016, November 5).

It was indeed unfortunate that the trip was cancelled, given President Widodo had been set to address a joint sitting of the Australian Parliament, as well as meet the Australian Governor-General, senior ministers, as well as business leaders. The address to the Australian Parliament had been seen as 'evidence the often frosty relationship between the neighbouring countries had turned the corner' (Topsfield, 2016, November 5). It was not long, however, for the Indonesian-Australian relationship to turn frosty again, when the Indonesian Military (*Tentara Nasional Indonesia*, or TNI) announced it was suspending cooperation with its counterparts over a perceived insult.

The decision was made by the Indonesian Military Commander General Gatot Nurmantyo in early January 2017, barely two months after the President's cancelled trip, and centered on offensive teaching material found at an Australian military camp in Perth. An Indonesian Special Forces (Komando Pasukan Khusus, or Kopassus) language instructor, who was there as part of a training exchange program, reported to his superiors back home about materials on display, ridiculing Indonesia's state ideology *Pancasila* by instead using the phrase '*Pancagila.*' It should be noted that '*gila*' translates as 'crazy', and as one media noted, the offensive phrase 'basically translate as "five crazy principles"' (Topsfield & Hunter, 2017, January 5). General Gatot Nurmantyo thus decided that 'all forms of cooperation have been suspended' (Doherty, 2017, January 4). Curiously, it soon became apparent the decision was made without the knowledge of the President or the Government. A spokesperson for Widodo stressed, '[t]his was not a decision of the President' (Topsfield & Hunter, 2017, January 5) whilst the Defense Minister Ryamizard Ryacudu tried to play down the incident stating, '[d]on't let insignificant rats disrupt the relationship between countries' (Topsfield & Rosa, 2017, January 5).

One Australian expert described the fact that General Gatot Nurmantyo had unilaterally suspended military cooperation without referring to the President as 'pretty extraordinary' and 'very strange stuff', especially since such decisions would normally be the responsibility of the civilian Government to make (Topsfield, 2017, January 5). In trying to explain the decision, speculation mounted that General Gatot Nurmantyo holds political ambitions of his own — including to be president or vice president — after he reaches the military's retirement age of 58 next year in 2018. The move was thus seen as an attempt to polish his nationalist credentials with the Indonesian public. Others pointed to General Gatot Nurmantyo's history of anti-Western sentiments. Nevertheless, military cooperation between Indonesia and Australia was restored a month later, in February 2017, after the Australian Defense Force extended an official apology during a high-delegation visit to Jakarta and handed over the results of an internal investigation into the incident that had offended the Indonesian Military.

That same month, President Widodo would make his rescheduled trip to Sydney, although without addressing a joint sitting of the Australian Parliament. Despite that, the President was invited to a private dinner at Prime Minister Malcolm Turnbull's residence, where the two leaders were able to talk casually. Continuing the informal nature of the visit, the two went for a morning walk around a park where they met with several members of the public. The move was seen as reciprocating the time President Widodo took his counterpart for a tour of the Tanah Abang market in central Jakarta to meet members of the Indonesian public, and marked the recovery of Jakarta–Canberra relations, after what had been a rollercoaster few months during President Widodo's third year in office. Arguably, those rollercoaster months were a vivid example of how the President's domestic struggles impacted his international standing.

## 3.2. *The Apprentice in the White House*

In contrast, the unexpected victory of Donald J. Trump as the U.S. President presented Widodo with a foreign policy challenge that was purely unrelated to his domestic struggles. As the world's preponderant superpower, any change of administration in Washington D.C. would unavoidably affect the rest of the world, including Indonesia. It should be noted that Indonesia had an unusually special connection with the outgoing Barack Obama — special given his childhood upbringing in Jakarta, unusual given that Jakarta had traditionally preferred Republicans in the White House as opposed to Democrats. As an editorial in *The Jakarta Post* (2016, November 8) noted on the day of the U.S. Presidential Elections, 'Traditionally, Indonesia prefers a Republican-led administration because they are more business-friendly and pay less attention to human rights issues, while Democrats are harder to please.'

However, as some observers have mentioned, Donald Trump is not a typical Republican, with his anti-free trade sentiments going against the party's pro-business cause, whilst his twice-divorced status and questionable attitude towards women challenging the GOP's traditional family values. In this sense, Donald Trump's rise to become the 45th President of the U.S. threatens to turn conventional norms — including Jakarta's usual preference for a Republican in the White House — upside down. Indeed, the former star of the reality television show, 'The Apprentice', has already begun to plunge the world, including the Asia-Pacific region that Indonesia belongs to, into uncertainty.

During his first 100 days in office, Donald Trump issued the so-called 'Muslim ban' as well as pulled the U.S. out of the Trans-Pacific Partnership (TPP) negotiations. While the seven Muslim countries targeted by the travel restriction issued on January 27, 2017 did not include Indonesia, as the world's most populous Muslim nation, it was unlikely for Jakarta to remain silent. One lawmaker deplored the new policy, adding the reasoning for the ban 'tends to put all Muslim's in a bad light by attaching the word 'terrorists' which clearly hurts them' (Siregar & Prasetyo, 2017, February 2). President Widodo attempted to brush aside the 'Muslim ban' by stating, 'We are not affected by the policy' (Ministry of Foreign Affairs, Republic of Indonesia, 2017, January 31) Indonesia also tried to brush aside any negative impact from the U.S. withdrawal from the TPP.

Like the 'Muslim ban', withdrawing from the TPP had been a key campaign pledge of Donald Trump and as such, policymakers in Jakarta would have been prepared in advance on its response. An official at the Indonesian Foreign Ministry merely pointed out that since Indonesia was not yet part of the TPP, the Donald Trump Administration's decision to withdraw from the negotiations would technically break up the regional trade agreement, making President Widodo's interest in joining no longer relevant (*Tempo* 2017, January 20). Jakarta's downplayed response stood in stark contrast to its neighbors, such as Singapore whose Prime Minister Lee Hsein Loong warned prior to the withdrawal, 'It is not just on trade, even on strategic issues...It is your credibility as an ally and as a deterrent. I do not think failing to ratify the TPP will strengthen that at all...' (Bremner, 2016, October 26).

Indonesia's muted reaction appeared to be part of a 'wait-and-see' approach put in place since Donald Trump's shock victory. As Foreign Minister Retno Marsudi explained, 'We will see if President Donald Trump will go through with his promised foreign policies or adjust them here and there. We will determine our stance once he's made up his mind' (Prasetyo, 2017, January 1). Arguably, the 'wait-and-see' approach could also be interpreted as Indonesia having yet to devise a strategy on how to deal with the new U.S. President and the consequences of his controversial actions. It remains to be seen how long Jakarta's measured approach will last, especially if Donald Trump goes through with his promise to recognise Jerusalem as the capital of Israel, an issue that will undoubtedly offend the Indonesian public.

Indeed, the Government was forced to come off the fence when Indonesia was included in a list of 16 countries that Donald Trump wanted investigated for their trade surplus with the U.S. The 90-day investigation was announced in April 2017 and aimed at 'identify[ing] every form of trade abuse and every non-reciprocal practice that contributes to the US trade deficit' as well as to explore whether the U.S. trade deficit 'is the result of cheating or other inappropriate behaviour' (Raj, 2017, April 3). The trade deficit with Indonesia stood at USD 13 billion, placing it in 15th place on the list (Raj, 2017, April 3). As one media noted, 'Officials in Jakarta were left scrambling' following the announcement with the Government announcing it would closely monitor the situation and evaluate what products might be affected (Salna & Purnomo, 2017, April 13). A visit by U.S. Vice President Mike Pence to Jakarta on April 20, 2017 saw deals worth USD 10 billion being signed between Indonesian and American companies in an effort by Jakarta to appease Donald Trump (Al Azhari, 2017, April 23).

Widodo would come face-to-face with the new U.S. President for the first time on the sidelines of the G20 meeting held in Hamburg, Germany, on July 8, 2017. With the discussion focused on trade issues, the latter told reporters, 'We've become friends and we're going to be doing a lot of deals together — trade deals' (U.S. Embassy & Consulates in Indonesia, 2017, July 8). Meanwhile, the former invited the U.S. President to Jakarta, playing up to Donald Trump's notorious ego by telling him, 'I need to deliver to you warm greetings from your millions of fans in Indonesia… They are only interested in one thing: When can they personally welcome you to Indonesia?' (U.S. Embassy & Consulates in Indonesia, 2017, July 8). Whilst the reference to millions of Donald Trump supporters in Indonesia was highly questionable, Widodo's performance at the G20 meeting in Hamburg was nevertheless widely praised. *The Jakarta Post* (2017, July 12), for example, noted the 'human yet popular approach of diplomacy a la President Joko 'Jokowi' Widodo, characterized by his 'wefie' sessions and video blogging with fellow world leaders.' It went on to argue that the President's attendance meant 'Indonesia's voice was loud and clear in asserting its national interests *vis-à-vis* the developed world' (*The Jakarta Post* 2017, July 12). Despite the President's performance, his attempt at flattery with Donald Trump appeared to have failed when Indonesia was not included as part of the American leader's upcoming trip to the Asia-Pacific in November 2017. Announced on October 16, 2017, Donald Trump's first trip to the region will take in Japan, South Korea, China, Vietnam, the Philippines, and Hawaii, lasting from November 3–14. In this sense, Indonesia's supposed millions of Donald Trump supporters will have to wait a little longer before they could welcome the American leader to Jakarta.

## 3.3. The Saudi King and His 1,500-Strong Entourage

One leader Indonesians had to wait a significant amount of time to welcome to their shores was that of King Salman bin Abdul Aziz of Saudi Arabia. Indeed, the visit to Indonesia was the first by a Custodian of the Two Holy Mosques in 47 years. Whilst Indonesia is accustomed to welcoming foreign visitors, arguably, no visit has sparked as much excitement among the Indonesian public quite like that of the Saudi monarch, with rolling news coverage of his every movement from the moment he landed on March 1, 2017. Part of a six-nation tour of the region, King Salman bin Abdul Aziz spent an extraordinary nine days in Indonesia, with March 1–3 spent in Jakarta for official state business, and March 3–9 spent in Bali for a personal holiday.

Prior to his arrival, much was made of the 1,500-strong entourage that would accompany the King, including 25 princes and 10 ministers (Smith, 2017, March 1). A fleet of luxury cars were prepared for the entourage, whilst the King himself brought two of his own elite Mercedes-Benz S600 as part of a reported 450 tons of cargo that travelled with the entourage (Smith, 2017, March 1). Indonesian officials also announced the visit would see trade deals worth USD 25 billion being signed between the two countries (Halim, 2017, February 22).

Unsurprisingly, President Widodo rolled out the red carpet for the Saudi King, offering the rare honor of personally welcoming his counterpart as he arrived on the tarmac at Halim Perdanakusuma airport

(*Tempo* 2017, March 1). The King was also invited to address the Indonesian House of Representatives — again an honor that few foreign leaders have been afforded. Embarrassingly though, whilst King Salman bin Abdul Aziz spoke on the serious issue of intensifying the fight against terrorism, Indonesia's lawmakers were more interested in taking 'selfies' with their guest of honor (Retaduari, 2017, March 2). The President, too, was not immune from the 'selfie' bug, uploading a video blog featuring himself and the Saudi King during a dinner reception (*Kompas* 2017, March 1).

More embarrassing, however, was when it became clear that the promised USD 25 billion-worth of deals with Indonesia would not materialize. In the end, only USD 6.71 billion was pledged by Saudi Arabia (Halim & Hermansyah, 2017, March 2). Adding insult to injury, it was revealed that Saudi Arabia agreed to invest USD 65 billion in China when King Salman bin Abdul Aziz continued his Asia trip to Beijing. President Widodo was reported to have felt let down by the news, telling reporters, 'I am surprised that when the King came to China he signed Rp 870 trillion [USD 65 billion]... I even held up the umbrella for the King, but we got a smaller amount. I am a little bit disappointed' (Hermansyah, 2017, April 14).

In this sense, it was the second time that President Widodo's attempts at wooing a foreign leader fell short, despite the special efforts that included holding an umbrella for the King of Saudi Arabia as the rain poured on a wet Jakarta day.

## 3.4. The Plight of the Rohingyans and Cracks in ASEAN

Elsewhere, the plight of the Rohingya became an issue, following a heavy-handed response by the Myanmar military that supposedly targeted the terrorist Arakan Rohingya Salvation Army (ARSA) but instead forced millions of civilians to flee their homes. The latest outbreak of violence in the restive Rakhine state began on October 9, 2016, when ARSA militants targeted several police posts in a coordinated attack that left nine police officers dead. The authorities responded with a security crackdown against the Rohingya Muslims that allegedly saw 'more than 100 people have been killed, hundreds have been detained by the military...dozens of women claim to have been sexually assaulted, more than 1,200 building appear to have been razed and at least 30,000 people have fled for their lives' (Solomon, 2016, November 21).

Given the religious elements to the violence, Muslims in the Southeast Asian region — including in Indonesia — put pressure on their governments to take a hard line against Naypyidaw's actions. However, the responses from Indonesia and Malaysia differed, with the latter describing Myanmar's actions as 'genocide', whilst the former opting to deploy diplomatic efforts in order to find a peaceful solution and prevent it from escalating into a regional crisis.

Indeed, it seemed that the potential regional crisis was not just over the possible large number of Rohingya refugees once again fleeing across the border into neighboring Southeast Asian countries, but also over the deep splits the issue was causing in ASEAN. Malaysia's Prime Minister Najib Razak made what many saw as a serious breach of diplomatic protocol when he spoke out against Myanmar's treatment of the Rohingya and described it as 'genocide' (Ng, 2016, December 4). The Malaysian Prime Minister went on to directly question the inaction of Myanmar's State Counsellor Aung San Suu Kyi, pointedly asking, 'What's the point of a Nobel Peace Prize?' and telling her, 'Enough is enough!' (Naidu, 2016, December 4).

Eyebrows were further raised when he called on President Widodo to join him, even making reference to the anti-Basuki Tjahaja Purnama demonstrations in the Indonesian capital, stating, 'Do not just protest against Ahok [Basuki Tjahaja Purnama]. The Rohingya should be defended in Indonesia' (Batu & Hermansyah, 2016, December 7). Such an act of megaphone diplomacy was almost unheard of among the ASEAN member-states, especially coming from an ASEAN Leader, and poses serious ramifications for the ASEAN region. Certainly, it threatened to open a Pandora's box whereby member-states start criticizing each other's domestic problems out in the open, damaging any sense of ASEAN unity.

Indeed, Naypyidaw predictably condemned Malaysia's interference in its domestic affairs, with Myanmar's President's Office warning, 'A member country [of ASEAN] does not interfere in other member countries' internal affairs' (Mon, 2016, December 2). Meanwhile, a commentary by *The Irrawaddy*'s editor-in-chief was headlined, 'Malaysia,

Don't Use Burma to Distract from Disquiet at Home' — alluding to the 1MDB (1 Malaysia Development Berhad) investment fund scandal rocking the Malaysian Prime Minister (Zaw, 2016, December 5). The commentary went on to suggest Najib Razak's strong stance was a political move aimed at both distracting the domestic public and burnishing his credentials among the Malay Muslim voters ahead of upcoming general elections in 2018 (Zaw, 2016, December 5).

The Myanmar government has since announced it was stopping its migrant workers from going to Malaysia, and Aung San Suu Kyi has further refused to meet Malaysia's foreign minister (*Reuters* 2016, December 7; Khalib, 2016, December 12). Policymakers in Jakarta would likely have been similarly unimpressed by Najib Razak's attempt to use Indonesia's domestic political situation to advance his own interests and agenda. Fortunately, Indonesia adopted a more nuanced approach, instead offering to dispatch humanitarian assistance to the Rohingya, and focusing on taking steps that would actually help those affected by the security crackdown. The humanitarian offer builds on Indonesia's previous efforts that have led to the building of schools and a hospital in Rakhine state, and illustrates Jakarta's understanding that such activities could not be conducted via megaphone diplomacy nor by offending Naypyidaw. In this sense, President Widodo politely ignored Najib Razak's call to join him, maintaining Indonesia's position as an honest broker pushing for an effective, long-lasting, and comprehensive solution that appeases all stakeholders, including the Rakhine Buddhists, the Rohingya Muslims, and the mostly Burman military (Almuttaqi, 2016, December 16).

In an effort towards finding that that solution, Foreign Minister Retno Marsudi would embark on shuttle diplomacy in September 2017, first paying a visit to Myanmar where she met with Myanmar's State Counsellor Aung San Suu Kyi, as well as the powerful Senior General U Min Aung Hlaing who heads the country's military, or *Tatmadaw*, before holding talks in Bangladesh with Prime Minister Sheikh Hasina and Foreign Minister Mahmood Ali. During her trip, Foreign Minister Retno Marsudi called on Myanmar to prioritize de-escalation efforts, and expressed Indonesia's willingness to help the Rohingya refugees that had fled to Bangladesh (Sheany, 2017, September 6). It remains to be seen however whether Widodo will keep such a nuanced approach if the situation in Rakhine state deteriorates or if it becomes an electoral issue among religious conservatives in Indonesia ahead of the Presidential Elections in 2019.

Aside from the diplomatic fallout from the plight of the Rohingya, a further crack appeared to emerge in ASEAN following the region's response — or lack thereof — to the assassination of Kim Jong-Nam, the half-brother of North Korean leader Kim Jong-Un, in Kuala Lumpur. The involvement of an Indonesian and a Vietnamese — allegedly duped by North Korean agents — did little to reverse ASEAN's indifference. Neither did the extraordinary diplomatic fallout between Pyongyang and Kuala Lumpur that saw North Korea ban Malaysian nationals from leaving the country and Malaysia responding in kind; a move that Malaysian Prime Minister Najib Razak described as 'effectively holding our citizens hostage' (*South China Morning Post* 2017, March 7).

An editorial by *The Jakarta Post* (2017, March 9) criticized the lack of solidarity among ASEAN Leaders, noting,

> 'It is regrettable that ASEAN leaders have not shown any kind of solidarity for Malaysia in facing North Korea's acts...It is disappointing to see ASEAN foreign ministers fail to issue a joint statement to at least express their concern about the killing.'

Whilst Jakarta did pledge to provide consular support to the Indonesian citizen alleged to have been involved, it was indeed interesting that the Government did not publicly join its counterparts in Malaysia in condemning the actions of North Korea.

## 3.5. *Siege of Marawi*

If the plight of the Rohingya presented a regional crisis that was arguably a diplomatic one — at least for ASEAN member-states — the siege of Marawi perhaps posed a much more serious crisis that threatened the safety and security of Southeast Asian countries. As many as 1,100 people died and 350,000 were displaced after terrorists affiliated to the Maute and Abu Sayyaf group established an Islamist foothold in the southern part of the Philippines in May 2017 (Petty, 2017, October 29). After 154 days of battle against Islamist terrorists, the Philippines declared victory on October 23, 2017. However, despite Philippine President Rodrigo Duterte's declaration of the 'liberation of Marawi', terrorist activity in the region is still dormant, and for the wider ASEAN region, there are continued fears that what took place in the southern Philippines may spread to neighboring Indonesia and Malaysia (Santos, 2017, October 17).

It should be noted that Marawi is only some 500 kilometres away from Indonesia's North Sulawesi province. It was in this sense that Indonesia deployed additional troops in the province in order to prevent any militants from crossing into Indonesia (Wardi, 2017, May 30). Worryingly, however, Indonesian citizens were among the foreign fighters reported to have taken part in the siege of Marawi. Speaking at a ceremony to mark ASEAN's 50th anniversary on August 6, 2017, President Widodo stated, 'The attack in Marawi is a wake-up call for all of us...We must unite to build cooperation and strengthen our synergy to combat terrorism' (Sheany, 2017, August 11). Indeed, a few months earlier, Indonesia would cooperate with Malaysia and the Philippines by launching the Indonesia–Malaysia–Philippines Trilateral Maritime Patrol (Indomalphi) on June 20, 2017.

The initiative involved 'increased intelligence sharing and joint patrols' with the three countries establishing a maritime command center in Tarakan (Indonesia), Tawau (Malaysia), and Bongao (the Philippines), as well as communication hotlines to ensure coordinated operations (Mckirdy, Quiano & Watson, 2017, June 19). The Indomalphi initiative also 'provides that naval personnel from any of the three nations may enter the maritime waters of the others in pursuit of suspected militants and criminals' (U.S. Library of Congress, 2017, June 30). A few months later, on October 13, 2017, an air element was added to the initiative with the launching of air patrols. A land component to the trilateral patrols is also planned for inclusion later on.

According to the Philippine Defense Secretary Delfin Lorenzana, the Indomalphi initiative has been a success. He noted, 'The maritime patrol is working very well. We have not had incidents, piracy or kidnappings in the maritime areas of common concern' (Wakefield, 2017, October 16). To what extent the decrease in incidents can be attributed to the Indomalphi initiative is perhaps too early to tell, although one expert has argued,

'There does seem to be evidence to support this assertion' (Macleod, 2017, October 29).

That is not to say that the initiative was not without its struggles. Possible trilateral cooperation between Indonesia, Malaysia, and the Philippines was first mooted on the sidelines of the ASEAN Defense Ministers Meeting (ADMM) in May 2016 and by July 2016, a Trilateral Cooperation Agreement was signed by the defense ministers from the three countries (Arshad, 2016, August 5). Despite that early momentum as well as promises to 'immediately begin' coordinated joint sea patrols, experts noted how almost a year on from the signing of the Trilateral Cooperation Agreement, there had been 'several postponements occurring' and that 'the path forward is still not quite that clear' (Parameswaran, 2017, June 5). Patrols had been 'slow to take off' and negotiations on a Standard Operating Procedure (SOP) had 'stalled' (Parameswaran, 2017, June 20; Guiang, 2017, September 30). Clearly, the siege of Marawi shook the governments in Jakarta, Kuala Lumpur, and Manila, and forced them into action.

## 3.6. *The North Natuna Sea and Panda Diplomacy*

If Indonesia was often on the back foot with regards to events in the Sulu Sea, Jakarta sought to take the initiative over its sovereignty over the waters surrounding the Natuna Islands. Unlike Widodo's second year in office which saw Indonesia and China face-off on a number of occasions over the latter's violation of Indonesia's Exclusive Economic Zone (EEZ), there was no such repeat incident during the President's halfway stage. That is not to say there were no diplomatic incidents. Jakarta would assert its ownership of the waters surrounding the Natuna Islands by taking the symbolic step of renaming it as the 'North Natuna Sea.' The announcement, made on July 14, 2018, was seen to 'send a clear message, both to the Indonesian people and diplomatically speaking' (Allard & Munthe, 2017, July 14). Beijing attempted to dismiss Indonesia's act by claiming, 'Some countries' so-called renaming is meaningless' (Connelly, 2017, July 19). The Indonesian Government would hit back, with Minister of Marine Affairs and Fisheries Susi Pudjiastuti stating, 'We have the right [to rename the waters], the North Natuna Sea is ours' (Sapiie, 2017, July 18).

Despite the diplomatic incident, Indonesia–China ties were not too disrupted, with Beijing engaging in its so-called 'panda diplomacy'. Two infant pandas were gifted on loan to Indonesia's Taman Safari zoo as 'a symbol of bilateral relations and peace between the two countries' (*Asian Correspondent* 2017, September 27). It should be noted, however, that although President Widodo and his Chinese counterpart President Xi Jinping were scheduled to personally welcome the arrival of the two pandas on September 28, 2017, in the end the task was delegated to Indonesia's Forestry Minister Siti Nurbaya and an official from the Embassy of China (Wijaya, 2017, September 28).

## 3.7. Reviewing Membership of International Organizations

For the third time in his presidency, Widodo skipped the U.N. General Assembly, with Vice President Jusuf Kalla representing Indonesia at the global gathering of world leaders in New York. The President's absence at the U.N. General Assembly the previous year had raised eyebrows, given that Indonesia was using that opportunity to launch its bid for a non-permanent seat at the U.N. Security Council. Widodo's decision back then was seen as risking Indonesia's chances, and the President's continued snub was arguably not helping matters. Further risking damage was Jakarta's decision to review its membership of a number of international organizations. On December 22, 2016, President Widodo held a limited cabinet meeting where he instructed his ministers to look into Indonesia's global participation. Noting that Indonesia was a member of 233 international organizations, the President stated, 'Do not let us join international organizations just for formalities sake' (Sekretariat Kabinet Republic Indonesia, 2016, December 22). Widodo instead insisted that Indonesia's membership should be based on benefitting its national interests.

Immediately following the instruction, Indonesia's Foreign Ministry reviewed an initial 75 unnamed international organizations, and identified six that Indonesia would possibly end its association with. Whilst a Foreign Ministry spokesman argued the move was in the interest of improving efficiency so that 'Indonesia's contribution will be larger and clearer for the international world', Cabinet Secretary Pramono Anung admitted the decision was financially motivated, noting official overseas trip to participate in international organizations were a major expenditure for the Government (Sofwan, 2016, December 23). As such, whilst Indonesia was looking to play a greater role in the international arena — most illustrated by its ambitions to secure a non-permanent seat on the U.N. Security Council — it would seem President Widodo was not prepared to put the proverbial money where his mouth was.

## 4. Summary and Conclusion

Joko Widodo has now reached the halfway stage of his presidency. Arguably, sufficient time has passed for the Indonesian public to judge the President's performance and to wonder whether he deserves a second term or not. Certainly, the Presidential Elections of 2019 is on everyone's minds, with nearly every issue or event being interpreted through the lens of whether it would improve or hurt Widodo's chances of reelection. This is especially true in terms of the President's response to domestic developments that seem to have placed Widodo on the back foot. As noted earlier, the defeat of his ally Basuki Tjahaja Purnama in the race to be the Governor of Jakarta and the emergence of a conservative Islamic movement determined to frustrate the President were major setbacks. Significantly, that movement has been buoyed by its success in the Gubernatorial Elections and may try to emulate the same playbook — exploiting religious and identity politics — in order to remove the incumbent Widodo who enjoys a corruption-free image and high approval ratings at the next Presidential Elections.

Widodo's response to this emerging threat was two-fold. On the one hand, the President has attempted to appease the religious conservatives. Sharing a stage with those calling for Basuki Tjahaja Purnama to be jailed was one telling example, as too was the authorities clamping down on affronts to the Islamic faith, including against LGBT, alcohol, pornography, and communism among others, that were supposedly at such alarming levels that Indonesia was in a state of emergency.

On the other hand, the President would also deploy the 'stick' to complement the aforementioned 'carrot', introducing a sweeping regulation that allowed the Government to disband any mass organizations without any judicial process. Notably, the first target of the Government's new 'draconian' instrument was an Islamic mass organization that had helped organize the series of anti-Basuki Tjahaja Purnama demonstrations. The President's threat to 'clobber' those that dare to challenge him outside the legal process, in addition to his various 'safari' visits to key military and police headquarters — where he gave coded messages warning any potential opponents of the military strength at the President's disposal — were additional examples of the 'stick' approach used by Widodo.

That 'stick' was swung amid strong rumors of a coup plot when several individuals were arrested on treason charges on the morning of one of the anti-Basuki Tjahaja Purnama demonstrations. How serious a threat their plot was to the Government is to some extent questionable, but it cannot be denied that it was a worrying time for the President, and suggested that the gains made by Widodo during his second year in office were under enormous strains during the halfway stage of his presidency. Widodo would also suffer a setback when the pro-government Golkar chairman was implicated in a graft case, putting at stake the President's majority in Parliament. The fact that Widodo met with his political opponent Prabowo Subianto on several occasions in an effort to calm the political temperature was demonstrative of the serious situation the President found himself in on the domestic stage.

Given that the President was wobbling domestically at his halfway stage, the question was how it would impact Widodo's international standing. Coping with an uncertain and unpredictable global environment was challenging enough for any national leader, let alone one hamstrung by domestic setbacks. As noted, one of the obvious impacts of a hamstrung President was when Widodo was forced to postpone his trip to Australia. The violence of the November 4 demonstration was so serious that it robbed the President of the opportunity to address a joint sitting of the Australian Parliament — an agenda that had been portrayed as a sign that Jakarta's frosty relationship with Canberra was turning a corner. Instead, Indonesia's relationship with Australia would deteriorate further when military cooperation was suspended. Curiously, that suspension was made neither by the President nor with his knowledge, but instead by the politically-ambitious Indonesian Military Commander General Gatot Nurmantyo. That the fate of Indonesia's relationship with its largest neighbor was determined by someone other than the President should raise serious questions about Widodo and his Government's control over the various tools of the State, including that of the military. As a democracy, it is clear there should be civilian supremacy — as embodied in the elected President of the Republic of Indonesia — over not just the military but also over the country's foreign policy. A repeat incident should not be allowed to happen during the remainder of Widodo's presidency.

Widodo's efforts at wooing foreign leaders during his third year in office would also fall flat, even if such failures were not necessarily caused by the President's domestic situation. On at least two occasions, the President appeared to go beyond what was expected of him in order to advance Indonesia's interests on the world stage. The first was his attempt at flattery with U.S. President Donald Trump, inviting the Leader of the Free World to visit Jakarta and greet his supposed millions of fans. Despite expressing interest, Donald Trump has not included Indonesia in his upcoming trip to Asia. The second was the red carpet the President rolled out for King Salman bin Abdul Aziz of Saudi Arabia, which included welcoming the visiting Saudi monarch on the tarmac upon his arrival to Indonesia and famously holding an umbrella to shield the King from the pouring rain. Whilst Indonesian officials had promised USD 25 billion of trade deals with Saudi Arabia, the President was left disappointed after it turned out only USD 6.71 billion was agreed. In contrast, Beijing was able to secure trade deals worth USD 65 billion with Saudi Arabia without any Chinese leaders going the extra mile to hold up any umbrella.

Speaking of the U.S., Jakarta's response to Donald Trump's controversies, which plunged the region and the wider world into uncertainty, was relatively muted and appeared to be part of a 'wait-and-see' approach. As noted earlier, this approach could be interpreted as Indonesia having yet to devise a strategy on how to deal with the new U.S. President, though it remains to be seen how long Jakarta's measured approach will last. Indeed, the wisdom of the 'wait-and-see' was called into question when Indonesian officials were left scrambling in search of a response after Indonesia was included in a list of 16 countries that Donald Trump wanted investigated for their trade surplus with the U.S. In order to avoid a situation whereby Indonesian officials are similarly left unprepared and ill-equipped, it was highly advisable that Jakarta promptly devise a strategy on dealing with the unpredictable and erratic Donald Trump.

Closer to home, events in the region either threatened to cause deep splits in ASEAN or posed a risk to the very safety and security of its member-states. These included the plight of the Rohingya and the assassination of the North Korea's Kim Jong-Un's half-brother, with the former event sparking a diplomatic war of words between Myanmar and Malaysia — during which Kuala Lumpur attempted to drag Jakarta into the mix — whilst the latter demonstrating a serious lack of ASEAN solidarity in spite of serious allegations that North Korea had committed an assassination on ASEAN soil and had then effectively held ASEAN citizens hostage. Meanwhile, the siege of Marawi in the southern part of the Philippines left an estimated 1,100 dead and 350,000 displaced and would, in the words of President Widodo, be 'a wakeup call' for the region to cooperate better to combat terrorism. Indonesia's response to these events included Foreign Minister Retno Marsudi's shuttle diplomacy to Naypyidaw and Dhaka, the offers of humanitarian assistance to the restive Rakhine state in Myanmar, and the launching of trilateral maritime patrols known as Indomalphi. However, just as in Widodo's previous year in office, it would seem Indonesia's foreign policy was largely reactionary, responding to regional events only when it became so serious it was difficult to ignore.

One area where this was not the case was when Jakarta pressed home its ownership of waters surrounding Natuna Islands by renaming it the North Natuna Sea, much to the annoyance of China's own claims to the South China Sea. Despite efforts by Beijing to dismiss Jakarta's move as meaningless and counterproductive, Indonesia would hold firm, and the fact that China would loan two infant pandas as part of its so-called 'panda diplomacy' to Indonesia suggested that Indonesia–China ties were not too disrupted by Jakarta's North Natuna Sea policy. Lastly, Widodo did not help Indonesia's chances of securing a non-permanent seat in the U.N. Security Council when, for the third time in his presidency, he skipped the U.N. General Assembly. Further risking damage to Indonesia's chances was the Government's decision to review its membership of a number of international organizations, with six already identified by Jakarta to possibly end association with. The admission by Cabinet Secretary Pramono Anung that the President's decision to review Indonesia's involvement in international organizations was financially motivated seemed to suggest that whilst Indonesia was looking to play a greater role in the international arena, President Widodo was not prepared to put the proverbial money where his mouth was.

At the half-way stage of his presidency, it could thus be said that Widodo was suffering from a mid-term wobble. The domestic gains the President had worked so hard for during his first two years in office appeared to have been wiped out by the series of events described above. If Widodo's domestic consolidation during his second year had left no doubt who was in charge, the third year saw old questions as to whether the President was in control being quietly asked again. At the very least, Widodo's control was being challenged. This was somewhat unfortunate from a foreign policy perspective. It had been hoped that if Widodo's second year was one of domestic consolidation, his third year should be that of foreign policy consolidation. This was clearly not the case, even if the President's shortcomings on the international stage were not always the result of his domestic situation. Indeed, some of the shortcomings were not too dissimilar to those from previous years of the Widodo presidency. These include his seemingly lack of interest with the U.N. General Assembly, the reactionary nature of Jakarta's foreign policy that only saw the Government respond to regional issues when they were too serious to ignore, and the lack of coordination that once again saw not all components of the State working on the same page. On this last point, it should be noted that if the lack of coordination in previous years was merely embarrassing for the Government and confusing for its external partners, it was deeply worrying that the Indonesian Military could make the decision to suspend bilateral cooperation (even if it was limited to military-to-military ones) without the President's knowledge.

If there was one improvement in Indonesia's foreign policy this year-round, it was perhaps the absent of any embarrassing reversals that had plagued Widodo's first two years. For the most part, Widodo would remain consistent, for example, holding firm in the face of China's opposition to Jakarta's renaming of the North Natuna Sea. That is not to say there were no foreign policy embarrassments, as noted in Widodo's failures *vis-à-vis* President Donald Trump and King Salman bin Abdul Aziz. With no signs that Donald Trump will moderate his erraticism any time soon, Widodo urgently needed to abandon the 'wait-and-see' approach and think of a new tactic in dealing with the world's sole superpower. This will perhaps be one of the most urgent foreign policy issues going into Widodo's fourth year. It would thus seem that, at the mid-term stage, Indonesia was still far off achieving the pressing goal of a coordinated, united, and sustainable foreign policy, let alone the original goal of an assertive, active, and effective foreign policy.

# References

Al Azhari, M. (2017, April 23). 'Good takeaways from Pence's visit, but can Indonesia get away from US trade hit list?' *Jakarta Globe*. Retrieved from: https://jakartaglobe.id/economy/good-takeaways-pences-visit-can-indonesia-get-away-us-trade-hit-list/

*Al Jazeera* (2017, July 19). 'Hizb ut-Tahrir Indonesia banned 'to protect unity'.' Retrieved from: https://www.aljazeera.com/news/2017/07/indonesia-hizbut-tahrir-group-banned-protect-unity-170719050345186.html

Allard, T. and Munthe, B.C. (2017, July 14). 'Asserting sovereignty, Indonesia renames part of South China Sea.' *Reuters*. Retrieved from: https://www.reuters.com/article/us-indonesia-politics-map/asserting-sovereignty-indonesia-renames-part-of-south-china-sea-idUSKBN19Z0YQ

Almuttaqi, A.I. (2016, December 16). 'Decoding Najib's megaphone diplomacy.' *The Jakarta Post*. Retrieved from: https://www.thejakartapost.com/academia/2016/12/16/decoding-najibs-megaphone-diplomacy.html

*Antara News* (2016, November 11). 'President seeks to ensure loyalty of military, police to state.' Retrieved from: https://en.antaranews.com/news/107740/president-seeks-to-ensure-loyalty-of-military-police-to-state

Arshad, A. (2016, August 5). 'Jakarta, KL and Manila to start joint patrols in Sulu Sea.' *The Straits Times*. Retrieved from: http://www.straitstimes.com/asia/se-asia/jakarta-kl-and-manila-to-start-joint-patrols-in-sulu-sea

*Asian Correspondent* (2017, September 27). 'Jokowi and Xi Jinping to personally welcome panda couple to Indonesian zoo.' Retrieved from: https://asiancorrespondent.com/2017/09/jokowi-xi-jinping-personally-welcome-panda-couple-indonesian-zoo/

Batu, S.L. and Hermansyah, A. (2016, December 7). 'Protest persecution of Rohingyas, not just Ahok: Malaysian PM.' Retrieved from: https://www. thejakartapost.com/news/2016/12/07/protest-persecution-of-rohingyas-not-just-ahok-malaysian-pm.html

*BBC Indonesia* 2016, November 7). 'Mengapa berhembus kabar SBY dibalik demo 4 November?' Retrieved from: https://www.bbc.com/indonesia/indonesia-37893315

*BBC Indonesia* (2016, November 17). 'Prabowo temui Jokowi di Istana: 'Saya tidak akan jegal Jokowi'.' Retrieved from: https://www.bbc.com/indonesia/indonesia-38009831

*BBC Indonesia* (2016, November 21). 'Kapolri deteksi rencana maker di balik demonstrasi 2 Desember.' Retrieved from: https://www.bbc.com/indonesia/indonesia-38048048

Bremner, I. (2016, October 26). 'Singapore's Lee Hsein Loong on the U.S. Election, Free Trade and Why Government Isn't a Startup.' *Time.* Retrieved from: http://time.com/4545407/lee-hsien-loong-singapore-globalization/

Burhani, A.N. (2017, September 19). 'The Banning of Hizbut Tahrir and the Consolidation of Democracy in Indonesia.' *ISEAS-Yusof Ishak Institute Perspective* Issue: 2017 No. 71. Retrieved from: https://www.iseas.edu.sg/images/pdf/ISEAS_Perspective_2017_71.pdf

Connelly, A. (2017, July 19). 'Indonesia's new North Natuna Sea: What's in a name?' *The Interpreter.* Retrieved from: https://www.lowyinstitute.org/the-interpreter/indonesia-s-new-north-natuna-sea-what-s-name

Doherty, B. (2017, January 4). 'Indonesia suspends military cooperation with Australia.' *The Guardian.* Retrieved from: https://www.theguardian.com/australia-news/2017/jan/04/indonesia-suspends-military-cooperation-with-australia

Faizal, A. (2016, November 19). 'Kapolri: Aksi 2 Desember Politis, Bukan Lagi soal Ahok.' *Kompas.* Retrieved from: https://regional.kompas.com/read/2016/11/19/15192241/kapolri.aksi.2.desember.politis.bukan.lagi.soal.ahok

Guiang, G. (2017, September 30). 'Are minilaterals the future of ASEAN security?' *East Asia Forum.* Retrieved from: http://www.eastasiaforum.org/2017/09/30/are-minilaterals-the-future-of-asean-security/

Gunn, G.C. (2018). 'Indonesia in 2017 — Shoring up the Pancasila State.' *Asian Survey* Vol. 58, No. 1, January/February, pp. 166–173. Retrieved from: http://as.ucpress.edu/content/58/1/166

Halim, H. (2017, February 22). 'Jokowi to welcome Saudi Arabia's King Salman, investment.' *The Jakarta Post.* Retrieved from: https://www.thejakartapost.com/news/2017/02/22/jokowi-welcome-saudi-arabia-s-king-salman-investment.html

Halim, H. and Hermansyah, A. (2017, March 2). 'No big deals from king's visit.' *The Jakarta Post.* Retrieved from: https://www.thejakartapost.com/news/2017/03/02/no-big-deals-from-king-s-visit.html

Halim, H. and Ramadhani, N.F. (2016, November 1). 'Jokowi, Prabowo call for calm ahead of rally.' *The Jakarta Post.* Retrieved from: https://www.thejakartapost.com/news/2016/11/01/jokowi-prabowo-call-for-calm-ahead-of-rally.html

Hamid, U. and Gammon, L. (2017, July 13). 'Jokowi forges a tool of repression.' *New Mandala.* Retrieved from: https://www.newmandala.org/jokowi-forges-tool-repression/

Hermansyah, A. (2017, April 14). 'I held up umbrella for King Salman, yet China gets the investment: Jokowi.' *The Jakarta Post.* Retrieved from: https://www.thejakartapost.com/news/2017/04/14/i-held-up-umbrella-for-king-salman-yet-china-gets-the-investment-jokowi.html

*The Jakarta Post* (2016, November 7). 'Ex-first lady says allegations are 'an extraordinary insult' to SBY.' Retrieved from: https://www.thejakartapost.com/news/2016/11/07/ex-first-lady-says-allegations-are-an-extraordinary-insult-to-sby.html

*The Jakarta Post* (2016, November, 8). 'The champion? No more.' Retrieved from: https://www.thejakartapost.com/news/2016/11/08/the-champion-no-more.html

*The Jakarta Post* (2016, December 3). 'Activist Sri Bintang Pamungkas detained over alleged treason.' Retrieved from: https://www.thejakartapost.com/news/2016/12/03/activist-sri-bintang-pamungkas-detained-over-alleged-treason.html

*The Jakarta Post* (2017, March 9). 'ASEAN solidarity.' Retrieved from: https://www.thejakartapost.com/news/2017/03/09/asean-solidarity.html

*The Jakarta Post* (2017, July 12). 'EDITORIAL: Jokowi's diplomacy.' Retrieved from: https://www.thejakartapost.com/academia/2017/07/12/editorial-jokowis-diplomacy.html

*The Jakarta Post* (2017, July 14). 'EDITORIAL: Perppu's slippery slope.' Retrieved from: https://www.thejakartapost.com/academia/2017/07/14/editorial-perppus-slippery-slope.html

*The Jakarta Post* (2017, July 17). 'KPK names Setya Novanto suspect in e-ID graft.' Retrieved from: https://www.thejakartapost.com/news/2017/07/17/kpk-names-setya-novanto-suspect-in-e-id-graft.html

Khalib, A.M. (2016, December 12). 'Myanmar's snub to Msia's megaphone diplomacy.' *Free Malaysia Today.* Retrieved from: https://www.freemalaysiatoday.com/category/opinion/2016/12/12/myanmars-snub-to-msias-megaphone-diplomacy/

KPU Provinsi DKI Jakarta (2017, February 26). Berita Acara Rekapitulasi Hasil Penghitungan Suara Tingkat Provinsi Pemilihan Gubernur dan Wakil Gubernur DKI Jakarta Tahun 2017. Retrieved from: https://kpujakarta.go.id/file_data/BA%20Hasil%20Perolehan%20Suara%20Pilgub%20Putaran%201.pdf

KPU Provinsi DKI Jakarta (2017, April 29). Berita Acara Rekapitulasi Hasil Penghitungan Perolehan Suara di Tingkat Provinsi Dalam Pemilihan Gubernur dan Wakil Gubernur DKIR Jakarta Tahun 2017 Putaran Kedua. Retrieved from: https://kpujakarta.go.id/file_data/BA%20Hasil%20Rekap%20Perolehan%20Suara%20Putaran%20Kedua%20ok.pdf

*Kompas* (2017, March 1). 'President Jokowi "Nge-vlog" Bareng Raja Salman.' Retrieved from: https://tekno.kompas.com/read/2017/03/01/21101437/presiden.jokowi.nge-vlog.bareng.raja.salman

Lamb, K. (2017, April 19). 'Muslim candidate beats Christian in divisive Jakarta governor vote.' *The Guardian.* Retrieved from: https://www.theguardian.com/world/2017/apr/19/divisive-campaign-for-jakarta-governor-sees-muslim-candidate-elected

Lamb, K. (2017, May 9). 'Jakarta governor Ahok sentenced to two years in prison for blasphemy.' *The Guardian.* Retrieved from: https://www.theguardian.com/world/2017/may/09/jakarta-governor-ahok-found-guilty-of-blasphemy-jailed-for-two-years

Lumbanrau, R.E. (2016, November 13). 'Perang Urat Syaraf Jokowi di Safari TNI-Polri.' *CNN Indonesia.* Retrieved from: https://www.cnnindonesia.com/nasional/20161113141646-32-172297/perang-urat-syaraf-jokowi-di-safari-tni-polri

Macleod, A. (2017, October 29). 'Under the Radar: Security in the Sulu Sea is set to improve.' *Global Risk Insights.* Retrieved from: https://globalriskinsights.com/2017/10/can-sulu-sea-become-secure-new-initiative/

Mckirdy, E., Quiano, K. and Watson, I. (2017, June 19). 'Indonesia, Malaysia and Philippines launch joint patrols to tackle ISIS threat.' *CNN.* Retrieved from: https://edition.cnn.com/2017/06/19/asia/indonesia-malaysia-philippines-isis/index.html

Ministry of Foreign Affairs, Republic of Indonesia (2016, November 5). 'President Jokowi Postponed his Visit to Australia.' Retrieved from: https://www.kemlu.go.id/en/berita/pages/President-Jokowi-Postponed-his-Visit-to-Australia.aspx

Ministry of Foreign Affairs, Republic of Indonesia (2017, January 31). 'President Jokowi: Indonesia Unaffected by President Trump's Immigration Policy Related to Seven Islamic Countries.' Retrieved from: https://www.kemlu.go.id/en/berita/pages/jokowi-indonesia-unaffected-trump-immigration-policy-seven-islamic-countries-.aspx

Mon, Y. (2016, December 2). 'Myanmar tells Malaysia not to interfere in internal issues.' *Myanmar Times*. Retrieved from: https://www.mmtimes.com/national-news/24018-myanmar-tells-malaysia-not-to-interfere-in-internal-issues.html

Naidu, S. (2016, December 4). 'Enough is enough' on Rohingya issue: Najib to Suu Kyi.' *Channel News Asia*. Retrieved from: https://www.channelnewsasia.com/news/asia/enough-is-enough-on-rohingya-issue-najib-to-suu-kyi-7639726

Ng, E. (2016, December 4). 'Malaysia's prime minister leads protest against 'genocide' against Muslims in Rohingya.' *Independent*. Retrieved from: https://www.independent.co.uk/news/world/genocide-of-rohingya-burma-aung-san-suu-kyi-malaysian-pm-najib-razak-leads-protest-against-a7454656.html

Nugroho, W. (2017, May 17). 'Jokowi: Kalau PKI Nonggol, Gebuk Saja.' *Kompas*. Retrieved from: https://nasional.kompas.com/read/2017/05/17/16433321/jokowi.kalau.pki.nongol.gebuk.saja

Ompusunggu, M. and Ramadhani, N.F. (2016, December 3). 'Anti-Jokowi figures charged with treason.' *The Jakarta Post*. Retrieved from: https://www.thejakartapost.com/news/2016/12/03/anti-jokowi-figures-charged-with-treason.html

Parameswaran, P. (2017, June 5). 'Sulu Sea Trilateral Patrols in the Spotlight at 2017 Shangri-La Dialogue.' *The Diplomat*. Retrieved from: https://thediplomat.com/2017/06/sulu-sea-trilateral-patrols-in-the-spotlight-at-2017-shangri-la-dialogue/

Parameswaran, P. (2017, June 20). 'What's Next for the New Sulu Sea Trilateral Patrols?' *The Diplomat*. Retrieved from: https://thediplomat.com/2017/06/whats-next-for-the-new-sulu-sea-trilateral-patrols/

Parlina, I. and Aritonang, M.S. (2016, November 11). 'Jokowi flexes muscles to maintain stability.' *The Jakarta Post.* Retrieved from: https://www. thejakartapost.com/news/2016/11/11/jokowi-flexes-muscles-to-maintain-stability.html

Patria, N. and Halim, H. (2017, May 18). 'Jokowi to 'clobber' intolerant groups.' *The Jakarta Post.* Retrieved from: https://www.thejakartapost.com/ news/2017/05/18/jokowi-to-clobber-intolerant-groups.html

Petty, M. (2017, October 29). 'Losses, looting as Philippine war's fortunate few return home.' *Reuters.* Retrieved from: https://www.reuters.com/article/ us-philippines-militants-return/losses-looting-as-philippine-wars-fortunate-few-return-home-idUSKBN1CY0GN

Prasetyo, E. (2017, January 1). 'Indonesia to take wait-and-see approach with president Trump's foreign policies.' *Jakarta Globe.* Retrieved from: https:// jakartaglobe.id/context/indonesia-take-wait-see-approach-president-trumps-foreign-policies

Raj, Y. (2017, April 3). 'Trump order investigation of countries with trade deficit with US, India on the list.' *Hindustan Times.* Retrieved from: https://www. hindustantimes.com/business-news/trump-orders-investigation-of-countries-with-trade-deficit-with-us-india-on-the-list/story-RkZjiCzHXvNmte9FbehT3L.html

*Republika* (2016, December 2). 'President Jokowi has Friday prayers with mass of 212 rally.' Retrieved from: https://www.republika.co.id/berita/en/national-politics/16/12/02/ohke1p414-president-jokowi-has-friday-prayer-with-mass-of-212-rally

Retaduari, E.A. (2017, March 2). 'Hebohnya Anggota DPR Bersalaman dan Selfie dengan Raja Salman.' *DetikNews.* Retrieved from: https://news.detik. com/berita/d-3436228/hebohnya-anggota-dpr-bersalaman-dan-selfie-dengan-raja-salman

*Reuters* (2016, December 7). 'Myanmar stops migrant workers going to Malaysia after Rohingya row.' Retrieved from: https://www.reuters.com/article/ us-myanmar-rohingya-malaysia-idUSKBN13W19X

Salna, K. and Purnomo, H. (2017, April 13). 'Indonesia Can't Figure Out Why it's on Trump's Trade Hit List.' *Bloomberg.* Retrieved from: https://www. bloomberg.com/news/articles/2017-04-12/indonesia-dazed-confused-by-u-s-trade-probe-before-pence-trip

Santos, E.P. (2017, October 17). 'Duterte declares liberation of Marawi.' *CNN Philippines*. Retrieved from: http://cnnphilippines.com/news/2017/10/17/Marawi-liberation-Duterte.html

Sapiie, M.A. (2017, July 18). 'Indonesia shrugs off China's protest over North Natuna Sea's name.' *The Jakarta Post*. Retrieved from: https://www.thejakartapost.com/news/2017/07/18/indonesia-shrugs-off-chinas-protest-over-north-natuna-seas-name.html

Sekretariat Kabinet Republic Indonesia (2016, December 22). 'Presiden Jokowi Minta Keanggotaan Indonesia di 233 Organisasi Internasional Dievaluasi.' Retrieved from: http://setkab.go.id/presiden-jokowi-minta-keanggotaan-indonesia-di-233-organisasi-internasional-dievaluasi/

Sheany (2017, August 11). 'Asean must unite to combat terrorism and transnational crime: Jokowi.' *Jakarta Globe*. Retrieved from: https://jakartaglobe.id/news/asean-must-unite-to-combat-terrorism-and-transnational-crime-jokowi/

Sheany (2017, September 6). 'Indonesia ready to help Bangladesh address refugee crisis: FM Retno.' *Jakarta Globe*. Retrieved from: https://jakartaglobe.id/foreign-affairs-news/indonesia-ready-help-bangladesh-address-refugee-crisis-fm-retno/

Siregar, H. and Prasetyo, E. (2017, February 2). 'Indonesia can be bridge between Muslim World and Trump Administration: Lawmaker.' *Jakarta Globe*. Retrieved from: https://jakartaglobe.id/news/indonesia-can-be-bridge-between-muslim-world-and-trump-administration-lawmaker/

Smith, N. (2017, March 1). '1,500 people, two Mercedes Benzes, 459 tonnes of luggage and a golden escalator: How the Saudi King travels.' *The Telegraph*. Retrieved from: https://www.telegraph.co.uk/news/2017/03/01/1500-people-two-mercedes-benz-459tonnes-luggage-golden-escalator/

Soeriaatmadja, W. and Arshad, A. (2016, November 4). 'Jakarta rally descends into chaos; Jokowi urges protestors to go home.' *The Straits Times*. Retrieved from: https://www.straitstimes.com/asia/se-asia/thousands-of-muslim-hardliners-to-rally-in-jakarta-over-alleged-blasphemy-by-governor

Sofwan, R. (2016, December 23). 'RI Pertimbangkan Keluar dari Enam Organisasi Internasional.' *CNN Indonesia*. Retrieved from: https://www.cnnindonesia.com/internasional/20161223141741-106-181763/ri-pertimbangkan-keluar-dari-enam-organisasi-internasional

Solomon, F. (2016, November 21). 'Something shocking is happening to Burma's Rohingya people. Take a look at this timeline.' *Time*. Retrieved from: http://time.com/4576079/burma-myanmar-arakan-rakhine-rohingya-tatmadaw-suu-kyi/

*South China Morning Post* (2017, March 7). 'North Korea is holding our citizens hostage, says Malaysia's PM Najib, after tit-for-tat travel bans.' Retrieved from: https://www.scmp.com/news/asia/diplomacy/article/2076656/pyongyang-bans-malaysians-leaving-north-korea-kcna

*The Straits Times* (2017, May 26). 'Threat to pluralism will be clobbered: Jokowi.' Retrieved from: https://www.straitstimes.com/asia/se-asia/jokowi-those-threatening-pluralism-will-be-clobbered

Taufiqqurahman, M. (2016, November 11). 'JK: Safari Militer Jokowi Dilalukan karena Dia Panglima Tertinggi.' *DetikNews*. Retrieved from: https://news.detik.com/berita/d-3343198/jk-safari-militer-jokowi-dilakukan-karena-dia-panglima-tertinggi

*Tempo* (November 5, 2016). 'Demo 4 November Rusuh, Jokowi Tuding Ada Aktor Politik.' Retrieved from: https://nasional.tempo.co/read/817903/demo-4-november-rusuh-jokowi-tuding-ada-aktor-politik

*Tempo* (2017, January 20). 'Indonesia Antisipasi Kebijakan Baru Presiden Donald Trump.' Retrieved from: https://dunia.tempo.co/read/838262/indonesia-antisipasikebijakan-baru-presiden-donald-trump/full&view=ok

*Tempo* (2017, March 1). 'Jokowi Tiba di Halim untuk Sambut Raja Salman.' Retrieved from: https://nasional.tempo.co/read/851359/jokowi-tiba-di-halim-untuk-sambut-raja-salman

*Tempo* (2017, July 18). 'House May Block Perppu on Mass Organization.' Retrieved from: https://en.tempo.co/read/892219/house-may-block-perppu-on-mass-organizations

Topsfield, J. (2016, November 5). 'Indonesia President Joko Widodo postpones visit to Australia.' *The Sydney Morning Herald*. Retrieved from: https://www.smh.com.au/world/indonesia-president-joko-widodo-postpones-visit-to-australia-20161105-gsiqdp.html

Topsfield, J. (2016, November 5). 'Violence in Jakarta as Muslims protest, demand Christian governor Ahok be jailed.' *The Sydney Morning Herald*. Retrieved from: https://www.smh.com.au/world/jakarta-protest-thousands-of-muslims-gather-to-demand-jailing-of-christian-governor-ahok-20161104-gsifnm.html

Topsfield, J. (2017, January 5). 'Why Indonesian general Gatot Nurmantyo halted military ties with Australia.' *The Sydney Morning Herald.* Retrieved from: https://www.smh.com.au/world/why-indonesian-general-gatot-nurmantyo-broke-off-military-relations-with-australia-20170105-gtmak3.html

Topsfield, J. and Hunter, F. (2017, January 5). 'Indonesia, Australia military co-operation on hold after training materials cause offence.' *The Sydney Morning Herald.* Retrieved from: https://www.smh.com.au/world/indonesia-australia-military-cooperation-on-hold-for-technical-reasons-20170104-gtltai.html

Topsfield, J. and Rompies, K. (2017, July 12). 'Indonesia introduces new power to ban mass organizations that threaten unity.' *The Sydney Morning Herald.* Retrieved from: https://www.smh.com.au/world/indonesia-introduces-new-power-to-ban-mass-organisations-that-threaten-unity-20170712-gx9sp8.html

Topsfield, J. and Rosa, A. (2017, January 5). 'Indonesian defence minister plays down diplomatic rift with Australia.' *The Sydney Morning Herald.* Retrieved from: https://www.smh.com.au/world/indonesian-defence-minister-plays-down-diplomatic-rift-with-australia-20170105-gtm2zc.html

Quiano, K. and Griffiths, J. (2016, December 2). 'Indonesia: 200,000 protest Christian governor of Jakarta.' *CNN.* Retrieved from: https://edition.cnn.com/2016/12/02/asia/jakarta-indonesia-protest-ahok/index.html

U.S. Embassy and Consulates in Indonesia (2017, July 8). Remarks by President Trump and President Widodo of Indonesia Before Bilateral Meeting. Retrieved from: https://id.usembassy.gov/remarks-president-trump-president-widodo-indonesia-bilateral-meeting/

U.S. Library of Congress (2017, June 30). 'Indonesia/Philippines/Malaysia: Agreement on Patrolling Shared Maritime Border.' Retrieved from: http://www.loc.gov/law/foreign-news/article/indonesiaphilippinesmalaysia-agreement-on-patrolling-shared-maritime-border/

Wakefield, F. (2017, October 16). 'PH, Malaysia, Indonesia launch trilateral air patrol vs terrorism.' *Manila Bulletin.* Retrieved from: https://news.mb.com.ph/2017/10/16/ph-malaysia-indonesia-launch-trilateral-air-patrol-vs-terrorism/

Wardi, R. (2017, May 30). 'Troops deployed in North Sulawesi to Stop Marawi Militants From Entering Indonesia.' *Jakarta Globe.* Retrieved from: https://jakartaglobe.id/terrorism/troops-deployed-north-sulawesi-stop-marawi-militants-entering-indonesia/

Westcott, B. (2017, June 1). "Never seen anything like this': Inside Indonesia's LGBT crackdown.' *CNN*. Retrieved from: https://edition.cnn.com/2017/05/31/asia/indonesia-lgbt-rights/index.html

Wijaya, C.A. (2017, May 9). 'Ahok gaily of blasphemy, sentenced to two years.' *The Jakarta Post*. Retrieved from: https://www.thejakartapost.com/news/2017/05/09/ahok-guilty-of-blasphemy-sentenced-to-two-years.html

Wijaya, C.A. (2017, September 28). 'Two giant pandas arrive in Indonesia.' *The Jakarta Post*. Retrieved from: https://www.thejakartapost.com/news/2017/09/28/two-giant-pandas-arrive-in-indonesia.html

Zaw, A. (2016, December 5). 'Malaysia, don't use Burma to distract from Disquiet at Home.' *The Irrawaddy*. Retrieved from: https://www.irrawaddy.com/opinion/commentary/malaysia-dont-use-burma-to-distract-from-disquiet-at-home.html

# Chapter IV

# Bad Omens in Jokowi's Fourth Year: Entering the Home Stretch for 2019

## 1. Introduction

President Joko 'Jokowi' Widodo's fourth year in charge was marked by a series of devastating natural disasters — ranging from earthquakes, volcanic eruptions, and even a tsunami — that unfortunately caused significant loss of lives in Indonesia. For the Javanese Widodo, it would not have gone unnoticed the traditional belief that such calamities were usually interpreted as a sign that a ruler had lost his ability to balance the so-called cosmic forces of the universe. Compounding the pressure on President Widodo was a series of terrorist attacks in Surabaya, as well as the financial storm that clouded the Indonesian economy and saw the Indonesian Rupiah dropped below the psychological level of 15.000 to the U.S. Dollar.

Having been dubbed by his most enthusiastic supporters as the '*Ratu Adil*' or the 'just king', that according to legend would bring peace, prosperity, and stability, the President's fourth year appeared to instead indicate that Indonesia had entered a period of disorder and chaos that would only end when the rightful 'just king' assumed the throne. Regardless of whether one subscribes to such traditional beliefs, Indonesia is gearing up for the 2019 elections, which, for the first time, will see both the Presidential and Parliamentary race be held simultaneously. An almost seven-month campaign period kicked off in September 2018, with Widodo officially registering to run for a second term and his rival Prabowo Subianto set to once again challenge him in the run-off. Like the regional elections the previous year, the June 2018 regional elections were similarly closely watched for any clues of the current and future political barometer of the Indonesian electorate. Worryingly, for Widodo, the last round of regional elections before next year's Presidential Elections saw setbacks for the ruling PDI-P whose gubernatorial candidates failed to come first in key provinces such as West Java and East Java.

Whilst the President's attention was clearly focused internally, Widodo's fourth year saw some notable achievements in the area of foreign policy. Despite minimal efforts on the President's part, Jakarta notched an impressive victory when Indonesia was chosen as a non-permanent member of the U.N. Security Council for the period of 2019–2020. Indonesia would also successfully host a number of major international events, including the Asian Games and the IMF–World Bank Annual Meetings, helping to raise the country's profile in the eyes of the international community, as well as to promote the image of President Widodo as a world statesman. It was in this regard that Indonesia would also host peace talks with religious clerics from Afghanistan and Pakistan that had initially saw the *Taliban* also invited, until they called for a boycott of the talks, leaving the President humiliated.

In ASEAN, the President pushed for the regional organization to have its own 'Indo-Pacific' concept in order to ensure ASEAN centrality amid competing visions from regional powers about the region's security architecture. Despite concerns that ASEAN's role was being undermined in the wider region, special Commemorative Summits held among the 10 ASEAN member-states, Australia, and India during Widodo's fourth year suggested that the regional organization would remain important. Progress was also made with Beijing over the South China Sea dispute, with the parties agreeing on a single draft on the long-awaited Code of Conduct (COC), although some critics pointed to the extremely slow pace of negotiations.

Elsewhere, President Widodo unadvisedly offered to host a historic summit between the U.S. President Donald Trump and North Korean Chairman Kim Jong-Un, only to be left embarrassed when the two leaders opted to meet in neighboring Singapore instead. Other shortcomings in President Widodo's foreign policy included Jakarta's aforementioned push for an ASEAN version of the Indo-Pacific concept, which despite a positive spin by Indonesian officials, received a somewhat mixed response, whilst its chairmanship of the MIKTA grouping (made up of Mexico, Indonesia, South Korea, Turkey, and Australia) went by mostly unnoticed. Meanwhile, Jakarta, like the rest of the world, has been negatively impacted by the trade war between the world's two largest economies, the U.S. and China, and appears unprepared on how to minimize the damage or even ensure it could take advantage of the situation.

As President Widodo enters the final straight towards the Presidential Elections of 2019, his fourth year at the helm of the world's third largest democracy was thus marked by ominous signs domestically but some significant achievements abroad, albeit with some shortcomings. How damaging were the calamities — both natural and economic — that struck Indonesia for Widodo? To what extent could the President's foreign achievements make up for his challenging domestic situation? Most importantly, will Joko Widodo win a second term in office and what would it mean for Jakarta's foreign policy outlook? It is in this sense that this chapter takes the topic of 'Bad Omens in Jokowi's Fourth Year: Entering the Home Stretch for 2019.'

## 2. The Domestic Scene: Disorder and Chaos?

### 2.1. *Earthquakes, Tsunamis, and Volcanic Eruptions*

Being geographically located on the so-called 'Ring of Fire', Indonesia is no stranger to natural disasters. Indeed, the National Disaster Mitigation Agency (Badan Nasional Penanggulangan Bencana, or BNPB) reported that on average, Indonesia was struck by 6,000 earthquakes in a year (Ali, 2018, January 24). However, the natural disasters that occurred during Widodo's fourth year in charge, covering the period October

2017–September 2018, were much stronger and deadlier than usual, shocking the archipelago and attracting widespread international coverage and offers of assistance. A strong 6.9 magnitude earthquake rocked the island of Lombok on August 5, 2018, leveling tens of thousands of homes, mosques, and businesses (*The Guardian*, 2018, August 19). As much as 564 people died and 20,000 more were made homeless by the quake that caused an estimated damage of IDR 7.45 trillion (USD 509 million) (Halim, 2018, October 1; *BBC*, 2018, August 6; and Tehusijarana, 2018, August 6).

Coincidentally, ministers from neighboring countries were gathered on the island as well as nearby Bali for regional meetings at the time the earthquake struck. Coordinating Minister for Political, Legal and Security Affairs Wiranto, who was hosting a Sub Regional Meeting on Counter Terrorism stated, '[w]e decided to postpone the meeting because of the earthquake and encourage delegates to return to their respective home countries immediately' (Erviani & Arbi, 2018, August 6). Singapore's Home Affairs and Law Minister K. Shanmugam shared photographs of the damage to his Lombok hotel room on social media, expressing his thoughts and prayers for the Indonesian people (Huiwen & Ng, 2018, August 6). Meanwhile, Australian Foreign Minister Julie Bishop, who was attending the Bali Process, thanked the Indonesian authorities for assisting the Australian delegations in Lombok and Bali (Erviani & Arbi, 2018, August 6).

Further disaster was to strike Indonesia only a few weeks later, on September 28, 2018 when a 7.5 magnitude earthquake struck the island of Sulawesi, triggering a tsunami that was reportedly as high as six meters (Lamb & Davidson, 2018, September 30). As many as 2,256 people died and another 223,751 people were displaced by the twin earthquake and tsunami that devastated the city of Palu and the regency of Donggala, and which also resulted in economic losses amounting to IDR 13.82 trillion (USD 911 million) (Tehusijarana, 2018, October 22). The Government came in for strong criticism after its initial tsunami warning was lifted only 34 minutes after it was first issued (*The Straits Times*, 2018 October 1). The confusion meant hundreds were still gathered at a beach festival and 'were unaware of the threat, so they were still carrying out their activities on the beach' (*News.com.au*, 2018, October 1). There was further fallout when it was revealed that a network of tsunami detection buoys installed after the Indian Ocean tsunami of 2004 had stopped working since 2012, and a replacement system had been postponed due to lack of funds (*The Star Online*, 2018, October 2). Government officials thus had to rely on modeling systems rather than live data to detect and monitor tsunami, which was likely a factor in the controversial early lifting of the tsunami warning.

In response to the devastating natural disasters, President Widodo paid several visits to Lombok and Sulawesi, including on September 2, 2018, when he skipped the closing ceremony of the Asian Games being held in the nation's capital to instead visit an evacuation camp in Lombok. The move was decried as a publicity stunt by opposition figures (Agung, 2018, September 4), though it should be noted that the President's trip to Lombok was his third since the island was rocked by seismic activities (Sekretariat Kabinet Republik Indonesia, 2018, September 2).

Despite the President's own efforts in the disaster response, there was further criticism over the Government's refusal to declare the Lombok earthquake as a 'national disaster'. Vice President Jusuf Kalla argued that the Lombok earthquake was not on the same scale as that of the Indian Ocean tsunami stating, 'We are still able to handle [the situation] and we do not need foreign aid' (Nugraha, 2018, August 21). The decision meant less international aid was being let through, and this led to accusations that the Government was afraid of the possible negative political and economic impact that declaring a national disaster would cause (Lipson, 2018, August 27). Cabinet Secretary Pramono Anung admitted as such, explaining,

'Once declared as a national disaster, tourists will be barred from entering the entire Lombok island, and that will cause even more losses...countries could issue travel warnings not only for Lombok but also for Bali. It could have overwhelming effect [on the whole tourism sector] that the public are not aware of' (*Tempo*, 2018, August 20).

The refusal to declare a national emergency seemed curiously at odds with the Government's previous penchant for declaring emergencies over issues such as LGBT, alcohol, pornography, and communism among others.

Other natural disasters were to occur in Widodo's fourth year, including volcanic eruptions at Mount Agung in November 2017 and Mount Sinabung in December 2017, as well as an earthquake off southern Java that also took place in December 2017. Whilst the frequency of natural disasters in Indonesia meant they sadly often rarely merit much mention beyond a few headlines, the timing of the Lombok earthquake and the Sulawesi tsunami so close to the start of the election campaign period meant they would unavoidably be politicized and be discussed with an eye on the Presidential Elections of 2019. It should be admitted, though, that some of the criticisms leveled against President Widodo and his Government were not just political point-scoring, but were actually justifiable complaints.

## 2.2. *Churches and the Police Under Attack*

If Indonesians were no stranger to natural disasters, they were sadly no stranger to acts of terrorism as well. A spate of bomb attacks against three churches and a police station in Surabaya was the latest in a long list of terrorism to occur in Indonesia. However, the Surabaya attacks was notable not only for being the deadliest seen in Indonesia in over a decade, but because the perpetrators came from three families, including their radicalized children who were as young as nine-years-old. Twenty-five people were reported to have died, 13 of which were the perpetrators, in the attacks that took place on May 13–14, 2018 (Boedhiwardhana, 2018, May 14).

National Police Chief Pol-Gen Tito Karnavian stated the attackers were believed to be members of *Jamaah Anshar Daulah* (JAD), an extremist group affiliated with the so-called Islamic State. He went on to reveal that the suicide bombing against the Surabaya Pentecostal Church was carried out by the father of one of the family, whilst his two teenage sons attacked the Saint Mary Immaculate Catholic Church, and his wife and two youngest daughters aged just 12 and nine targeted the Diponegoro Indonesian Christian Church (Kahfi, Andapita & Boedhiwardhana, 2018, March 13). CCTV video capturing the moments the terrorists struck shocked the nation, especially the sight of the young children seemingly participating in the attacks willingly, and sparked deep soul searching in the country. President Widodo, who flew to Surabaya to visit the victims, condemned the attacks stating, 'This is the act of cowards, undignified and barbaric' (Ellis-Petersen & Lamb, 2018, May 14), adding it should serve as 'a wake-up call how families have become indoctrination targets for terrorism ideology' (Maulia, 2018, May 25). The President went on to promise that Parliament would pass a new anti-terrorism legislation to tackle the threat posed by Islamist militants.

Indeed, a few days earlier on May 8, 2018, a major prison riot took place at the police's paramilitary Mobile Brigade (Brigade Mobil, or Brimob) headquarters in Depok that was being used to hold convicted Islamist militants and other terrorist inmates. Five police officers were killed and a further four were injured in the disturbances that surprisingly lasted for almost 40 hours before order was restored (Anggraeni, 2018, May 10). JAD, the same group involved in the Surabaya attacks, was suspected to be behind the riot, and it was revealed that the fallen police officers had their throats gruesomely slit by the rioters (Lamb, 2018, May 10; Siddiq, 2018, May 13).

Making good on the President's promise, the House of Representatives passed Law No. 5 Year 2018 empowering the police to hold terror suspects for up to three weeks (from the previous limit of one week) as well as giving the military a greater role in counter terror efforts (Maulia, 2018, May 25). The second point was somewhat contentious given that the police had traditionally taken the lead role in the fight against terrorism. However, it was the President himself who insisted that since terrorism was an 'extraordinary crime', therefore 'extraordinary action' was needed (Sani, 2018, May 22). Indeed, President Widodo threatened to issue a regulation in lieu of law (*Peraturan Pemerintah Pengganti Undang-Undang*, or Perppu) if Parliament failed to pass stronger legislation (Febriana, 2018, May 14). Widodo would also approve plans to revive the military's Joint Special Operations Command (Komando Operasi Khusus Gabungan, or Koopsusgab) as a super elite counter terror unit, similar to the police's Densus 88 (Detasemen Khusus 88, or Special Detachment 88) anti-terror unit, thus raising questions about their potentially overlapping roles (Sapiie, 2018, May 18). The Government insisted, however, that the police would still take the lead role, and the military's involvement would only be utilized in situations where the police was overwhelmed, such as the aforementioned prison riot (Prasetia, 2018, May 18). Critics, though, saw the move as further evidence that the military was increasingly entering the civilian realm under President Widodo's watch.

Speaking of the Indonesian Military (Tentara Nasional Indonesia, or TNI), the President would install a new Commander in December 2017, replacing General Gatot Nurmantyo with Air Chief Marshal Hadi Tjahjanto. Whilst changes to the military's top rank were nothing unusual, some eyebrows were raised at the installation of Air Chief Marshal Hadi Tjahjanto. For one thing, General Gatot Nurmantyo still had three months to go before reaching the military's retirement age. It was noted that the outgoing Commander had 'issued a number of controversial statements and policies that reportedly discomfited the President' (Razak, 2017, December 11), whilst it was also widely rumored that General Gatot Nurmantyo had presidential ambitions of his own. Meanwhile, the speed at which the change was made was also somewhat unusual. President Widodo submitted a letter recommending General Gatot Nurmanyto be honorably dismissed, and proposed the Air Chief Marshal's name to Parliament on December 5, 2017, which immediately carried out a 'fit and proper' test the next day. On December 7, a plenary session of the House of Representatives gave its approval to Widodo's sole choice and the next day, the new Commander was officially inaugurated by the President at the Merdeka Palace, becoming the first from the Air Force to serve the role.

## 2.3. *Economic Woes — Falling Rupiah and Stumbling IHSG*

Completing the dark clouds overshadowing Widodo's fourth year in office was the financial storm that saw the Indonesian Rupiah drop below the psychological level of 15.000 to the U.S. Dollar. The threshold was a sensitive one for Indonesians, bringing back painful memories of the Asian Financial Crisis of 1998 when the Rupiah was changing at 16.650 to the U.S. Dollar. Having broken the psychological level on October 2, 2018, it would weaken further to 15.217 to the U.S. Dollar on October 26, 2018 (Setiaji, 2018, October 2; *Bloomberg*, n.d.). The Government was initially slow to respond to the struggling Rupiah, with Coordinating Minister for Economic Affairs Darmin Nasution appealing for time stating, 'I have to go home. I want to study [the issue]… We have to closely look into [all factors]. We do not need to hurry to comment on it' (*The Jakarta Post*, 2018, October 3). The Governor of Bank Indonesia Perry Warjiyo called for calm, dispelling the notion that the Rupiah's fall to 15.000 to the U.S. Dollar was some kind of '*kiamat*' (doomsday), pointing out that the currencies of other emerging economies had suffered worst (Putera, 2018, October 3). Blame was later attributed to external factors such as the U.S. Federal Reserve's decision to increase its fund rate, global uncertainty as a result of the trade war between the world's two largest economies, the U.S. and China, as well as negative sentiments from the European continent after Italy posted a larger than expected budget deficit (*The Jakarta Post*, 2018, October 4; Setiawan, 2018, October 4).

The Indonesia Composite Index (*Indeks Harga Saham Gabungan*, or IHSG) also witnessed a similarly negative trend during the President's fourth year. Having closed at 6355.65 basis points on the last day of trading in 2017 — an all-time high that Widodo noted was 'beyond our expectations' (*Antara*, 2017, December 30) — it would fall to 5694.91 basis points on July 6, 2018, representing an almost 10.4 percent fall in value since the beginning of the year (*Tribun Bisnis*, 2018, July 6). After a short-lived rally, the IHSG would fall again on October 5, 2018, closing the day's trade at 5731.94 basis points (*CNN Indonesia*, 2018, October 5). Once again, the Government would blame external factors, underlining its argument that the fundamentals of the Indonesian economy were strong (Sentana, 2018, October 9). Despite such arguments, the falling Rupiah and IHSG appeared to hurt President Widodo's approval ratings, as it dipped to 65.3 percent in October 2018, having been at 70.8 percent 12 months earlier and an all-time high of 72.2 percent in April 2018 (*Kompas*, 2018, October 23). Critics of the President looked set to focus on the country's economic woes as a key battleground in the upcoming Presidential Elections, and this became apparent when the presidential candidates were registered in August 2018.

## 2.4. *#Jokowi2Periode versus #2019GantiPresiden*

On the evening of August 9, 2018, months of speculation finally came to an end after President Widodo and his rival Prabowo Subianto confirmed they would once again run in next year's elections. However, whilst it was clear for some time that the President would run again — he was officially named by the ruling PDI-P as its candidate on February 23, 2018, having already secured the support of Golkar, Hanura, PKB, PPP, and NasDem — it was not so certain with the former Special Forces commander (Aritonang, 2018, February 23). Observers questioned the latter's announcement at a Gerindra gathering in April 2018, arguing, 'Prabowo is genuinely ambivalent about running for president again and is hedging his bet' (Gammon, 2018, April 12).

Particular attention was paid to his statement, 'If the Gerindra Party orders me to run as a candidate in the upcoming presidential election, I am ready to take on that task' as well as to his caveat, 'There is one condition. Even if the party orders me [to run], I need the support of friendly parties' (Triyogo, 2018, April 11; Aritonang & Tehusijarana, 2018, April 12). That caveat alluded to the requirement that the only political parties allowed to nominate a candidate for the Presidential Elections were those that had (either on their own or in a coalition) secured 20 percent of parliamentary seats or 25 percent of the votes in the previous General Elections. With Gerindra only commanding 73 seats in the House of Representatives (i.e., 13.03 percent) and 11.81 percent of the public vote, it fell way short of the requirement. Furthermore, it was not guaranteed that the other opposition parties would support the Gerindra chairman, thus sparking months of horse-trading as parties sought a vice presidential ticket in return for their support.

Prabowo Subianto appeared to struggle with the challenge, which was made more complicated by former president Susilo Bambang Yudhoyono's Partai Demokrat and their late approach to the Prabowo Subianto camp. Their push for the former president's son, Agus Harimurti Yudhoyono, to be Prabowo Subianto's running mate drew protests from other political parties — namely PKS and PAN — that had long supported the Gerindra chairman's bid and felt they should be rewarded for their loyalty. PKS officials hinted, 'It is not Prabowo's character to abandon his loyal friends, let alone to betray them', suggesting Agus Harimurti Yudhoyono be a minister first rather than aim for the vice president role (Prasetia, 2018, July 24; Putra, 2018, July 27). Consequently, Prabowo Subianto would wait until the very final hours of August 9, 2018 — one day before the deadline to officially register with the General Elections Commission (Komisi Pemilihan Umum, or KPU) — before announcing that the Deputy Governor of Jakarta Sandiaga Uno would be his running mate. The choice was seen as a compromise, though an interesting if not controversial one, since Sandiaga Uno was a Gerindra party member. It was only during Prabowo Subianto's announcement that it was revealed the Deputy Governor would be leaving the party in order to avoid accusations Gerindra had monopolized the ticket (Erdianto & Rachan, 2018, August 9). Whilst it was enough to appease PKS and PAN, Partai Demokrat was left furious, notably failing to turn up at Prabowo Subianto's announcement. The party's Deputy Secretary-General Andi Arief went further, labelling Prabowo Subianto a 'cardboard general' and accused Sandiaga Uno of paying a political dowry of IDR 500 billion (USD 34.6 million) to PKS and PAN to support his candidacy (Aritonang & Sapiie, 2018 August 9). The accusation was never proven, and Partai Demokrat would eventually decide to support the Prabowo Subianto–Sandiaga Uno ticket.

President Widodo's search for a running mate was no less eventful. However, having secured the early support of Golkar, Hanura, PKB, PPP, and NasDem, he was in an already strong position when PDI-P Chairperson Megawati Sukarnoputri announced the ruling party would also name Widodo as its candidate. It should be noted here that despite the pro-Widodo Setya Novanto being found guilty of corruption charges, Golkar's new chairman, Airlangga Hartarto, declared his party would continue to support the President thus giving Widodo some breathing space. In this sense, the President was under less pressure with regards to his vice presidential candidate with none of the parties in any position to place conditions on the incumbent. Indeed, the various party leaders made numerous public references to Widodo's prerogative right to decide his running mate. For his part, Widodo engaged in a public guessing game, hinting he had already decided on his running mate but declined to reveal the name.

There were strong suggestions that Widodo's preferred choice was his current Vice President Jusuf Kalla who had previously served as Susilo Bambang Yudhoyono's deputy from 2004–2009. The meaning behind the Constitution's vague stipulation that the president and vice president 'may subsequently be reelected to the same office for one further term only' was challenged by Jusuf Kalla's supporters in the Constitutional Court who questioned whether it meant an individual was banned from serving more than two terms in general or specifically two successive terms.[1] The Constitutional Court rejected the initial challenge on June 29, 2018, stating that only a 'related party' (i.e., an individual seeking more than two terms or a party backing that individual) could file for a judicial review (*The Straits Times,* 2018, June 29). In response, the United Indonesia Party (Partai Persatuan Indonesia, or Perindo) made its own request for a judicial review, with Jusuf Kalla expressing his willingness to testify as a 'related party' (Aritonang, 2018, July 20). However, the path was shut for the Vice President after it became clear the Constitutional Court would not hear the case before the August 10 deadline to register candidates (Nurita, 2018, August 9).

Having waited until the very last possible moment in the hopes that the Constitutional Court would permit Jusuf Kalla to run for another term, Widodo was forced to look for alternatives. Strong speculation fell on former Chief Justice Mahfud M.D. Indeed, in the hours leading up to the President's announcement, Mahfud M.D. was spotted by the news media donning Widodo's trademark white shirt and waiting not far from a restaurant in central Jakarta where the President had gathered with party leaders ahead of the big announcement (Stefanie & Sasongko, 2018, August 9). It thus came as a shock to many when the chairman of the Indonesian Ulema Council (Majelis Ulama Indonesia, or MUI) Ma'ruf Amin emerged beside Widodo as the chosen running mate.

Just as was the case with Prabowo Subianto, Widodo's pick was not without its controversy. Ma'ruf Amin's role in issuing a *fatwa* (i.e., religious edict) declaring the actions of Widodo's ally, Basuki Tjahaja Purnama — popularly known as Ahok — as blasphemous two years earlier raised plenty of eyebrows among the President's supporters. Some, especially the so-called 'Ahokers', threatened to '*golput*' (or abstain), refusing to vote in the upcoming Presidential Elections as a sign of protest against Ma'ruf Amin's role in Basuki Tjahaja Purnama's jailing as well as

---

[1] Do note that there was a gap between Jusuf Kalla's first and second terms as Vice President.

his conservative views on minority groups and other issues (*BBC*, 2018, August 14). The jailed former Governor of Jakarta was reportedly surprised by Widodo's choice but nonetheless pledged to support his ally (Mediani, 2018, August 16). There were also concerns about the religious cleric's age at 75-years-old and whether he could appeal to the country's younger voters. The Widodo camp tried to downplay such worries, making the questionable suggestion that Ma'ruf Amin was a millennial at heart, adding, 'Millennial is not just about age. It is about actions and attitudes' (*The Jakarta Post*, 2018, August 10). The Prabowo Subianto camp similarly tried to downplay concerns about the lack of religious credentials on its ticket by making the questionable suggestion that Sandiaga Uno was a '*santri post-Islamisme*' (post-Islamism religious student), despite having never attended a religious boarding school (*The Jakarta Post*, 2018, August 30).

There were two main explanations behind Widodo's choice. First, it was interpreted as a strategic attempt to win over Muslim voters amid continued questions over the President's religious credentials. By selecting one of the key figures associated with the conservative '212' movement that had so successfully influenced the Jakarta Gubernatorial Elections in 2017, the President hoped to neutralize the threat they posed. Secondly, it was interpreted as a compromise to appease the pro-Widodo parties who feared that the chosen running mate would be the front runner in the Presidential Elections of 2024. By selecting someone who was already 75-years-old, it was unlikely that Ma'ruf Amin would be a viable presidential candidate in five years time, thus ensuring the longer-term presidential ambitions of the various pro-Widodo party leaders would not be threatened. This may also explain why Mahfud M.D. was discarded at the very last moment, with one expert noting, 'Mahfud's vice presidential nomination can open a path for him to run for presidency in 2024, something that some political parties would want to avoid' (*The Conversation*, 2018, August 10).

In terms of the presidential-vice presidential candidates and the possible implications on Indonesia's foreign policy, Widodo's pick seemed to confirm his disinterest in international affairs. Whilst Ma'ruf Amin is a respected religious scholar, he has almost no international experience and will likely be unknown to Washington D.C., Beijing,

Moscow, or Canberra, among others. Given that the President often tasked his current Vice President Jusuf Kalla to represent Indonesia at international summits such as the U.N. General Assembly or important ASEAN retreats, it is difficult to see Ma'ruf Amin taking up the same role, and his aforementioned conservative views on minority groups and other issues appear at odds with the modern and pluralistic image that Indonesia wishes to project abroad. Admittedly, his religious credentials may give Indonesia greater weight with the Muslim world and international groupings such as the Organization for Islamic Cooperation (OIC).

Meanwhile, Prabowo Subianto's pick arguably has the greater international experience, having held senior positions with companies in Singapore and Canada, and holding a postgraduate degree from George Washington University in the U.S. However, it should be noted that constitutionally, the vice president has very little powers other than to 'assist' the president in exercising his/her duties, and it is up to each individual president to decide how much he/she wishes to delegate powers to their number two. Being almost 20 years Prabowo Subianto's junior, it is unlikely that the Prabowo Subianto–Sandiago Uno partnership will be one of equals, and it can be assumed that foreign policy under a Prabowo Subianto–Sandiaga Uno government will thus be dominated by the former soldier. This may be problematic as it is no secret that several foreign governments are uneasy by the prospect of working with an individual tainted by alleged human rights abuses, including the abduction of dozens of student activists back in 1998. However, with a seven-month campaign period before the Presidential Elections is held on April 17, 2019, it remains to be seen whether the strategic picks made by Widodo and his rival Prabowo Subianto will be enough to sway voters.

It should be noted, however, that Indonesians will not only go to the polls on April 17, 2019 to decide their president and vice president for 2019–2024, but also to determine who will sit in the 575-seat House of Representatives (expanded due to population changes). Having initially lacked a majority in Parliament, Widodo struggled to push his legislative agenda in his first year in office, thus underlining the importance that pro-Widodo parties also do well in the General Elections. The regional elections of 2018 were thus closely watched for any clues about the current and future political barometer of the Indonesian electorate. This was especially so since over 150 million voters were registered to take part in the June 27 polls, representing more than half of the country's entire electorate (Soeriaatmadja & Yulisman, 2018, June 27). Worryingly for President Widodo, the last round of regional elections before next year's Presidential and General Elections saw setbacks for the ruling PDI-P whose gubernatorial candidates failed to come first in the key provinces of West Java and East Java. The frontpage headline of *The Jakarta Post* on the morning after the regional elections read 'Jokowi gains, PDI-P loses', and described the ruling party as 'clearly one of the biggest losers' (Aritonang & Ramadhani, 2018, June 28). In the country's most populous province, West Java, where the President's rival Prabowo Subianto secured almost 60 percent of votes in the Presidential Elections four years earlier, the ruling PDI-P's candidate for the gubernatorial race, Tubagus Hasanuddin, came a distant last with less than 13 percent of the vote (Heriyanto, 2018, June 27; Aritonang & Ramadhani, 2018, June 28). Elsewhere, the PDI-P's candidate for the gubernatorial race in East Java, Saifullah Yusuf — who ran with Puti Guntur Soekarno, the niece of PDI-P's chair Megawati Sukarnoputri — lost to Khofifah Indar Parawansa, who had served as Social Affairs Minister in the Widodo Government but left the Cabinet in order to run. It was only in the PDI-P's traditional strongholds of Central Java and Bali that the ruling party managed victories, whilst its preferred choice in the North Sumatra gubernatorial race, former Jakarta Governor Djarot Saiful Hidayat, also lost.

Observers though were quick to point out that translating the results of the regional elections in terms of what it meant for next year's Presidential and General Elections was more difficult. This was especially so since 'parties fluidly join or oppose each other in different regions with no clear ideological distinction' (Sheany & Ganesha, 2018, July 6). For example, in the gubernatorial race in East Java, PDI-P and Gerindra both backed Saifullah Yusuf, whilst in the gubernatorial race in North Sumatra, the pro-Widodo parties of Golkar, Nasdem, and Hanura joined the pro-Prabowo Subianto parties of Gerindra, PKS, and PAN in supporting Edy Rahmayadi over the PDI-P candidate Djarot Saiful Hidayat.

Nevertheless, the controversial use of a '*2019 Ganti Presiden*' (2019 Change the President) t-shirt during a televised debate featuring candidates for the West Java gubernatorial race underlined the fact that the Presidential

Elections of 2019 was very much on everyone's mind. For his part, President Widodo expressed irritation at the growing popularity of the Twitter hashtag #2019GantiPresiden that was increasingly found emblazoned on t-shirts worn by his opponents, commenting, 'As if a t-shirt can change the President? Only the people can change the President' (Jordan, 2018, April 7). Moreover, the police banned a number of #2019GantiPresiden-themed events, which resulted in accusations of political bias (Walden, 2018, September 21). Meanwhile, the President's supporters attempted to popularize alternative Twitter hashtags such #Jokowi2Periode ("Jokowi 2 Terms"), #2019TetapJokowi ("2019 Still Jokowi"), and #DiaSibukKerja ("He's Busy Working"), though they arguably did not go as viral as #2019GantiPresiden.

Facing natural disasters, terrorist attacks, economic woes, and political setbacks, President Widodo's chances of re-election are arguably far from certain. What is clear though, is that the ominous signs domestically have damaged the President, at least to the extent that the Opposition is confident enough to fancy their chances in taking on Widodo in the upcoming Presidential Elections in 2019. When at one point it seemed a second term was a foregone conclusion — to the extent there were genuine fears the President Widodo would be the sole candidate (*The Straits Times,* 2018, March 12) — the race for the Merdeka Palace in 2019 is all to play for. In this sense, could the President's foreign achievements, if any, help strengthen Widodo's case for another term to lead Indonesia and make up for his domestic setbacks?

## 3. Indonesia's Foreign Achievements: So Much Winning?

### 3.1. *Securing a Non-Permanent Seat on the U.N. Security Council*

Undoubtedly, Indonesia's most notable foreign policy achievement under Widodo — not only during the President's fourth year in office but arguably throughout his entire first term — was when on June 8, 2018, it was selected to be a non-permanent member of the U.N. Security Council for the period of 2019–2020. Joining Germany, Belgium, South Africa, and the Dominican Republic, Indonesia will for the fourth time in its history serve on the United Nation's principal organ that is tasked with the primary responsibility of maintaining international peace and security. However, unlike the other non-permanent members, Indonesia's bid to represent the Asia-Pacific region was contested by the Maldives, triggering a vote at the U.N. General Assembly. Despite minimal effort on the President's part — Widodo has famously never attended the U.N. General Assembly — Indonesia, which campaigned on the theme of 'A true partner for world peace', would win 144 votes compared to the Maldives' 44 votes (Sheany, 2018, June 9).

Large credit should go to Foreign Minister Retno Marsudi who engaged in intensive lobbying in the run-up to the vote. In the weeks running up to the crucial vote, Foreign Minister Retno Marsudi visited the capitals of Guyana, Argentina, and Peru, among others, in an effort to secure support for Indonesia's candidacy (Septiari, 2018, May 29). Moreover, in the days before the June 8 vote, she hosted a diplomatic reception at the U.N. Headquarters in New York, as well as held meetings with U.S. Secretary of State Mike Pompeo and senior diplomats from Italy, Singapore, the Gambia, Algeria, Comoros, the Netherlands, Bolivia, Liberia, Tanzania, Sweden, and Nauru, among others (*The Nation,* 2018, June 9). The efforts clearly paid off for the Foreign Minister, giving Indonesia the opportunity to play a greater role in the international arena.

President Widodo highlighted Indonesia's feat in his State Address two months later, noting,

'Our capacity and reputation are respected by the world. The recognition speaks volumes that on 8 June 2018, Indonesia was elected as a non-permanent member of the United Nations Security Council for 2019–2020. We have to uphold the trust we have got from the world' (Sekretariat Kabinet Republik Indonesia, 2018, August 16).

The President would go on to declare that 'Palestine becomes the main priority of Indonesia's term as a non-permanent of the United Nations Security Council' (*Jakarta Globe,* 2018, August 16), building on from the Government's previous efforts to advance the Palestinian cause. However, it remains to be seen what Jakarta can really achieve, given the likelihood that certain permanent members of the U.N. Security Council — in particular, the U.S. — have regularly exercised their veto powers to hinder efforts to resolve the question of Palestine. This was most demonstrated in December 2017, when the U.S. was the sole dissenting vote on a U.N. Security Council resolution calling on U.S. President Donald Trump to cancel controversial plans to recognize Jerusalem as the capital of Israel. A furious U.S. Ambassador to the United Nations, Nikki Haley, famously warned, 'The president will be watching this vote carefully and has requested I report back on those who voted against us' (Beaumont, 2017, December 20). In response to the U.S.' controversial move, Indonesia expressed its condemnation, summoning the U.S. Ambassador in Jakarta to convey its deep objections (Sheany, 2018, February 26). Given the clear differences between Jakarta and Washington D.C. on the issue of Palestine — and their seeming refusal to budge on the issue, it will be interesting to see what happens if the Palestine issue becomes heated again during Indonesia's non-permanent membership.

Curiously, the issue of the Rohingya in Myanmar's restive Rakhine State was not mentioned in President Widodo's State Address as an Indonesian priority at the U.N. Security Council, despite the fact Indonesia has previously been vocal on the issue at the regional level, especially in ASEAN. Indeed, one observer writing an opinion article to *The Jakarta Post* asked, 'Will Indonesia bring Rohingya to Security Council?' (Tobing, 2018, June 21). It was also notable that the South China Sea issue was absent. Another observer noted, 'While some have wondered whether Indonesia will raise the South China Sea issue, this seems exceedingly unlikely' (Troath, 2018, July 2).

Indeed, it is perhaps advisable that Jakarta lowers its expectations and aim for more realistic goals. Indonesia should also be mindful that its larger international profile will bring with it not only greater responsibilities but also increased scrutiny, both abroad and at home. President Widodo would do well to remember the backlash his predecessor Susilo Bambang Yudhoyono faced when Indonesia abstained on a U.N. Security Council resolution to impose sanctions against Iran the last time it was a non-permanent member in 2007–2008. A similar backlash in the first few months after Indonesia takes up its seat on January 1, 2019 may have disastrous consequences on the President's popularity ahead of the all-important Presidential Elections of 2019.

## 3.2. The Energy of Asia

If securing a non-permanent seat on the U.N. Security Council was the President's most significant foreign policy achievement during his first term — providing Jakarta with the opportunity to showcase its soft power diplomacy — Indonesia's hosting of the Asian Games did little to hurt the country's international profile. Set in the capital city as well as Palembang, the regional sporting event featured some 12,000 athletes and officials from 45 nations competing in 40 sports. Indeed, it was dubbed as the 'Olympics+' due to the huge numbers involved (*BBC,* 2018, August 14). In his State Address a few days before the opening of the Asian Games, President Widodo described the event as 'a golden opportunity to show the world our excellence and achievement' (Sekretariat Kabinet Republik Indonesia, 2018, August 16). The President went on to call on his fellow countrymen 'to show the world that Indonesia is a gracious host, a winning nation, a triumphant nation, that upholds fair play. We have to show that Indonesia is ready to be at the forefront to boost Asia's position in the world' (Sekretariat Kabinet Republik Indonesia, 2018, August 16).

A highly praised opening ceremony set the tone for the two-week extravaganza that saw the host nation beat all expectations. Having targeted 16 gold medals and a top-10 finish in the medal table, Indonesia came away with 31 gold, 24 silver, and 43 bronze, putting Indonesia in fourth place (behind only China, Japan, and South Korea) and going down as its best ever performance at the Asiad (Bayuni, 2018, September 3). Boosted by this success, President Widodo announced Indonesia would submit a bid to host the Olympics in 2032, a move that was welcomed by the President of the International Olympic Committee (IOC) Thomas Bach, who said, 'With the great success of the Asian Games, Indonesia has demonstrated it has all the ingredients to organize [the] Olympic Games in a very successful way' (*Nikkei Asian Review*, 2018, September 1). It should be noted that Indonesia had less time to prepare for the Asian Games given it was initially awarded to Vietnam who then pulled out in 2013 citing financial concerns, and moreover Indonesia requested the Asiad be moved a year earlier from its original schedule of 2019 in order to avoid the Presidential Elections. In this sense, praise of Indonesia's successful hosting of the Asian Games was certainly warranted.

That is not to say the Asiad went without a hitch. Ticketing problems would blight the initial first few days after public enthusiasm heightened following the opening ceremony, whilst the promised launching of the long-awaited Mass Rapid Transit (MRT) system in Jakarta was postponed to after the Asian Games. Meanwhile, the Government's effort to literally hide a problem under a carpet was widely panned after a polluted river near the newly-constructed athlete's village in Kemayoran, central Jakarta, was covered by a black mesh net (Lamb, 2018, July 26).

More controversial were the accusations of a violent crackdown by the police against criminals in the run up to the Asian Games. Human rights group Amnesty International claimed that at least 77 people had been shot dead by the police since the beginning of 2018, with 31 of those fatalities occurring in the host cities of Jakarta and Palembang, adding, 'We have seen the police shooting and killing dozens of people with almost zero accountability for the deaths…The hosting of an international sporting event must not come at the price of abandoning human rights' (*BBC,* 2018, August 17). Police, though, rejected the allegations, stating that law enforcement officers only opened fire on those that resisted arrest. With 100,000 police officers deployed to secure the Asian Games, it was clear the Government would not tolerate any threats to the Asiad (Wright, 2018, August 14). Given the spate of terrorist attacks that took place earlier in the year, it was thus a relief that the regional sporting event passed peacefully.

## 3.3. *Progress on the Korean Peninsula*

Speaking of peace, the Asian Games also witnessed a significant milestone when a unified Korean team marched into the Gelora Bung Karno stadium during the opening ceremony. The move followed on from earlier in the year when the two Koreas also marched together under the unification flag at the opening of the Winter Olympics hosted in Pyeongchang, South Korea. However, whilst the two Koreas agreed to compete as a unified Korea in only the women's ice hockey event in Pyeongchang, the Asian Games saw 60 athletes compete as a united 'Korea' in three sports, including rowing and basketball (Baynes, 2018, August 18). Indeed, they would taste success when, for the first time, a united Korean team won gold in the 500-meters women's dragon boat race event (*BBC*, 2018, August 26). The unified Korean team would also secure one silver and two bronze at the Asiad. In this sense, Indonesia could claim to have played a role in the unexpected recent progress on the Korean peninsula that came about after North Korea's Kim Jong-Un made overtures, declaring Pyongyang was 'open to dialogue' in his New Year's address (*Al Jazeera*, 2018, January 1).

Indeed, President Widodo had long been keen for Indonesia to take advantage of its good relations with the two Koreas in the hopes of bringing peace. On April 30, 2018, the President invited the ambassadors of South Korea and North Korea to the Merdeka Palace to discuss the issue. The invitation came after South Korean President Moon Jae-In and North Korea's Kim Jong-Un met a few days earlier for a historic third inter-Korean Summit — the first in over a decade — at the Korean Demilitarized Zone (DMZ). During a press conference following the meeting with the two ambassadors, President Widodo told reporters, 'We fully support peace process between North Korea and South Korea. The follow-up from leaders of the countries also has been conveyed to me' (Saputri & Almas, 2018, April 30).

Unfortunately, President Widodo would then unadvisedly offer to host a summit between the North Korean leader and U.S. President Donald Trump, after the White House announced the Leader of the Free World 'will accept the invitation to meet with Kim Jong-Un at a place and time to be determined' (Fifield, Nakamura & Kim, 2018, March 8). There was much speculation over where the historic summit would take place, with the only known detail being it was scheduled to take place before the end of May. It was thus somewhat questionable when on May 1, 2018, President Widodo publicly expressed his readiness to host a meeting between the two leaders who, only a year earlier, had famously called each other a 'mentally deranged dotard' and 'little rocket man.'

At the aforementioned Merdeka Palace meeting with the ambassadors of the two Koreas, Widodo told reporters, 'We are offering, if there is a meeting plan between Leader Kim Jong Un and President Donald Trump, it can be held here in Indonesia' (Sapiie & Septiari, 2018, May 1). However, Widodo conceded it was not guaranteed that his offer would be accepted, noting, 'We still don't know, he [the North Korean Ambassador] still has to deliver it there first (Sapiie & Septiari, 2018, May 1). The wisdom of publicly revealing Indonesia's offer without any indication it would be taken seriously by Pyongyang or Washington D.C. was highly questionable, and left the President exposed to embarrassment. One observer labeled President Widodo's offer as 'belated' and 'among the outlier contenders', adding 'it's not clear what Jakarta would be adding to Singapore's offer of good offices, other than extra mileage and Bali's charms' (Graham, 2018, May 6).

It was also questionable why the President felt the need to throw Indonesia's name into the ring, given that a few days earlier, U.S. news media were already reporting Mongolia and eventual host Singapore as the 'final two sites under consideration' (*CBS News,* 2018, April 28). It should be noted that back in 2015, it was initially reported that Kim Jong-Un would travel to Indonesia for his first official overseas trip to attend the 60th commemoration of the Asian-African Conference, before it was later announced the plan was cancelled (*Kompas,* 2015, January 25; Armenia, 2015, March 26). That earlier incident should have made President Widodo more careful about making public announcements regarding foreign leaders, yet it was further reported that the Indonesian leader had again tried to invite Kim Jong-Un together with his South Korean counterpart President Moon Jae-in to the opening ceremony of the Asian Games (Yong-Soo & Jin-Kyu, 2018, June 27). Unfortunately for President Widodo, the opening ceremony was instead attended by South Korean Prime Minister Lee Nak-yon and North Korean Vice Premier Ri Ryong Nam (*News.com.au,* 2018, August 19). That it was the third occasion the North Korean leader had failed to travel to Indonesia made it difficult to interpret it as anything other than an embarrassing coincidence at best, or a humiliating snub at worst for President Widodo. In any case, it is perhaps advisable for Widodo and his Government to take into consideration the likelihood of their proposed invitations before making it public in order to avoid such interpretations.

### 3.4. *Hostess with the Mostess*

Whilst the President failed in his bid to host the Donald Trump–Kim Jong-Un Summit, Indonesia did play host to a number of important international events during Widodo's fourth year in office. As noted earlier, ministers from the region were in Indonesia when an earthquake struck the island of Lombok in August 2018 affecting both a Sub Regional Meeting on Counter Terrorism and a Bali Process gathering. However, in addition to those earthquake-affected meetings as well as the Asian Games, Indonesia would also host the IMF–WB (International Monetary Fund–World Bank Group) Annual Meetings in October 2018, the Our Ocean Conference (OOC) also in October, an Indonesia–Afghanistan–Pakistan trilateral meeting of *ulemas* (religious clerics) in May 2018, as well as held the chairmanship of the MIKTA grouping (made up of Mexico, Indonesia, South Korea, Turkey, and Australia).

The IMF–WB Annual Meetings saw heads of states, central bankers, finance ministers, business executives, representatives from civil society, as well as academics come together to 'discuss issues of global concern, including the world economic outlook, poverty eradication, economic development, and aid effectiveness' (Annual Meetings, 2018 Indonesia, n.d). Traditionally, the event takes place in Washington D.C. for two consecutive years before moving to another country in the third year. In this sense, 2018 saw the turn of Indonesia to play host with the annual meeting taking place on the island of Bali from October 8–14, 2018. Among the 34,000 attendants from more than 189 countries that took part in the week-long event were the 10 ASEAN Leaders as well as IMF Managing Director Christine Lagarde, World Bank President Jim Young Kim, U.S. Treasury Secretary Steven Mnuchin, the Governor of the U.S. Federal Reserve Jerome Hayden Powell, the Governor of the European Central Bank Mario Draghi, and business leaders Jack Ma and Bill Gates (Sheany, 2018, October 5; Aisyah, 2018, October 7; and Primadhyta, 2018, October 5).

Speaking at the IMF–WB Annual Meetings, President Widodo told the audience, 'With all the problems that the global economy currently face, it is appropriate to say that 'winter is coming'.' (Gorbiano, 2018, October 12). The President's reference to the popular TV drama 'Game of Thrones' may have been an unorthodox way of warning about the rise of protectionism and trade wars that was spooking the global economy, but it nonetheless drew applause and 'sparked raucous laughter' (*Rappler,* 2018, October 12). Indeed, it was the second time that Widodo made a popular cultural reference, having a month earlier cited a Hollywood film, 'Avengers: Infinity War', at a World Economic Forum held in Hanoi. On that occasion, the President told the audience, 'Not since the Great Depression of the 1930s have trade wars erupted with the intensity that they have today...But rest assured, myself and my fellow Avengers stand ready to prevent Thanos from wiping out half the world's population' (*Reuters,* 2018, September 12). The reference to the film's villain — who destroyed half the world's population in order to solve the issue of limited resources — was similarly warmly received by the audience, and drew laughter and applause.

Some, however, suspected Widodo's popular cultural references were an attempt to appeal to Indonesia's younger voters, especially given that the election campaign period had already kicked off. Indeed, the IMF–WB Annual Meetings would become politicized, with the Prabowo Subianto camp criticizing the Government's 'lavish' spending and calling for the gathering to be cancelled (Renaldi, 2018, October 10; Putri, 2018, October 5). Noting the earlier mentioned natural disasters that had affected Lombok and Sulawesi, a spokesperson for the Opposition argued, 'This is really unsettling for the coalition and it is embarrassing. Why? Because in the midst of a disaster yet we party in Bali' (Anggriawan, 2018, October 6).

The Government would dismiss such criticisms, pointing out that the IMF–WB Annual Meetings resulted in Indonesia securing 19 investment deals worth IDR 200 trillion (USD 13.6 billion) (*Kompas,* 2018, October 12). Indeed, the gathering was labeled a success, with IMF Managing Director Christine Lagarde describing it as an 'incredible achievement' and Indonesian Finance Minister Sri Mulyani Indrawati adding, 'No one gave me any — even small — complaint about this event... So it's very successful. Amazing' (*The Straits Times,* 2018, October 15). Indonesia's hosting of the fifth Our Ocean Conference (OOC) a few weeks later on October 29–30, 2018, was similarly seen as successful. The two-day gathering, also on the island of Bali, was attended by some 1,900 government and civil society participants, and saw 287 commitments aimed at preserving the oceans agreed upon (Parlina & Cahya, 2018, October 31).

Unfortunately for the President, not all events hosted by Indonesia during his fourth year in office were as successful as the two events in Bali. One notable example was the Indonesia–Afghanistan–Pakistan trilateral meeting of *ulemas* (religious clerics) held in Bogor on May 11, 2018. A statement issued by Indonesia's Foreign Ministry described the event as 'historic and momentous', noting it was the first ever meeting of religious scholars from the three Muslim-majority countries (Ministry of Foreign Affairs, Republic of Indonesia 2018, May 10). The statement further added that under the theme of 'Islam as *Rahmatan lil Alamin*,[2] Peace and Stability in Afghanistan' the trilateral conference aimed to discuss the role of religious clerics in 'sowing the seed for peace and stability in Afghanistan' (Ministry of Foreign Affairs, Republic of Indonesia, 2018, May 10). The idea behind the gathering came as a result of an earlier state visit that President Widodo paid to Afghanistan and Pakistan in January 2018. Indeed, the President appeared to be enthusiastically behind the event, not only opening the event but allowing it to take place at the presidential Bogor Palace. In his opening remarks, Widodo told the religious clerics,

> 'This meeting is part of Indonesia's commitment to promote the ulemas' role [in creating peace]... We know our efforts to create peace are never easy, but as people of faith, we must believe in help from God. Hence, we should not lose hope or give up' (Anya & Sapiie, 2018, May 11).

However, although it resulted in a declaration denouncing terrorism and suicide attacks, the trilateral conference was boycotted by the *Taliban*, despite having earlier been expected to participate. A statement issued on the *Taliban*'s website criticized Indonesia's initiative that they argued would only 'legitimize the presence of infidel invaders in the Islamic country of Afghanistan' (*Reuters*, 2018, March 10). The statement went on to warn participants to 'not afford an opportunity to the invading infidels in Afghanistan to misuse your name and participation in this conference as means of attaining their malicious objective (*Reuters*, 2018, March 10). An editorial in *The Jakarta Post* (2018, March 14) described the *Taliban* as having 'humiliated' the President and called the Afghan issue 'a bridge too far for Indonesia.' Meanwhile, Vice President Jusuf Kalla attempted to brush off the controversy by explaining, 'There were

---

[2] *Rahmatan lil Alamin* refers to the concept of "blessings for the universe".

no ulama representatives from the Taliban, because this conference was proposed by the countries' ulema councils and their respective governments. So the Taliban are not yet part of this' (Sheany, 2018, May 16). Whether the President genuinely believed in such an account of events or it was a merely a face-saving excuse is not known; however, it is unlikely that Widodo was not embarrassed by the boycott.

Another example where Indonesia came up short as an international host was its chairmanship of the MIKTA grouping. Assuming the rolling chairmanship on December 13, 2017, Indonesia was the last among the five middle powers to take the leading role after it was first initiated in 2012. That fact alone was seen as indicative of Indonesia's lack of enthusiasm for the initiative. Taking up the theme of 'Fostering Creative Economy and Contributing to Global Peace', Indonesia held a number of public activities, including the launching of a MIKTA-themed book, a culinary program, and campus visits (Ministry of Foreign Affairs, Republic of Indonesia, 2018, September 28). Despite such efforts, it could be argued that Indonesia's leadership of MIKTA went by largely unnoticed. Indeed, it was somewhat telling that President Widodo did not deem his country's chairmanship of the MIKTA grouping important enough to warrant mention in his State Address. It was also notable that Indonesia's national news agency, *Antara*, only featured three articles on MIKTA during the duration of Widodo's fourth year, despite chairing the grouping (*Antara*, n.d.).

## 3.5.  Owning the 'Indo-Pacific'

If Indonesia's chairmanship of MIKTA attracted little attention — both domestically and internationally — the same could not be said of Jakarta's push to advance its 'Indo-Pacific' vision. The term has attracted plenty of attention after it was used by U.S. President Donald Trump during his trip to Asia in November 2017 that included visits to Japan, South Korea, China, Vietnam, and the Philippines (Nelson, 2017, November 7). The U.S. President's frequent use of the term during his 11-day tour was 'a departure from [the] language employed by previous administrations' — i.e., the 'Asia-Pacific' — and was seen to signal a re-definition of Washington D.C.'s geopolitical view of the Asian region (Jaipragas, 2018, July 20). As opposed to a China-dominated 'Asia-Pacific', the U.S. saw the 'Indo-Pacific' as one strategically bound by India to the west, the U.S. to the east, Japan to the north, and Australia to the south. The deliberate framing of the region as one defined by the so-called Quadrilateral countries (also known as the Quad) has been interpreted by many as an attempt to counter China's dominance of the region (Jaipragas, 2018, July 20). Certainly, Beijing — which prefers the term 'Asia-Pacific' — voiced uneasiness with the new concept, seeing it as an attempt to encircle China and prevent its rise. Chinese Foreign Minister Wang Yi made a coded warning, stating, 'Contrary to the claims... that the Indo-Pacific Strategy aims to contain China, the four countries official position is that it targets no one... I hope they mean what they say and their action will match their rhetoric' (Birties, 2018, March 8). Meanwhile, for the other Quad countries, the 'Indo-Pacific' is seem as a statement of their intention to play a larger role — moving from the periphery to the center — and to firmly attach themselves to the region. For example, for India, the concept complements Indian Prime Minister Narendra Modi's 'Act East' policy, whilst for Australia, the 'Indo-Pacific' provides an opportunity for an 'outward-looking Australia [that is] fully engaged with the world [which] is essential to our future security and prosperity' (Australian Government, 2017).

However, for all the recent hype surrounding the 'Indo-Pacific', it is worth remembering that the term is not a new concept. Indeed, back in 2013, the then-Indonesian Foreign Minister Marty Natalegawa put forward the idea of an Indo-Pacific Treaty of Friendship and Cooperation that was modelled on ASEAN's Treaty of Amity and Cooperation (Georgieff, 2013, May 17). Unfortunately, the Indonesian initiative fell by the wayside after its chief champion, Natalegawa, was not asked to serve in Widodo's Government. Fast forward to four years later, the U.S.' resurrection of the idea raises questions about Indonesia's place. Traditionally, Indonesia has long pushed for an ASEAN-led regional architecture, being strong supporters of the ASEAN Plus Three, ASEAN Regional Forum (ARF), and East Asian Summit (EAS) mechanisms. The 'Indo-Pacific' concept potentially threatens the 'ASEAN Centrality' that Jakarta views as critical for the peace and security of the region.

It was in this sense that at the 32$^{nd}$ ASEAN Summit held in Singapore in April 2018, President Joko Widodo proposed that the regional organization take ownership of the 'Indo-Pacific' and play an active part in developing the concept. Speaking at the ASEAN Summit, the President told his Southeast Asian counterparts, 'ASEAN must be able to play a role in developing the framework of Indo-Pacific cooperation [...] which is important for ASEAN to stay relevant and maintain its centrality' (Sapiie, 2018, April 29). Consequently, Indonesia prepared a concept paper to be discussed by the other 10 member-states of ASEAN, with the plan being to present it at the East Asian Summit later in November 2018. Among the key aspects of Indonesia's concept of the 'Indo-Pacific' is that it should be 'open, transparent and inclusive, promoting the habit of dialogue, promoting cooperation and friendship, and upholding international law' (Anya, 2018, May 9). Notably, the emphasis on 'inclusive' meant that unlike the Quad countries' understanding of the 'Indo-Pacific' that sought to exclude Beijing, Indonesia would seek to involve ASEAN's strategic partner to the north. Foreign Minister Retno Marsudi made clear, 'The concept should not be used as a containment strategy' (Shekhar, 2018, July 16). One observer added, 'For Indonesia, and much of the ASEAN, China is simply too big and important to be realistically excluded from any regional order' (Heydarian, 2018, June 13).

The reaction to Indonesia's push, however, appeared mixed. After Jakarta's concept of the 'Indo-Pacific' was shared at the Eighth East Asian Summit (EAS) Foreign Ministers' Meeting in Singapore on August 4, 2018, Foreign Minister Retno Marsudi told reporters, 'Most of the 18 countries of [the] EAS expressed their support toward Asean's centrality' (Sheany & Nathalia, 2018, August 5). A statement on the Foreign Ministry's website added that the EAS Foreign Ministers' Meeting had 'assessed that the Indo-Pacific Indonesia concept carried principles that could be accepted by all parties and prioritized ASEAN's centrality in order to get a lot of support from EAS participating countries' (Ministry of Foreign Affairs, Republic of Indonesia, 2018, August 6). Despite Indonesia's positive spin, it was notable that the Chairman's Statement produced after the meeting only stated,

'The Ministers exchanged views on the various Indo-Pacific concepts. The Ministers looked forward to further discussion on the various Indo-Pacific concepts, which should embrace key principles such as ASEAN

Centrality, openness, transparency, inclusivity, and rules-based approach, while contributing to mutual trust, mutual respect and mutual benefit' (ASEAN Secretariat, 2018, August 4).

It was also telling that despite much fanfare surrounding President Widodo bringing up the issue of the 'Indo-Pacific' at the 32$^{nd}$ ASEAN Summit and his aforementioned call for the regional organization to play a role in developing it, the Chairman's Statement following the ASEAN Leaders' gathering only stated, 'We look forward to further discussion on recent initiatives, including the Indo-Pacific concept' (ASEAN Secretariat, 2018, April 28). Clearly, more work is needed to get the other 10 member-states of ASEAN as well as regional powers to sign up to Indonesia's concept of the 'Indo-Pacific'. However, having personally and publicly pushed for an open, transparent, and inclusive 'Indo-Pacific', President Widodo risks being embarrassed if Jakarta's concept fails to gain acceptance from others in the region. Moreover, there are no guarantees that the Donald Trump Administration's 'Indo-Pacific' will not go the same way as the predecessor Barack Obama's 'Pivot to Asia.' Again, having personally and publicly pushed for an open, transparent, and inclusive 'Indo-Pacific', President Widodo risks being embarrassed if the currently trending 'Indo-Pacific' is altogether abandoned by regional powers such as the U.S. It would seem that the lessons from Indonesia's failed foreign policy ventures *vis-à-vis* Afghanistan and the Korean Peninsula — which left the President humiliated — have yet to be fully learned.

## 3.6. *Regional Dynamics in ASEAN*

Speaking of ASEAN, there was much dynamics that took place in Indonesia's own backyard. These included a new ASEAN Secretary-General, progress on the South China Sea issue, stalled talks on the Regional Comprehensive Economic Partnership (RCEP), key elections in Southeast Asian countries, as well as special Commemorative Summits with Australia and India, among others. Starting with changes at the top of the ASEAN Secretariat, the former Permanent Secretary at the Bruneian Ministry of Foreign Affairs and Trade Dato Lim Jock Hoi officially assumed the position of ASEAN Secretary-General on January 5, 2018. On that same day, the new ASEAN Secretary-General, together with Foreign Minister Retno Marsudi, inaugurated a groundbreaking ceremony to expand the ASEAN Secretariat building in Jakarta. Fully funded by the Indonesian Government, Foreign Minister Retno Marsudi declared, 'The construction of this building is a manifestation of Indonesia's contribution so that the ASEAN Secretariat will be able to perform its tasks well in the next 50 years' (Ministry of Foreign Affairs, Republic of Indonesia, 2018, January 9). ASEAN Secretary-General Dato Lim Jock Hoi would later pay a courtesy call to President Widodo at the Merdeka Palace on March 23, 2018, where it was promised that the construction for the new building would be completed in just over a year (Sekretariat Kabinet Republik Indonesia, 2018, March 23).

It was not, however, the first time that the President met with the newly appointed ASEAN Secretary-General. Indeed, a few weeks after the latter took up his new position, Dato Lim Jock Hoi would join President Widodo together with the other nine leaders of ASEAN to attend India's Republic Day ceremony, as well as a special ASEAN–India Commemorative Summit in New Delhi. Held in conjunction with the 25th year of ASEAN–India relations, it was the first time that multiple Heads of States/Governments were invited to be the chief guest of honor for the Republic Day celebrations, and underlined the importance that regional powers placed in ASEAN (Parashar, 2018, January 25). A few months later, President Widodo would again attend a special commemorative summit with an ASEAN Dialogue Partner — this time with Australia. Held in Sydney from March 17–18, 2018, the ASEAN–Australia Special Summit reciprocated a similar gathering that took place in Vientiane in September 2016, and marked the first time it was held on Australian soil — demonstrating Canberra's continued commitment as ASEAN's oldest Dialogue Partner.

That is not to say that all was well in Indonesia's own backyard of ASEAN. Observers wondered whether Indian Prime Minister Narendra Modi's push towards ASEAN was being driven largely by the desire to counter the rise of Beijing (Almuttaqi, 2018, January 26). So frequent was China referred to in media articles leading up to the special ASEAN–India Commemorative Summit that an editorial in the Chinese *Global Times*

(2018, January 25) noted, 'Repeated reports by some Indian media that New Delhi has launched a diplomatic offensive against Beijing are baffling to the Chinese public.' In any case, it seemed to demonstrate the way in which ASEAN–India relations were being pushed by the China factor, rather than pulled by the merits and opportunities of closer ASEAN–India cooperation. Meanwhile, in the case of the ASEAN–Australia Special Summit, Cambodia's Prime Minister Hun Sen threatened to boycott the event due to international scrutiny over allegations that elections that were to be held in July 2018 would be far from free or fair (Sokhean & Nachemson, 2018, February 21). Indeed, responding to a planned protest by Cambodians living in Australia, Prime Minister Hun Sen publicly threatened to 'pursue them to their houses and beat them up' (Sokhean & Nachemson, 2018, February 21). Notably, in the run up to the elections the main opposition party was dissolved, its leader imprisoned, and a major independent newspaper critical of the government was shut down — moves that virtually guaranteed the ruling Cambodian People's Party won the general elections later in July.

Whilst the Cambodian leader did in the end attend the ASEAN–Australia Special Summit, Philippine President Rodrigo Duterte decided to skip the event due to 'developments at home' — although the more likely reason was international criticism over Manila's 'War on Drugs' (Mendez, 2018, March 6). It should be noted that a report released by the U.S. Office of the Director of National Intelligence identified Philippine President Rodrigo Duterte as a 'threat to democracy in Southeast Asia' (Esguerra, 2018, February 21). The report pointed to Duterte's 'War on Drugs' which by some estimates have claimed 12,000 lives, as well as his suggestions to suspend the constitution, declare a 'revolutionary government', and impose nationwide martial law (Esguerra, 2018, February 21). The same report also highlighted the situation in Thailand, where a military junta has been in power since 2014 and has repeatedly postponed planned elections that would return the country back to civilian rule (Esguerra, 2018, February 21). For example, in February 2018, Thai Prime Minister Prayuth Chan-ocha declared that general elections would take place 'no later' than February 2019, having earlier promised to hold it in November 2018 — the latest in a string of unrealized promises (Hariraksapitak, 2018, February 27).

Amid the democratic decline taking place in Southeast Asia, Indonesia appeared silent. Jakarta did not join the international chorus condemning the controversial elections in Cambodia, with President Widodo instead congratulating Cambodian Prime Minister Hun Sen for his re-election. In a letter the President sent to his Cambodian counterpart, Widodo expressed, 'I would like to congratulate all the people of Cambodia for the peaceful and successful organization of Cambodia's 2018 General Election' (*Fresh News*, 2018, September 29). Meanwhile, far from condemning Philippine President Rodrigo Duterte's 'War on Drugs', Indonesia appeared keen to emulate it. As one observer wrote,

'It is not hard to draw a parallel to the bloody war on drugs in the Philippines which to date has claimed the lives of more than 13,000 civilians. President Joko "Jokowi" Widodo shows no hesitation in expressing his strong stance against what he claims to be a narcotics 'emergency': "Gun them down. Show no mercy," he says of drug traffickers' (Blokhuizen, 2017, October 24).

Whilst the death toll in Indonesia is far below that in the Philippines, the aforementioned pre-Asian Games crackdown on crime resulted in at least 77 people shot dead by the police since the beginning of 2018.

In the case of Thailand, Jakarta said little about the continued delay to the long-promised general elections. A commentary in *The Jakarta Post* (Purba, 2018, July 31) called on President Widodo to ensure Thailand would not assume the ASEAN Chair in 2019 until the military junta finally held free and fair elections. The commentary led to an angry response from Thai Prime Minister Prayut Cha-ocha who when asked about the piece hit back, 'The Jakarta Post is not Indonesia... Did the Indonesian government say that?' (Nanuam, 2018, August 6). Interestingly, the Indonesian Government remained silent, refusing to respond to either *The Jakarta Post*'s article or the Thai Prime Minister's question.

The one outlier bucking the declining democracy narrative in Southeast Asia was that of Malaysia which, in May 2018, witnessed the first ever change of government since it gained independence. Former Malaysian Prime Minister Mahathir Mohamad came out of retirement at the age of 92-years-old to lead the opposition *Pakatan Harapan* (Alliance of Hope) coalition to inflict the first ever electoral defeat on the ruling *Barisan Nasional* (National Front) that had previously governed the country for 61 unbroken years. The return of one of the so-called 'titans of ASEAN' (the others being the late Soeharto from Indonesia and the late Lee Kuan Yew from Singapore) has already ruffled feathers in the region, with Malaysia pledging to take a firmer stance with Beijing over the South China Sea (Heydarian, 2018, May 20). Indeed, in June 2018, the Malaysian Prime Minister called on Beijing to withdraw its warships, noting, 'If China wants to participate with small boats, they are welcome. Anybody, even the US if they want to participate — but don't bring battleships here' (Jaipragas, 2018, June 19). Despite the Malaysian Prime Minister's call, some progress has arguably been made in the long-running regional dispute in the South China Sea.

In particular, the 51$^{St}$ ASEAN Foreign Ministers' Meeting and Related Meetings held in Singapore in August 2018 saw ASEAN and China announcing an agreement on a single draft negotiating text that will 'be the basis of future COC [Code of Conduct] negotiations' (Yong, 2018, August 3). Whilst Singapore's Foreign Minister Vivian Balakrishnan described it as 'yet another milestone' (*Reuters,* 2018, August 2), some critics pointed to the extremely slow pace of negotiations. It should be noted that 16 years have passed since ASEAN and China first agreed on a non-binding Declaration on the Conduct of Parties in the South China Sea (DOC) back in 2002 and committed to developing a more binding COC. In this sense it is highly questionable that almost two decades on the two sides have only agreed 'the basis to conduct future negotiations.' Indeed, it could be argued that the 'milestone' progress appeared little more than lip service that will do little to change the facts on the ground, including Beijing's continued refusal to abide by the Permanent Court of Arbitration's (PCA) landmark ruling of July 12, 2016, as well as its ongoing reclamation of features in the South China Sea and installation of military facilities on its manmade islands. These developments have left many observers pessimistic about the future prospect of the South China Sea, with control over the disputed area seemingly being handed over to Beijing.

On the part of Indonesia, it has continued to maintain its position as a non-claimant to the South China Sea dispute, even though the wisdom of Jakarta's strategic ambivalence was somewhat exposed in previous years, after a series of standoffs between Indonesia and China over incidents of illegal fishing by Chinese boats in Indonesian waters. Unfortunately, despite the new Malaysian government's hardened position *vis-à-vis* China, Indonesia seems reluctant to seize the opportunity to work together and push back against China's over-excessive claims to the South China Sea. For example, during a joint press conference with her Malaysian counterpart, Indonesia's Foreign Minister Retno Marsudi stated that both Jakarta and Kuala Lumpur would work together to strengthen ASEAN centrality and unity. However, it was notable that the issue of the South China Sea was not explicitly mentioned (Almuttaqi, 2018, August 6). Instead, the two listed their joint commitment to resolve ongoing border negotiations, to enhance protection for Indonesian migrant workers in Malaysia, and to counter attempts by the EU to restrict their palm oil industry. The lack of any serious maritime incidents between Indonesia and China during President Widodo's fourth year in office appeared to have curbed Jakarta's activeness in the South China Sea and suggested the reactionary nature of Indonesia's foreign policy has yet to be fully overcome.

## 4. Summary and Conclusion

The month of October 2018 marked the end of President Widodo's fourth year, with minds now fully concentrated on the upcoming Presidential Elections. Set to take place on April 17, 2019, the elections will no doubt dominate — and largely determine — the fifth and final year of Widodo's first term. Should he win the April polls, the President's fifth year will likely see a status quo situation. Should he lose, Widodo's final year may be characterized by a lame duck situation. The question for Indonesian voters on April 17, 2019 is therefore which of the two situations they prefer? In making that choice, voters will no doubt be guided by the President's performance, with the achievements and failures of his fourth year in charge particularly fresh in their minds. That fourth year was one marked by ominous signs domestically with some significant achievements abroad.

Whilst the President could not be faulted for the series of devastating natural disasters, including earthquakes, volcanic eruptions, and even a tsunami that hit Indonesia during his fourth year, Widodo's responses were up for analysis. The President made the right call to visit the affected regions — even foregoing the closing ceremony of the Asian Games — but the Government's refusal to declare the Lombok earthquake a 'national disaster' was highly questionable. So too was the Government's failure to replace the network of tsunami detection buoys that for years had stopped functioning and was arguably a dereliction of responsibility on the Government's part. Similarly, whilst Widodo could not be faulted for the spate of terrorist attacks in Surabaya, his hard security reaction raised eyebrows, including forcing Parliament to pass tougher counter-terror legislation and opening the space for the Indonesian Military to play a greater role. This was despite ongoing concerns about the military's increasing activeness in the civilian sphere.

Meanwhile, the economy appeared to falter with the Indonesian Rupiah dropping below the psychological level of 15.000 to the U.S. Dollar and the Indonesian Composite Stock losing almost 10.4 percent of its value from the beginning of 2018. Whilst fluctuations in the economy are normal, the economic storm came at a politically sensitive time for the President and hurt Widodo's approval ratings, which dropped to 65.3 percent in October 2018 from 70.8 percent a year earlier. The opposition would seize on the underperforming Indonesian currency and stock exchange, positioning it as a key campaign issue for the upcoming Presidential Elections.

That was made clear on the evening of August 9, 2018, when Widodo and his rival Prabowo Subianto confirmed they would once again run in next year's race for the presidency. The former selected Ma'ruf Amin, chairman of the Indonesian Ulema Council (Majelis Ulama Indonesia, or MUI) as his running mate, whilst the latter chose Sandiaga Uno, Deputy Governor of Jakarta as his number two. The choices were not without its controversies. The President first flirted with the idea of running with current Vice President Jusuf Kalla — only for the Constitutional Court to shut down that possibility — before then considering former Chief Justice Mahfud M.D., and finally settling on the ageing religious cleric that may alienate Widodo's more liberal and millennial supporters. Meanwhile, his opponent Prabowo Subianto appeared reluctant to run at first, and when he did eventually decide to enter would then struggle to find a running mate triggering months of horse trading with other opposition parties. Prabowo Subianto's final decision to go with someone from his own Gerindra party appeared to infuriate the other opposition parties who felt they deserved some reward, having long-supported the former Special Forces commander.

In search of an early indication of how Indonesians would vote in 2019, observers looked to the results of the regional elections held in June 2018. The last round of regional elections before the all-important Presidential Elections saw setbacks for the ruling PDI-P, whose gubernatorial candidates failed to win in key provinces except for their traditional strongholds of Central Java and Bali. The PDI-P's less than impressive performance should worry President Widodo in the event he wins a second term only to be constrained by a Parliament where he lacks a majority. Widodo's irritation at the *#2019GantiPresiden* hashtag was perhaps an indication that a second term was far from secure. In this sense, it could be argued that the natural disasters, terrorist attacks, economic woes, and political setbacks that occurred during the fourth year have indeed hurt President Widodo, at least to the extent that the Opposition is confident enough to fancy their chances in taking on the incumbent in 2019.

As such, Widodo may look to play up his foreign policy achievements to the Indonesian electorate in order to compensate for the challenging domestic situation. Certainly, there were some significant achievements in the President's fourth year, not least securing a non-permanent seat on the U.N. Security Council as well as the successful hosting of the Asian Games. Both were interpreted as recognition of Indonesia's growing clout on the world stage. However, given the increased scrutiny that Indonesia will be under following its larger international profile, Jakarta would be best advised to lower its expectations and aim for more realistic goals. An unpopular decision at the U.N. Security Council may cause a public backlash, whilst an unrealistic initiative may result in humiliation if it were to be blocked by other members of the United Nations' principal organ — the last things President Widodo needs in the run up to the elections. Having said that, Indonesia also successfully hosted important events such as the IMF–WB Annual Meetings and the Our Ocean Conference (OOC) in October 2018, that not only saw Jakarta secure a number of important investment deals but also promote the image of President Widodo as a world statesman.

That is not to say there were no shortcomings in President Widodo's foreign policy. On several occasions the President was left embarrassed when a number of his initiatives did not receive the response he hoped for. These included Indonesia's push for ASEAN to take ownership of the 'Indo-Pacific', the offer to host a summit meeting between U.S. President Donald Trump and North Korean leader Kim Jong-Un, the invitation for the two Korean leaders to attend the opening ceremony of the Asian Games, and the offer extended to the *Taliban* to take part in the Indonesia–Afghanistan–Pakistan trilateral meeting of *ulemas* (religious clerics). These initiatives received either a mixed response, were politely ignored, or in the worst case, disparagingly rejected. That it happened on at least four different occasions during Widodo's fourth year should raise serious question marks as to why the President was allowed to put himself in such a potentially embarrassing position. Too often it appeared that Jakarta had failed to consider the likelihood of its initiatives being accepted by external partners before making it public, leaving President Widodo's credibility on the line.

Lastly, Indonesia was once again silent in response to the regional dynamics that took place in its own backyard. Rather than joining the international chorus condemning the controversial elections in Cambodia, President Widodo instead congratulated Cambodian Prime Minister Hun Sen. Meanwhile, far from condemning the Philippines' deadly 'War on Drugs', Indonesia appeared keen to emulate it. And when Thailand's Prime Minister Prayuth Cha-ocha angrily responded to an Indonesia journalist's call that Thailand to not be given the ASEAN Chairmanship in 2019 until the military junta delivered on its promise to hold elections, the Indonesian Government refused to comment. The few bright spots in the region were the largely smooth change of government in Malaysia as well as the so-called progress on the South China Sea issue. However, despite Malaysia seemingly taking up a more hardened position *vis-à-vis* China, Indonesia seemed reluctant to seize the opportunity to work together and push back against China's over-excessive claims to the South China Sea. Given the absence of any major maritime incidents between Jakarta and Beijing, a valid question was whether Indonesia's curbed activeness in the South China Sea during President Widodo's fourth year indicative of the view that Indonesia's foreign policy was still reactionary in nature.

Entering the home straight in the race that is the Presidential Elections of 2019, it can be summarized that the ominous domestic signs that marked Widodo's fourth year have certainly damaged the President to some extent. President Widodo's approval ratings have dipped — even if they remained relatively high — the ruling PDI-P suffered setbacks during regional elections, and moreover, the Opposition appeared confident enough to fancy their chances on taking the President on. It can also be summarized that the President's foreign policy achievements may not be enough to compensate for his challenging domestic situation. Whilst there were some significant achievements, there were also a few embarrassments for Widodo. On balance, the achievements appear to outweigh the embarrassments, at least in the sense that the President will more likely play up his foreign policy successes and surprisingly, the Opposition has yet to highlight his failures to any noticeable extent. This may be simply due to the relegated position that foreign policy tends to hold as an electoral campaign issue, and if true, is the reason why the President's foreign policy achievements may not be enough to compensate for his challenging domestic situation.

It remains to be seen, however, if this will change in the run up to the Presidential Elections, and only time will tell if a major incident were to occur that puts President Widodo's foreign policy achievements and shortcomings in the electoral spotlight. In this sense, Indonesia's non-permanent seat on the U.N. Security Council may be a double-edged sword for the President. On the one hand, it may be taken as evidence of Indonesia's growing international clout; however, on the other hand, it may also be a stage for the President to be embarrassed in front of a global audience — something that happened far too frequently in Widodo's fourth year. If the President's third year had seen an improvement in Indonesia's foreign policy in the sense there were no more embarrassing reversals that had plagued the first two years, the past 12 months saw them returning — albeit in different 'clothes'. The 'flip-flops' have now become self-inflicted 'own-goals', with the Government too eager to make big announcements without first considering the likelihood of it being accepted. In this sense, it is questionable whether any progress has been made in either achieving last year's pressing goal of a coordinated, united, and sustainable foreign policy, let alone the original goal of an assertive, active, and effective foreign policy. Whether that matters in the Presidential Elections will be up for the Indonesian electorate to decide. At this stage, the only thing certain is that the outcome of next year's race for Merdeka Palace is no longer the foregone conclusion it had seemed at one point.

# References

Almuttaqi, A.I. (2018, January 26). 'China, the push factor for ASEAN-India relations?' *The Jakarta Post.* Retrieved from: https://www.thejakartapost. com/news/2018/01/26/china-push-factor-asean-india-relations.html

Almuttaqi, A.I. (2018, August 6). 'Renewed ASEAN position on South China Sea?' *The Jakarta Post.* Retrieved from: https://www.thejakartapost.com/ news/2018/08/06/renewed-asean-position-south-china-sea.html

*Antara* (n.d.). 'News search: MIKTA, 6 News found.' Retrieved from: https:// en.antaranews.com/search?q=mikta

Anya, A. (2018, May 9). 'East Asia to hear about Indo-Pacific idea.' *The Jakarta Post.* Retrieved from: https://www.thejakartapost.com/news/2018/05/09/ east-asia-hear-about-indo-pacific-idea.html

Anya, A. and Sapiie, M.A. (2018, May 11). 'President Jokowi opens trilateral ulema meeting at Bogor Palace.' *The Jakarta Post.* Retrieved from: https:// www.thejakartapost.com/news/2018/05/11/president-jokowi-opens-trilateral-ulema-meeting-at-bogorpalace.html

Agung, B. (2018, September 4). 'Fadli Zon Sindir Aksi Jokowi Tutup Asian Games dari Lombok.' *CNN Indonesia.* Retrieved from: https://www. cnnindonesia.com/nasional/20180904034745-32-327348/fadli-zon-sindir-aksi-jokowi-tutup-asian-games-dari-lombok

Aisyah, R. (2018, October 7). 'Annual Meetings participants surpasses govt target.' *The Jakarta Post.* Retrieved from: https://www.thejakartapost.com/ news/2018/10/07/annual-meetings-participants-surpasses-govt-target.html

*Al Jazeera* (2018, January 1). 'North Korea's Kim Jong-un 'open to dialogue' with South.' Retrieved from: https://www.aljazeera.com/news/2018/01/ north-korea-kim-jong-open-dialogue-south-180101085743276.html

Ali, M. (2018, January 24). 'BNPB: Dalam Setahun, Indonesia Diguncang 6.000 Kali Gempa.' *Liputan6*. Retrieved from: https://www.liputan6.com/news/read/3236506/bnpb-dalam-setahun-indonesia-diguncang-6000-kali-gempa

Anggraeni, K. (May 10, 2018). '40 Hours Riot in Mako Brimob Detention Center Ends.' *Tempo*. Retrieved from: https://en.tempo.co/read/918315/40-hours-riot-in-mako-brimob-detention-center-ends

Anggriawan, R.D. (2018, October 6). 'Prabowo`s Camp Deem IMF-World Bank Meeting an Embarrassment.' *Tempo*. Retrieved from: https://en.tempo.co/read/922293/prabowos-camp-deem-imf-world-bank-meeting-an-embarrassment

Annual Meetings 2018 Indonesia (n.d.). 'About.' Retrieved from: https://meetings.imf.org/en/2018/Annual/About

*Antara* (2017, December 30). 'President Jokowi closes IDX trade for 2017.' Retrieve from: https://en.antaranews.com/news/114047/president-jokowi-closes-idx-trade-for-2017

Aritonang, M. (2018, February 23). 'BREAKING: PDI-P officially endorses Jokowi for 2019 presidential election.' *The Jakarta Post*. Retrieved from: https://www.thejakartapost.com/news/2018/02/23/breaking-pdi-p-officially-endorses-jokowi-for-2019-presidential-election.html

Aritonang, M. (2018, July 20). 'Kalla to testify about his right to run for VP again.' *The Jakarta Post*. Retrieved from: https://www.thejakartapost.com/news/2018/07/20/kalla-to-testify-about-his-right-to-run-for-vp-again.html

Aritonang, M.S. and Ramadhani, N.F. (2018, June 28). 'Jokowi gains, PDI-P loses.' *The Jakarta Post*. Retrieved from: https://www.thejakartapost.com/news/2018/06/28/jokowi-gains-pdi-p-loses.html

Aritonang, M. and Sapiie, M.A. (2018 August 9). 'Democratic Party politician calls Prabowo 'cardboard general'.' *The Jakarta Post*. Retrieved from: https://www.thejakartapost.com/news/2018/08/09/democratic-party-politician-calls-prabowo-cardboard-general.html

Aritonang, M. and Tehusijarana, K.M. (2018, April 12). 'It's official: Prabowo to join 2019 race.' *The Jakarta Post*. Retrieved from: https://www.thejakartapost.com/news/2018/04/12/its-official-prabowo-to-join-2019-race.html

Armenia, R. (2015, March 26). 'Kim Jong-un Batal Hadiri KAA, Utus Tangan Kanannya ke Jakarta.' *CNN Indonesia*. Retrieved from: https://www.cnnindonesia.com/nasional/20150326202656-20-42216/kim-jong-un-batal-hadiri-kaa-utus-tangan-kanannya-ke-jakarta

ASEAN Secretariat (2018, April 28). *Chairman's Statement of the 32nd ASEAN Summit, Singapore, 28 April 2018.* Retrieved from: https://asean.org/wp-content/uploads/2018/04/Chairmans-Statement-of-the-32nd-ASEAN-Summit.pdf

ASEAN Secretariat (2018, August 4). *Chairman's Statement of the 8th East Asia Summit Foreign Ministers' Meeting, Singapore, 4 August 2018.* Retrieved from: https://asean.org/storage/2018/08/8th-EAS-FMM-Chairmans-Statement-Final-Clean.pdf

Australian Government (2017). *2017 Foreign Policy White Paper.* Retrieved from: https://www.fpwhitepaper.gov.au/foreign-policy-white-paper

Bayuni, E. (2018, September 3). 'Commentary: Asian Games: Badly needed confidence booster for our nation.' *The Jakarta Post.* Retrieved from: https://www.thejakartapost.com/academia/2018/09/03/commentary-asian-games-badly-needed-confidence-booster-for-our-nation.html

Baynes, C. (2018, August 18). 'Unified Korean athletes cheered by thousands as they parade together at Asian Games opening ceremony.' *Independent.* Retrieved from: https://www.independent.co.uk/news/world/asia/unified-korea-athletes-asian-games-opening-ceremony-north-south-kim-jong-un-a8497521.html

*BBC* (2018, August 6). 'Lombok quake: Thousands evacuated after dozens die on Indonesian island.' Retrieved from: https://www.bbc.com/news/world-asia-45081508?intlink_from_url=https://www.bbc.com/news/topics/c34zx89q9wkt/lombok-earthquakes&link_location=live-reporting-story

*BBC* (2018, August 14). 'Asian Games — Is this eclectic mix of 40 events the Olympics+?' Retrieved from: https://www.bbc.com/sport/45180298

*BBC* (2018, August 14). 'Golput 'bisa menggerus' perolehan suara Jokowi-Ma'ruf Amin di Pilpres 2019.' Retrieved from: https://www.bbc.com/indonesia/indonesia-45161027

*BBC* (2018, August 17). 'Asian Games: Indonesia police kill dozens in criminal crackdown.' Retrieved from: https://www.bbc.com/news/world-asia-45223495

*BBC* (2018, August 26). 'Asian Games: Unified Korea boating team win historic gold.' Retrieved from: https://www.bbc.com/news/world-asia-45314674

Beaumont, P. (2017, December 20). 'US will 'take names of those who vote to reject Jerusalem recognition'.' *The Guardian.* Retrieved from: https://www.

theguardian.com/us-news/2017/dec/20/us-take-names-united-nations-vote-to-reject-jerusalem-recognition

Birties, B. (2018, March 8). 'China mocks Australia over 'Indo-Pacific' concept it says will 'dissipate'.' *ABC News*. Retrieved from: https://www.abc.net.au/news/2018-03-08/china-mocks-australia-over-indo-pacific-concept/9529548

Blokhuizen, I. (2017, October 24). 'Indonesia can win its war on drugs, by ending it.' *The Jakarta Post*. Retrieved from: https://www.thejakartapost.com/academia/2017/10/24/indonesia-can-win-its-war-on-drugs-by-ending-it.html

*Bloomberg* (n.d.). 'USDIDR:CUR.' Retrieved from: https://www.bloomberg.com/quote/USDIDR:CUR

Boedhiwardhana, W. (2018, May 14). '25 killed in East Java attacks, including 13 suicide bombers.' *The Jakarta Post*. Retrieved from: https://www.thejakartapost.com/news/2018/05/14/25-killed-in-east-java-attacks-including-13-suicide-bombers.html

*CBS News* (2018, April 28). 'Mongolia, Singapore are final 2 sites under consideration for Trump-Kim Jong Un meeting.' Retrieved from: https://www.cbsnews.com/news/trump-kim-jong-un-summit-location-mongolia-singapore/

*The Conversation* (2018, August 10). 'Political compromise behind Indonesia's vice presidential nominees: Experts respond.' Retrieved from: http://theconversation.com/political-compromise-behind-indonesias-vice-presidential-nominees-experts-respond-101382

*CNN Indonesia* (2018, October 5). 'IHSG 'Meringkuk' di Zona Merah ke Level 5.731.' Retrieved from: https://www.cnnindonesia.com/ekonomi/20181005162408-92-336103/ihsg-meringkuk-di-zona-merah-ke-level-5731

Ellis-Petersen, H. and Lamb, K. (2018, May 14). 'Surabaya blast: Family of five carried out bomb attack on Indonesia police station.' *The Guardian*. Retrieved from: https://www.theguardian.com/world/2018/may/14/indonesia-car-bomb-surabaya-police-station-attacked

Erdianto, K. and Rachman, D.A. (2018, August 9). 'Jadi Cawapres Prabowo, Sandiaga Keluar dari Gerindra.' *Kompas*. Retrieved from: https://nasional.kompas.com/read/2018/08/09/23573541/jadi-cawapres-prabowo-sandiaga-keluar-dari-gerindra

Erviani, N.K. and Arbi, I.A. (2018, August 6). 'Australian delegates, minister 'safe' following Lombok earthquake.' *The Jakarta Post*. Retrieved from:

https://www.thejakartapost.com/news/2018/08/06/australian-delegates-minister-safe-following-lombok-earthquake.html

Esguerra, A.Q. (2018, February 21). 'US Intelligence Community: Duterte is one of threats to democracy in Southeast Asia.' *Inquirer*. Retrieved from: https://globalnation.inquirer.net/164455/us-intelligence-community-duterte-one-threats-democracy-southeast-asia?utm_expid=.XqNwTug2W6nwDVUSgFJXed.1

Febriana, B. (2018, May 14). 'Jokowi Ancam Keluarkan Perppu Anti Terorisme.' *Gatra*. Retrieved from: https://www.gatra.com/rubrik/nasional/pemerintahan-pusat/322452-Jokowi-Ancam-Keluarkan-Perppu-Anti-Terorisme

Fifield, A., Nakamura, D. and Kim, S.M. (2018, March 8). 'Trump accepts invitation to meet with North Korean leader Kim Jong Un.' *The Washington Post*. Retrieved from: https://www.washingtonpost.com/world/asia_pacific/north-korean-leader-kim-jong-un-has-invited-president-trump-to-a-meeting/2018/03/08/021cb070-2322-11e8-badd-7c9f29a55815_story.html?noredirect=on&utm_term=.7ef03119dab0

*Fresh News* (2018, September 29). 'Indonesian President Congratulates PM Hun Sen on Election's Victory.' Retrieved from: http://m.en.freshnewsasia.com/index.php/en/11339-2018-09-29-08-43-33.html

Gammon, L. (2018, April 12). 'Prabowo didn't just announce a presidential run.' *New Mandala*. Retrieved from: https://www.newmandala.org/prabowo-didnt-just-announce-presidential-run/

Georgieff, J. (2013, May 17). 'An Indo-Pacific treaty: An idea whose time has come?' *The Diplomat*. Retrieved from: https://thediplomat.com/2013/05/an-indo-pacific-treaty-an-idea-whose-time-has-come/

*Global Times* (2018, January 25). 'India's geopolitical bluff baffles China.' Retrieved from: http://www.globaltimes.cn/content/1086643.shtml

Graham, E. (2018, May 6). 'Trump–Kim summit: What's in the venue?' *The Interpreter*. Retrieved from: https://www.lowyinstitute.org/the-interpreter/trump-kim-summit-what-s-venue

Gorbiano, M.I. (2018, October 12). 'Winter is coming, Jokowi tells fiscal, monetary policymakers.' *The Jakarta Post*. Retrieved from: https://www.thejakartapost.com/news/2018/10/12/winter-is-coming-jokowi-tells-fiscal-monetary-policymakers.html

*The Guardian* (2018, August 19). 'Lombok: Magniture-6.3 earthquake rocks Indonesian island.' Retrieved from: https://www.theguardian.com/

world/2018/aug/19/lombok-magnitude-63-earthquake-rocks-indonesian-island

Halim, D. (2018, October 1). 'Hampir 2 Bulan Berlalu, Ini "Update" Korban Gempa Lombok dari BNPB.' *Kompas.* Retrieved from: https://nasional. kompas.com/read/2018/10/01/21091241/hampir-2-bulan-berlalu-ini-update-korban-gempa-lombok-dari-bnpb

Hariraksapitak, P. (2018, February 27). 'Thai PM now says election to be held no later than Feb 2019.' *Reuters.* Retrieved from: https://www.reuters.com/article/us-thailand-politics/thai-pm-now-says-election-to-be-held-no-later-than-feb-2019-idUSKCN1GB0QS

Heriyanto, D. (2018, June 27). '2018 regional elections: The basics.' *The Jakarta Post.* Retrieved from: https://www.thejakartapost.com/news/2018/06/22/2018-regional-elections-the-basics.html

Heydarian, R. (2018, May 20). 'How 'polarising' former strongman Mahathir Mohamad could bring unity to Southeast Asia.' *South China Morning Post.* Retrieved from: https://www.scmp.com/news/china/diplomacy-defence/article/2146650/how-polarising-former-strongman-mahathir-mohamad-could

Heydarian, R.J. (2018, June 13). 'The Indo-Pacific age is beginning.' *China US Focus.* Retrieved from: https://www.chinausfocus.com/peace-security/the-indo-pacific-age-is-beginning

Huiwen, N. and Ng, C. (2018, August 6). 'Lombok quake: Shanmugan and Singapore delegation arrive back in Singapore.' *The Straits Times.* Retrieved from: https://www.straitstimes.com/singapore/k-shanmugam-waiting-for-flight-out-of-lombok-after-70-magnitude-quake

Jaipragas, B. (2018, June 19). 'Forget the warships: Malaysian PM Mahathir's peace formula for South China Sea.' *South China Morning Post.* Retrieved from: https://www.scmp.com/week-asia/geopolitics/article/2151403/forget-warships-malaysian-pm-mahathirs-peace-formula-south

Jaipragas, B. (2018, July 20). 'Why is the US calling Asia-Pacific the Indo-Pacific? Donald Trump to 'clarify'.' *South China Morning Post.* Retrieved from: https://www.scmp.com/week-asia/politics/article/2118806/why-us-calling-asia-pacific-indo-pacific-trump-clarify

*Jakarta Globe* (2018, August 16). 'World Recognizes Indonesia's Diplomatic Achievements: Jokowi.' Retrieved from: https://jakartaglobe.id/context/world-recognizes-indonesias-diplomatic-achievements-jokowi/

*The Jakarta Post* (2018, March 14). 'EDITORIAL: Afghanistan: A bridge too far.' Retrieved from: https://www.thejakartapost.com/academia/2018/03/14/editorial-afghanistan-a-bridge-too-far.html

*The Jakarta Post* (2018, August 10). 'Will 'millennial' Ma'ruf and 'santri' Sandiaga change Prabowo vs Jokowi game?' Retrieved from: https://www.thejakartapost.com/news/2018/08/10/will-millennial-maruf-and-santri-sandiaga-change-prabowo-vs-jokowi-game.html

*The Jakarta Post* (2018, August 30). 'Post-Islamism what? Sandiaga confused by PKS campaign slogan.' Retrieved from: https://www.thejakartapost.com/news/2018/08/30/post-islamism-what-sandiaga-confused-by-pks-campaign-slogan.html

*The Jakarta Post* (2018, October 3). 'Economic chief needs time to explain rupiah drop.' Retrieved from: https://www.thejakartapost.com/news/2018/10/03/economic-chief-needs-time-to-explain-rupiah-drop.html

*The Jakarta Post* (2018, October 4). 'It's not doomsday, says BI boss on rupiah depreciation.' Retrieved from: https://www.thejakartapost.com/news/2018/10/04/its-not-doomsday-says-bi-boss-on-rupiah-depreciation.html

Jordan, R. (2018, April 7). 'Jokowi Sindir #2019GantiPresiden: Masak Kaus Bisa Ganti Presiden?' *Detik*. Retrieved from: https://news.detik.com/berita/3958859/jokowi-sindir-2019gantipresiden-masak-kaus-bisa-ganti-presiden

Kahfi, K., Andapita, V. and Boedhiwardhana, W. (2018, March 13). '[UPDATED] Surabaya church bombings: What we know so far.' *The Jakarta Post*. Retrieved from: https://www.thejakartapost.com/news/2018/05/13/surabaya-church-bombings-what-we-know-so-far.html

*Kompas* (2015, January 25). 'Kim Jong-un Dijadwalkan Hadiri Peringatan KAA ke-60 di Bandung.' Retrieved from: https://internasional.kompas.com/read/2015/01/25/11543881/Kim.Jong-un.Dijadwalkan.Hadiri.Peringatan.KAA.ke-60.di.Bandung

*Kompas* (2018 October 12). 'Pertemuan Tahunan IMF-Bank Dunia di Bali, Apa yang Didapat Indonesia?' Retrieved from: https://ekonomi.kompas.com/jeo/pertemuan-tahunan-imf-bank-dunia-di-bali-apa-yang-didapat-indonesia

*Kompas* (2018, October 23). 'Survei "Kompas": Apresiasi Kinerja Pemerintahan Jokowi-JK Turun.' Retrieved from: https://nasional.kompas.com/read/2018/10/23/11052661/survei-kompas-apresiasi-kinerja-pemerintahan-jokowi-jk-turun

Lamb, K. (2018, May 10). 'Indonesian prison riot leaves five officers and one prisoner dead.' *The Guardian*. Retrieved from: https://www.theguardian. com/world/2018/may/10/indonesian-prison-riot-leaves-five-officers-and-one-prisoner-dead

Lamb, K. (2018, July 26). 'Cover-up: Jakarta hides foul river with giant net before Asian Games.' *The Guardian*. Retrieved from: https://www. theguardian.com/cities/2018/jul/26/cover-up-jakarta-hides-foul-river-with-giant-net-before-asian-games

Lamb, K. and Davidson, H. (2018, September 30). 'Death toll from Sulawesi tsunami reaches 384.' *The Guardian*. Retrieved from: https://www. theguardian.com/world/2018/sep/28/tsunami-hits-indonesian-cities-after-powerful-earthquake

Lipson, D. (2018, August 27). 'Declaring a natural disaster after Lombok earthquakes would have led to more aid, says critics of President.' *ABC News*. Retrieved from: https://www.abc.net.au/news/2018-08-27/criticism-of-government-response-to-lombok-earthquakes/10169218

Maulia, E. (2018, May 25). 'Indonesia passes tougher terror law after Surabaya attacks.' *Nikkei Asian Review*. Retrieved from: https://asia.nikkei.com/ Politics/Indonesia-passes-tougher-terror-law-after-Surabaya-attacks

Mediani, M. (2018, August 16). 'Ahok Kaget Jokowi Pilih Ma'ruf Amin Jadi Cawapres.' *CNN Indonesia*. Retrieved from: https://www.cnnindonesia.com/ nasional/20180816190626-20-322891/ahok-kaget-jokowi-pilih-maruf-amin-jadi-cawapres

Mendez, C. (2018, March 6). 'President Duterte to skip Asean-Australia summit this March.' *The Philippine Star*. Retrieved from: https://www.philstar.com/ headlines/2018/03/06/1793968/president-duterte-skip-asean-australia-summit-march

Ministry of Foreign Affairs, Republic of Indonesia (2018, January 9). *2018 Annual Press Statement of the Minister for Foreign Affairs of the Repubilc of Indonesia — H.E. Retno L.P. Marsudi, Jakarta, 9 January 2018*. Retrieved from: https://www.kemlu.go.id/id/pidato/menlu/Pages/PPTM2018%20 MENLU%20RI%20ENG.pdf

Ministry of Foreign Affairs, Republic of Indonesia (2018, May 10). 'Collaboration for Peace: Indonesia hosts the Trilateral Ulema Conference of Indonesia, Afghanistan and Pakistan.' Retrieved from: https://www.kemlu.go.id/en/

berita/Pages/Collaboration-for-Peace-Indonesia-hosts-the-Trilateral-Ulema-Conference-of-Indonesia,-Afghanistan-and-Pakistan.aspx

Ministry of Foreign Affairs, Republic of Indonesia (2018, August 6). 'Introducing the Indo-Pacific Concept, Indonesia Set the Tone at the East Asia Summit.' Retrieved from: https://www.kemlu.go.id/en/berita/pages/Introducing-the-Indo-Pacific-Concept,-Indonesia-Set-the-Tone-at-the-East-Asia-Summit.aspx

Ministry of Foreign Affairs, Republic of Indonesia (2018, September 28). 'Foreign Ministers Commemorated the 5th Anniversary of MIKTA.' Retrieved from: https://www.kemlu.go.id/en/berita/pages/Foreign-Ministers-Commemorated-the-5th-Anniversary-of-MIKTA.aspx

Nanuam, W. (2018, August 6). 'Prayut: Jakarta Post does not speak for Indonesia.' *Bangkok Post*. Retrieved from: https://www.bangkokpost.com/news/politics/1516822/prayut-jakarta-post-does-not-speak-for-indonesia

*The Nation* (2018, June 9). 'Superheroes of Indonesian diplomacy on UNSC sea mission.' Retrieved from: https://www.pressreader.com/thailand/the-nation/20180609/281642485869664

Nelson, L. (2017, November 7). 'In Asia, Trump keeps talking about Indo-Pacific.' *Politico*. Retrieved from: https://www.politico.com/story/2017/11/07/trump-asia-indo-pacific-244657

*News.com.au* (2018, August 19). 'North Korea, South Korea march together at Asian Games 2018 opening ceremony.' Retrieved from: https://www.news.com.au/world/asia/north-korea-south-korea-march-together-at-asian-games-2018-opening-ceremony/news-story/d9928181ebab7c3821d0cdcf4ae094ac

*News.com.au* (2018, October 1). 'Tsunami warning systems in Indonesia missed the giant wave that killed more than 800 people.' Retrieved from: https://www.news.com.au/world/asia/tsunami-warning-systems-in-indonesia-missed-the-giant-wave-that-killed-more-than-800-people/news-story/86ba323ec2508ffba90a1698c6aa4d0a

*Nikkei Asian Review* (2018, September 1). 'Indonesia to bid for 2032 Olympics after Asian Games success.' Retrieved from: https://asia.nikkei.com/Politics/Indonesia-to-bid-for-2032-Olympics-after-Asian-Games-success

Nugraha, P. (2018, August 21). 'Govt won't declare Lombok quakes 'national disaster'.' *The Jakarta Post*. Retrieved from: https://www.thejakartapost.com/news/2018/08/21/govt-wont-declare-lombok-quakes-national-disaster.html

Nurita, D. (2018, August 9). 'Jusuf Kalla can no longer run for Jokowi's VP in 2019 election.' *Tempo.* Retrieved from: https://en.tempo.co/read/920672/jusuf-kalla-can-no-longer-run-for-jokowis-vp-in-2019-election

Parashar, S. (2018, January 25). 'India to invite heads of 10 Asean nations for Republic Day celebrations.' *Time of India.* Retrieved from: https://timesofindia.indiatimes.com/india/india-to-invite-heads-of-10-asean-nations-for-republic-day-celebtations/articleshow/59497883.cms

Parlina, I. and Cahya, G.H. (2018, October 31). 'Our Ocean Conference ends with new confidence.' *The Jakarta Post.* Retrieved from: https://www.thejakartapost.com/news/2018/10/31/our-ocean-conference-ends-with-new-confidence.html

Prasetia, A. (2018, May 18). 'Jokowi akan Aktifkan Antiteror 'Super Elite' TNI dengan Catatan.' *DetikNews.* Retrieved from: https://news.detik.com/berita/4027396/jokowi-akan-aktifkan-antiteror-super-elite-tni-dengan-catatan

Prasetia, F.A. (2018 July, 24). 'PKS: Bukan Karakter Prabowo Mengkhianati Teman Setia.' *Tribun News.* Retrieved from: http://www.tribunnews.com/nasional/2018/07/24/pks-bukan-karakter-prabowo-mengkhianati-teman-setia

Primadhyta, S. (2018, October 5). '10 Bintang 'Bersinar' di Pertemuan IMF-World Bank di Bali.' *CNN Indonesia.* Retrieved from: https://www.cnnindonesia.com/ekonomi/20181001191739-532-334765/10-bintang-bersinar-di-pertemuan-imf-world-bank-di-bali

Purba, K. (2018, July 31). 'Commentary: Don't let Thai junta chief chair ASEAN next year.' *The Jakarta Post.* Retrieved from: https://www.thejakartapost.com/academia/2018/07/31/commentary-dont-let-thai-junta-chief-chair-asean-next-year.html

Putera, A.D. (2018, October 3). 'Rupiah Rp 15.000 Gubernur BI Sebut Belum "Kiamat".' *Kompas.* Retrieved from: https://ekonomi.kompas.com/read/2018/10/03/154500426/rupiah-rp-15.000-gubernur-bi-sebut-belum-kiamat-

Putra, P.M.S. (2018, July 27). 'PKS: AHY Sebaiknya Jadi Menteri Saja Dulu.' *Liputan 6.* Retrieved from: https://www.liputan6.com/news/read/3602055/pks-ahy-sebaiknya-jadi-menteri-saja-dulu

Putri, B. U. (2018, October 5). 'Prabowo Demands Halt for IMF-World Bank Meeting.' *Tempo.* Retrieved from: https://en.tempo.co/read/922274/prabowo-demands-halt-for-imf-world-bank-meeting

*Rappler* (2018, October 12). ''Winter is coming,' Indonesian leader warns amid economic gloom.' Retrieved from: https://www.rappler.com/world/regions/

asia-pacific/indonesia/bahasa/englishedition/214152-winter-is-coming-widodo-warns-economic-gloom

Razak, I. (2017, December 11). 'Commentary: Change of guard in TNI and President's leadership style.' *The Jakarta Post*. Retrieved from: https://www. thejakartapost.com/academia/2017/12/11/commentary-change-of-guard-in-tni-and-presidents-leadership-style.html

Renaldi, E. (2018, October 10). 'Indonesia's Opposition slams 'lavish' IMF-World Bank meeting in Bali amid quake disaster.' *ABC News*. Retrieved from: https://www.abc.net.au/news/2018-10-09/imf-world-bank-meeting-in-bali-criticised/10350818

*Reuters* (2018, March 10). 'Afghan Taliban urge religious scholars to boycott peace conference.' Retrieved from: https://www.reuters.com/article/us-afghanistan-taliban/afghan-taliban-urge-religious-scholars-to-boycott-peace-conference-idUSKCN1GM0CL

*Reuters* (2018, August 2). 'ASEAN, China agree 'milestone' text as basis for South China Sea talks.' Retrieved from: https://www.reuters.com/article/us-asean-singapore-southchinasea/asean-china-agree-milestone-text-as-basis-for-south-china-sea-talks-idUSKBN1KN14V

*Reuters* (2018, September 12). 'Indonesia's 'Avengers' president stands ready to defeat trade wars.' Retrieved from: https://www.reuters.com/article/us-wef-vietnam-indonesia-avengers/indonesias-avengers-president-stands-ready-to-defeat-trade-wars-idUSKCN1LS1KL

Sani, A.F.I. (2018, May 22). 'Jokowi asks to take extraordinary measures in fighting terrorism.' *Tempo*. Retrieved from: https://en.tempo.co/read/918662/jokowi-asks-to-take-extraordinary-measures-in-fighting-terrorism

Sapiie, M.A. (2018, April 29). 'Indonesia wants ASEAN to take central role in developing Indo-Pacific cooperation.' *The Jakarta Post*. Retrieved from: https://www.thejakartapost.com/seasia/2018/04/29/indonesia-wants-asean-to-take-central-role-in-developing-indo-pacific-cooperation.html

Sapiie, M.A. (2018, May 18). 'Jokowi agrees to revive Koopsusgab special forces.' *The Jakarta Post*. Retrieved from: https://www.thejakartapost.com/news/2018/05/18/jokowi-agrees-to-revive-koopsusgab-special-forces.html

Sapiie, M.A. and Septiari, D. (2018, May 1). 'Indonesia offers to host Trump-Kim talk.' *The Jakarta Post*. Retrieved from: https://www.thejakartapost.com/news/2018/05/01/indonesia-offers-to-host-trump-jong-un-talk.html

Saputri, D.S. and Almas. P. (2018, April 30). 'Jokowi invites two Korean ambassadors.' *Republika*. Retrieved from: https://www.republika.co.id/ berita/en/national-politics/18/04/30/p7zy18414-jokowi-invites-two-korean-ambassadors

Sekretariat Kabinet Republik Indonesia (2018 March 23). 'President Jokowi Ensures New ASEAN Secretariat Building Completed in Early 2019.' Retrieved from: https://setkab.go.id/en/president-jokowi-ensures-new-asean-secretariat-building-completed-in-early-2019/?yop_poll_tr_id=&yop-poll-nonce-1_yp5abc53734268a=6ba744fde9

Sekretariat Kabinet Republik Indonesia (2018, August 16). *State Address of the President of the Republic of Indonesia on the Occasion of the 73rd Anniversary of the Proclamation of Independence of the Republic of Indonesia before the Joint Session of the House of Representatives of the Republic of Indonesia and the Regional Representatives Council of the Republic of Indonesia.* Retrieved from: https://setkab.go.id/en/state-address-of-the-president-of-the-republic-of-indonesia-on-the-occasion-of-the-73rd-anniversary-of-the-proclamation-of-independence-of-the-republic-of-indonesia-before-the-joint-session-of-the-ho/

Sekretariat Kabinet Republik Indonesia (2018, September 2). 'President Jokowi Visits Quake-Hit Lombok Again to Meet Survivors, Children.' Retrieved from: https://setkab.go.id/en/president-jokowi-visits-quake-hit-lombok-again-to-meet-survivors-children/

Sentana, I.M. (2018, October 9). 'Indonesia's economy will emerge from market turbulence stronger, finance minister says.' *Wall Street Journal*. Retrieved from: https://www.wsj.com/articles/indonesias-economy-will-emerge-from-market-turbulence-stronger-finance-minister-says-1539061915

Septiari, D. (2018, May 29). 'Indonesia to ramp up lobbying for UN Security Council seat.' *The Jakarta Post*. Retrieved from: https://www.thejakartapost.com/news/2018/05/29/indonesia-to-ramp-up-lobbying-for-un-security-council-seat.html

Setiaji, H. (2018, October 2). 'Sah, Dolar AS Tembus Rp 15.000!' *CNBC Indonesia*. Retrieved from: https://www.cnbcindonesia.com/market/20181002105403-17-35640/sah-dolar-as-tembus-rp-15000

Setiawan, K. (2018, October 4). 'Sri Mulyani: Mayoritas Pemicu Melemahnya Rupiah Faktor Eksternal.' *Tempo*. Retrieved from: https://bisnis.tempo.co/

read/1132933/sri-mulyani-mayoritas-pemicu-melemahnya-rupiah-faktor-eksternal

Sheany (2018, February 26). 'Indonesia Condemns US Plan to Open Embassy in Jerusalem in May.' *Jakarta Globe.* Retrieved from: https://jakartaglobe.id/context/indonesia-condemns-us-plan-to-open-embassy-in-jerusalem-in-may/

Sheany (2018, May 16). 'Ulema from three countries meet in West Java, Denounce Terrorism, Suicide Attacks.' *Jakarta Globe.* Retrieved from: https://jakartaglobe.id/context/trilateral-ulema-meeting-in-bogor-first-step-toward-peace-in-afghanistan

Sheany (2018, June 9. 'Indonesia wins UN security council seat.' *Jakarta Globe.* Retrieved from: https://jakartaglobe.id/context/indonesia-wins-un-security-council-seat/

Sheany (2018, October 5). 'Asean leaders to meet on sidelines of IMF-WB Annual Meetings in Bali.' *Jakarta Globe.* Retrieved from: https://jakartaglobe.id/context/asean-leaders-to-meet-on-sidelines-of-imf-wb-annual-meetings-in-bali/

Sheany and Ganesha, A. (2018, July 6). 'Regional elections set new precedent for 2019.' *Jakarta Globe.* Retrieved from: https://jakartaglobe.id/context/regional-elections-give-parties-precedent-for-2019

Sheany and Nathalia, T. (2018, August 5). 'Most EAS members support Asean Centrality in Indo-Pacific concept: FM.' *Jakarta Globe.* Retrieved from: https://jakartaglobe.id/context/most-eas-member-countries-in-support-of-asean-centrality-for-indo-pacific-concept-fm-retno/

Shekhar, V. (2018, July 17). 'Is Indonesia's 'Indo-Pacific cooperation' strategy a weak play?' *PacNet.* Number 47. Retrieved from: https://www.pacforum.org/sites/default/s3fs-public/publication/180717_PacNet_47.pdf

Siddiq, T. (2018, May 13). 'Serangan Mako Brimob, Polisi: Ada Komunikasi Pimpinan JAD dari LP.' *Tempo.* Retrieved from: https://nasional.tempo.co/read/1088450/serangan-mako-brimob-polisi-ada-komunikasi-pimpinan-jad-dari-lp

Soeriaatmadja, W. and Yulisman, L. (2018, June 27). 'Peaceful start to Indonesia's regional elections seen as test for next year's presidential polls.' *The Straits Times.* Retrieved from: https://www.straitstimes.com/asia/se-asia/indonesian-regional-polls-kick-off-peacefully-amid-tight-security

Sokhean, B. and Nachemson, A. (2018, February 21). 'Hun Sen threatens to boycott Asean summit proceedings if faced with 'pressure'.' *The Phnom*

*Penh Post*. Retrieved from: https://www.phnompenhpost.com/national/hun-sen-threatens-boycott-asean-summit-proceedings-if-faced-pressure

*The Star Online* (2018, October 2). 'Blame game over Indonesia's tsunami warning system and disaster at Palu, Sulawesi.' Retrieved from: https://www.thestar.com.my/news/regional/2018/10/02/blame-game-over-indonesias-tsunami-warning-system-and-disaster-at-palu-sulawesi/

Stefanie, C. and Sasongko, J.P. (2018, August 9). 'Mahfud MD Sambangi Restoran Dekat Pertemuan Jokowi.' *CNN Indonesia*. Retrieved from: https://www.cnnindonesia.com/nasional/20180809175456-32-320981/mahfud-md-sambangi-restoran-dekat-pertemuan-jokowi

*The Straits Times* (2018, March 12). 'Voters need more presidential candidates: The Jakarta Post.' Retrieved from: https://www.straitstimes.com/asia/se-asia/voters-need-more-presidential-candidates-the-jakarta-post

*The Straits Times* (2018, June 29). 'Indonesia's Constitutional Court refuses to pave way for V-P Jusuf Kalla to seek third term.' Retrieved from: https://www.straitstimes.com/asia/se-asia/indonesias-constitutional-court-refuses-to-pave-way-for-v-p-jusuf-kalla-to-seek-third

*The Straits Times* (2018 October 1). 'Criticism online over early lifting of tsunami warning.' Retrieved from: https://www.straitstimes.com/asia/se-asia/criticism-online-over-early-lifting-of-tsunami-warning

*The Straits Times* (2018, October 15). 'IMF-World Bank meetings billed a success by officials.' Retrieved from: https://www.straitstimes.com/asia/se-asia/imf-world-bank-meetings-billed-a-success-by-officials

Tehusijarana, K.M. (2018, August 6). '[UPDATED] What you need to know about the Lombok earthquake.' *The Jakarta Post*. Retrieved from: https://www.thejakartapost.com/news/2018/08/06/what-you-need-to-know-about-the-lombok-earthquake.html

Tehusijarana, K.M. (2018, October 22). 'Central Sulawesi quake, tsunami inflicted US$911 million in losses: Govt.' *The Jakarta Post*. Retrieved from: https://www.thejakartapost.com/news/2018/10/21/central-sulawesi-quake-tsunami-inflicted-us911-million-in-losses-govt.html

*Tempo* (2018, August 20). 'Govt Says Lombok Quake Not National Disaster.' Retrieved from: https://en.tempo.co/read/920968/govt-says-lombok-quake-not-national-disaster

Tobing, D.H. (2018, June 21). 'Will Indonesia bring Rohingya to Security Council?' *The Jakarta Post*. Retrieved from: https://www.thejakartapost.

com/academia/2018/06/21/will-indonesia-bring-rohingya-to-security-council.html

*Tribun Bisnis* (2018, July 6). 'Akhir Pekan, IHSG Ditutup Terkoreksi ke Level 5.694.' Retrieved from: http://www.tribunnews.com/bisnis/2018/07/06/akhir-pekan-ihsg-ditutup-terkoreksi-ke-level-5694

Triyogo, A.W. (2018, April 11). '2019 Presidential Election, Prabowo Ready to Face Jokowi.' *Tempo.* Retrieved from: https://en.tempo.co/read/917504/2019-presidential-election-prabowo-ready-to-face-jokowi

Troath, S. (2018, July 2). 'Commentary: Indonesia has won a seat on the United Nations Security Council. Now what?' *Channel News Asia.* Retrieved from: https://www.channelnewsasia.com/news/commentary/indonesia-opportunity-on-united-nation-security-council-10459048

Walden, M. (2018, September 21). 'Indonesian opposition movement accuses president of authoritarianism.' *VOA.* Retrieved from: https://www.voanews.com/a/indonesian-opposition-movement-accuses-president-of-authoritarianism/4581207.html

Wright, S. (2018, August 14). 'Indonesia deploys 100,000-strong force to secure Asian Games, image.' *The Sydney Morning Herald.* Retrieved from: https://www.smh.com.au/world/asia/indonesia-deploys-100-000-strong-force-to-secure-asian-games-image-20180814-p4zxf3.html

Yong, C. (2018, August 3). 'Asean, China agree on text to negotiate South China Sea code.' *The Straits Times.* Retrieved from: https://www.straitstimes.com/politics/asean-china-agree-on-text-to-negotiate-south-china-sea-code

Yong-Soo, J. and Jin-Kyu, K. (2018, June 27). 'Indonesia wants Koreas' leaders at Asian Games.' *Korea Joongang Daily.* Retrieved from: http://koreajoongangdaily.joins.com/news/article/article.aspx?aid=3049866

# Epilogue

# Five More Years

## 1. Some Final Words

At the time this book was completed — May 2019 — the official result of Indonesia's Presidential and General Elections had just been announced. According to the General Elections Commission (Komisi Pemilihan Umum, or KPU), the presidential–vice presidential pairing of Joko Widodo–Ma'ruf Amin won with 55.50 percent of the votes, whilst the rival pairing of Prabowo Subianto–Sandiaga Uno only received 44.50 percent (*CNN Indonesia*, 2019, May 21a). Given the choice between five more years or a new beginning, the Indonesian electorate clearly opted for the former as they casted their votes on April 17, 2019.

It should be noted that the logistical challenge of holding a vote involving some 190 million registered voters and 800,000 polling stations across the vast archipelago was hugely daunting. Added to this was the fact that both the Presidential and General Elections were held on the exact same day, with almost 20,000 positions at the national, provincial, and local levels contested. For many though, all eyes were on the vote that determined who will occupy Merdeka Palace for 2019–2024. As Indonesians headed to the voting booth, the key question they faced was — does Joko Widodo deserve five more years or should Prabowo Subianto be given a chance?

Quick count results — based on a sample of the results from selected polling stations across the country — had suggested that Joko Widodo was on course to secure a second term. *Kompas'* (n.d.) quick count results, for example, showed that Widido has secured 54.45 percent of the votes whilst Prabowo Subianto only managed 45.55 percent. Other pollsters had similar results with the former securing between 54–56 percent and the latter trailing with around 44–46 percent of the votes. The official results, announced a month after the elections, confirmed these findings, and President Widodo is on course to be inaugurated for a second term in October 2019.

Having said that, it is worth remembering that despite being ahead in several surveys in the lead up to the April 17 vote, a Widodo second term was far from guaranteed on the morning of the vote. Indeed, the official results show that Widodo barely improved from 2014 when he secured 53.15 percent. Certainly, many of the President's supporters had expressed disappointment with his performance over the past five years. Widodo had not been the great champion of human rights that activists hoped for back in 2014, the economy was nowhere near the seven percent GDP growth he famously campaigned on, and the choice of Ma'ruf Amin as his running mate put off some millennial and ethnic minority voters. Calls for the electorate not to *golput*, or abstain, was perhaps indicative of the concern that many of Widodo's voters would simply not turn up on April 17, 2019. Meanwhile, Prabowo Subianto's supporters had appeared the more motivated, with a so-called reunion of the '212' demonstrations, attracting between 40,000 to 100,000 people recently in December 2018. The online discourse also suggested it would be a close contest, with the followers of the two candidates engaged in passionate — if not at times unhealthy — arguments.

Having said that, online posts do not necessarily translate into physical votes and neither does leading in the surveys. In other words, turnout was always going to be key. Which of the two candidates was more successful in getting their supporters to actually go to the polling stations would determine who would be handed the keys to Merdeka Palace. Important too were the relatively sizeable undecided voters leading up to April 17, and whether they would lean towards Widodo or Prabowo Subianto or maybe even not be bothered to take part. Fortunately, turnout was reportedly a record high, reaching approximately 80 percent. This was up compared to the previous Presidential Elections in 2014 when turnout was

69 percent. It would seem Widodo's supporters did not abandon him as some had feared in the lead up to the vote nor did the undecided voters choose to opt out of their civic duty as many thought they would. This was somewhat surprising given that the campaign season — including a series of televised presidential–vice presidential debates — was a relatively dull affair with arguably none of the candidates doing enough to convince the undecided voters to back them.

With regards to foreign policy, whilst one of the televised debates was on the topic, it did not appear to feature much in the minds of the Indonesian voters in making their decision, who instead focused on more pressing issues such as the economy, corruption, and religion. Traditionally, Indonesia's foreign policy holds a relegated position as an election campaign issue, as indicated by the fact foreign policy was lumped together with ideology, governance, defense, and security as the theme for the fourth televised debate. Even in cases where foreign policy did get any spotlight during the election campaign, it was always the case that neither Widodo nor Prabowo Subianto would significantly differ from one another. Predictably, both made normative commitments to Indonesia's *bebas-aktif* (free and active) foreign policy, with the former pledging to advance the Palestinian cause whilst the latter pledging to make Indonesia strong and respected abroad, and both candidates promised to make Indonesia take up its rightful place in the international community, just like they did back in 2014.

However, unlike the election campaign in 2014, where Widodo was a newcomer lacking sufficient foreign policy experience and knowledge, the circumstances were now different. As the incumbent, President Widodo could be judged on his foreign policy track record over the past few years. This book attempted to do just that, arguing, for example, that Widodo's first year in office appeared to be a step backwards. Indonesia's strong stance on illegal fishing and drugs smuggling angered other governments in the region that withdrew their ambassadors, warned of diplomatic consequences, and even refused to accept the credentials of Indonesian representatives. Meanwhile, the second year saw foreign policy characterized by a reactionary approach with the President seemingly intervening only when an issue became unavoidable. This was especially the case when Jakarta's sovereignty was at stake. On other occasions, the Government's ventures on the world stage during the President's second year were confusing. Widodo's surprise announcement that Indonesia intended to join the TPP was at odds with the country's long refrain from committing to the mega free trade agreement, and the announcement of so-called liaison ministers appeared to undermine the position of Widodo's own foreign minister.

There did appear to be improvements in the third year, at least in the sense that there were no more embarrassing foreign policy reversals that had plagued Widodo's first two years. For the most part, Widodo would remain consistent, for example, holding firm in the face of China's opposition to Jakarta's renaming of the North Natuna Sea. However, there were other foreign policy embarrassments, such as Widodo's failed attempts *vis-à-vis* U.S. President Donald Trump and King Salman bin Abdul Aziz of Saudi Arabia. The fourth year meanwhile, saw further embarrassment with the Government too eager to make big announcements without first considering the likelihood of it being accepted. This was seen in the case of Indonesia's push for ASEAN to take ownership of the 'Indo-Pacific', the offer to host a summit meeting between U.S. President Donald Trump and North Korean leader Kim Jong-Un, the invitation for the two Korean leaders to attend the opening ceremony of the Asian Games, and the offer extended to the *Taliban* to take part in the Indonesia–Afghanistan–Pakistan trilateral meeting of *ulemas* (religious clerics).

Considering the above, it could be argued that Widodo's first term did not reach the same high point in Indonesia's foreign policy when compared to the Susilo Bambang Yudhoyono presidency. However, it cannot be said that Widodo's first term represented a low point either. Just as Indonesia secured a non-permanent seat on the U.N. Security Council during Susilo Bambang Yudhoyono's presidency, so too did it win a seat during Widodo's first term. Just as the then-Foreign Minister Marty Natalegawa engaged in shuffle diplomacy over a regional crisis, so too did the Widodo-appointed Retno Marsudi, when the Southeast Asian region was in the spotlight over the Rohingya issue. And just as Susilo Bambang Yudhoyono tried and came up short in his attempts to lead ASEAN towards a certain direction, so too has President Widodo so far struggled in his own efforts to push the regional organization towards adopting its own 'Indo-Pacific' concept.

In this sense, President Widodo perhaps deserved the same praise and criticisms leveled at Susilo Bambang Yudhoyono. In the case of the former president, the decade under Susilo Bambang Yudhoyono was remembered for an assertive and active Indonesia in the field of foreign policy, but due to several shortcomings and failures, was not always effective. Looking back over the almost five years of the Widodo presidency, not much has really changed. For some, this may be disappointing. For others, given the inexperience and lack of foreign policy interest from President Widodo, this was no mean feat.

Following the April 17 vote, the Indonesian people have spoken, and the message is clear: Indonesians *do* want five more years of the same. Encouragingly, in addition to securing the presidency, the President will be helped by pro-Widodo parties who will command a majority of seats in the new Parliament. Of the seven parties that supported Widodo's candidacy, five have passed the national threshold (four percent) to sit in the House of Representatives (DPR). Collectively, the five parties secured 54.90 percent of the popular vote in the General Election (*CNN Indonesia*, 2019, May 21b). An editorial by *The Jakarta Post* (2019, April 22) noted 'Jokowi's anticipated second term (October 2019 to 2024) holds great promise for Indonesia', and went on to describe the likelihood of a 'more confident Jokowi who... will be more assertive and dare to stand up against pressure from political parties, businesses and trade lobbies in introducing bold reforms that promise long-term benefits but inflict short-term costs.' It remains to be seen whether he will take advantage of his parliamentary majority to push through his legislative agenda.

Certainly, he failed to do so in his first term, despite eventually controlling the lower House of Representatives after Golkar switched camps during Widodo's second year in office. The President would be wise not to waste this golden opportunity and should take heed of the lessons from his predecessor Susilo Bambang Yudhoyono. Despite a thumping victory in 2009 where he secured 60.8 percent of the votes in just the first round and his coalition gained 59.45 percent of the popular vote in the legislative election, Susilo Bambang Yudhoyono was widely regarded as failing to fully utilize the strong position he found himself in at the start of his second term. President Widodo should thus reflect on how to avoid a similar fate and ensure his legacy remains intact beyond his second term.

In order to do so, it would be advisable for Widodo to reassess what went right and what went wrong during his first term. That the President barely improved on the 53.15 percent of the votes he secured in 2014 should be some cause for concern. Clearly, a wake-up call is needed to examine why, despite his massive infrastructure push and bureaucratic reforms as well as his choice of religious cleric Ma'ruf Amin as his running mate, Widodo's electoral numbers did not improve significantly, if at all.

Noting that the two presidential candidates campaigned on the themes of '*Indonesia Maju*' (Indonesia Advances) and '*Indonesia Menang*' (Indonesia Wins), it could be argued that following the success of the simultaneous Presidential and General Elections, Indonesia has arguably both *maju* and *menang*. If former U.S. President Bill Clinton famously stated, 'The people have spoken, but it will take some time to determine what exactly they said', it could be rephrased for the Indonesian context, as such: 'The people have spoken, now is the time for all Indonesians to work together in delivering the country's advancement and victory for 2019–2024.' This is true not only for the domestic front but also in terms of Indonesia's foreign policy. May Widodo's second term be a success.

# References

*CNN Indonesia* (2019, May 21a). 'KPU Tetapkan Jokowi-Ma'ruf Pemenang Pilpres.'. Retrieved from: https://www.cnnindonesia.com/nasional/20190521020825-32-396686/kpu-tetapkan-jokowi-maruf-pemenang-pilpres-2019

*CNN Indonesia* (2019, May 21b). 'Gerindra Peringkat Dua Pemenang Pileg, NasDem Lima Besar.' Retrieved from: https://www.cnnindonesia.com/nasional/20190521071249-32-396719/gerindra-peringkat-dua-pemenang-pileg-nasdem-lima-besar

*Kompas* (n.d.). 'Hitung Cepat Pemilihan Presiden 2019.' Retrieved from: https://pemilu.kompas.com/quickcount

*The Jakarta Post* (2019, April 22). 'Jokowi's reelection buoys economy.' Retrieved from: https://www.thejakartapost.com/academia/2019/04/22/jokowis-reelection-buoys-economy.html

# About the Author

A. Ibrahim Almuttaqi works for the Jakarta-based think tank, The Habibie Center. Having first joined in February 2012, he is currently the Head of its ASEAN Studies Program, leading its development into one of the flagship programs of The Habibie Center. He is a regular contributor to national newspapers, including The Jakarta Post, providing opinion articles and comments on important foreign policy issues affecting Indonesia and the wider region. He is often invited to speak at conferences and seminars — both in Indonesia and abroad — to share his expertise on ASEAN regionalism, Indonesia's foreign relations and international politics. He has also taught part-time at BINUS (Bina Nusantara) University International on courses including Southeast Asian Culture and Competitive Strategy in ASEAN.

In 2015, A. Ibrahim Almuttaqi was a recipient of an Australia Award (Short Course) as well as participated in the ASEAN–ROK Next-Generation Opinion Leaders Program. In 2016, he successfully completed a Professional Fellows Exchange Program organized by the U.S. Department of State, Bureau of Educational & Cultural Affairs.

A. Ibrahim Almuttaqi read International Masters in ASEAN Studies at the Asia-Europe Institute, University of Malaya, Kuala Lumpur, where he attained a Pass with Distinction in 2011, and also holds a First Class Honours Degree from the School of Oriental & African Studies, University of London, London, in BA History & Politics, which he obtained in 2009. He can be followed on Twitter at: @ibrahim_id

www.ingramcontent.com/pod-product-compliance
Lightning Source LLC
Chambersburg PA
CBHW071103280326
41928CB00051B/2794